# Haunted Liverpool 23

Tom Slemen

The Tom Slemen Press

Copyright © 2013 Tom Slemen

All rights reserved.

ISBN-10: 1492184918
ISBN-13: **978-1492184911**

# DEDICATION

For my uncle Frank Slemen

# CONTENTS

| | |
|---|---|
| Introduction | 1 |
| The Joker | 6 |
| Future Rave | 24 |
| Can You See Them Too? | 29 |
| The White Train Mystery | 37 |
| The Vanishing Hippies | 42 |
| The 3am Effect | 48 |
| Cast Iron Shaw | 70 |
| The Doppelgangers | 73 |
| Communicating Across Time | 83 |
| Visiting Hours | 96 |
| More Werewolf Reports | 99 |
| Renshaw Street's Faceless Ghost | 118 |

| | |
|---|---|
| Trapped Between Worlds? | 122 |
| Esma Doon | 127 |
| The Ghostly Admirers | 131 |
| Our Haunted Roads | 135 |
| The Stilt Man | 155 |
| The Jüdel | 158 |
| Through A Train Window | 167 |
| The Secret in the Cellar | 170 |
| Two Mysterious Animals | 194 |
| Witches over Strawberry Fields | 213 |
| Ghostly Warplanes | 217 |
| The Druid's Chair | 220 |
| Lady Willpower | 232 |
| The Light in the Distance | 236 |
| Crosby's Crawling Men | 254 |
| Flight Into Hell | 259 |
| Rodney Street's Nosy Ghost | 263 |

| | |
|---|---|
| Death Overdue | 269 |
| Ain't Nobody | 274 |
| Bilocating Betty | 285 |
| Written in the Stars | 291 |
| Eye in the Sky | 311 |
| The Blacklers Ghost | 316 |
| The Barber's Haunted Looking Glass | 321 |
| Timewarp Boutique | 329 |
| When Women Rule the Earth | 345 |
| An Angel on Havelock Street | 354 |
| The Morba | 360 |
| Woolton Road's Phantom Park | 375 |
| Jaggaroo | 385 |
| A Tragic Echo | 388 |
| The Shadow on the Grass | 392 |
| Some Walton Ghosts | 394 |
| The Eye in the Sink | 402 |

| | |
|---|---|
| The Other One | 408 |
| Helter Skelter | 411 |
| Young Love | 416 |

# INTRODUCTION

**Many years ago** when I was an altar boy at St Anne's Church, Edge Hill, I talked to a troubled priest who had learned of a great secret. Before I go further, let me colour you in on the background to this secret. In a subterranean labyrinth of corridors and vaults beneath the Vatican in Rome there is a large safe containing various documents which the Vatican has hidden from the light of day. Most of the records in the Vatican Archives are hundreds of years old and are classed as heretical. Among the yellowed, timeworn manuscripts are Henry VIII's application for divorce, a dossier on the subversive activities of one Galileo Galilei, compiled by the spies of the Inquisition, and, according to an enduring legend, the Vatican safe also holds a small pale-blue-coloured envelope that bears the Papal seal. Within this innocuous-looking envelope is a mysterious document known as the Vatican Letter, reputed to contain prophesies of a terrifying, apocalyptic nature. The story of the Vatican Letter began in the year 1917. In the little Portuguese town of Fatima, three youngsters were looking after their families' sheep. The shepherds, Lucia dos Santos, aged nine, Francisco Marto, aged eight, and his six-year-old sister, Jacinta, were astounded to witness the appearance of the radiant figure of a boy who looked about fifteen years of age. The vision told the children to pray, then vanished.

The youngsters were sure they had encountered an angel, but decided to keep the unearthly meeting a secret. As Portugal's irreligious political leaders had vowed to stamp out Catholicism "within two generations", it was hardly the time to report the sighting of a heavenly messenger.

On 13 May that year the children were out in the fields again, tending their families' flocks, when they witnessed another apparition that appeared after a flash of strange summer lightning lit up the skies. The shepherds expected thunder and rain, and ran for shelter, but no thunder rolled and no rain fell. Instead, a woman in white suddenly appeared, inexplicably, nearby. The "lady" told the children that she was from heaven and said, "Continue to come here on the thirteenth of each month. In October I will say who I am and what I desire and will perform a miracle all shall see so that they believe."

As soon as the heavenly visitant had vanished, the children agreed that the encounter with the lady must be kept secret. However, upon reaching home, little Jacinta could not contain her excitement and blurted out her account of the meeting with the unearthly woman, whom she believed to be the Virgin Mary.

News of the vision quickly spread and crowds descended on Fatima. They followed the shepherd children everywhere and, on the thirteenth day of each month, the multitudes pursued them to the site of the rendezvous with the apparition. When the lady appeared, as she had promised, most of the crowd couldn't see her, although many did report seeing "a strange bright cloud" hanging low in the sky directly over the shepherds.

When 13 August arrived, Lucia, Francisco and Jacinta could not keep their appointment with the lady; the children had been kidnapped and jailed by the civil authorities. The youngsters were interrogated over their conversation with the invisible entity and, when the young shepherds remained tight-lipped, an official warned them that they would be "boiled alive" if they refused to denounce their vision. The brave children remained silent and were subsequently released. Six days later, the lady appeared to the young shepherds again, telling them that they would only see her one more time on this planet.

On 13 October a raging rainstorm hit Fatima, but the 80,000 people who had made a pilgrimage to the town endured the inclement weather and concentrated on the three shepherds. The observers were not disappointed. The rain stopped, the skies glowed and flashed with incandescent colours that were much richer than those of the usual rainbow. Shortly afterwards, the children appeared to be talking to an unseen presence. When the skies darkened again, a sensational rumour rippled through the crowds; the lady had handed a letter to Lucia.

It is alleged that officials took the letter from Lucia

and were so horrified at the predictions it contained that they literally became reformed people overnight, subsequently passing the epistle on to the Pope himself. According to rumours, various individuals inside the Vatican have claimed that Pope John XXIII suffered a minor stroke when he read the contents of the Vatican Letter in 1963 and, for some unknown reason, the soon-to-be-assassinated US President John F. Kennedy was afterwards summoned to the Vatican by the Pope - who also died that year. Months after Kennedy's clandestine meeting with Pope John, a German newspaper published the purported "complete text" of the Vatican Letter and the religious authorities refused to confirm or deny the validity of the scoop. The German newspaper story claimed that the letter mentioned the outbreak of two world wars, the attempted assassination of a reigning Pope, a global plague, and a nuclear war on the Asian subcontinent which would escalate and wipe out three entire nations. The letter was said to end with a warning that each of the aforementioned events would surely come to pass if humanity failed to change its "wicked, evil ways".

I talked to a priest when I was about 13 years of age about the Vatican Letter, as I had heard my mother mention it once, and the priest said he had been shown part of it once. He told me that an evil force would spread around the world and corrupt and pervert people's minds. This force would result in all sorts of depravities before a final conflict between good and bad. Not only would there be global devastation because of this force, the priest told me, but the minds of people would be torn apart with the most disgusting and immoral thoughts. That priest was transferred to another parish and I heard that he later died.

I truly believe that Armageddon could arrive within our lifetime – not necessarily in the form of some all-out nuclear war, but a war on the minds and souls of decent people. I feel that something very dark and demonic is at large today, and I suspect it is using every sort of medium to infect the minds of people. As I write, I have just heard of a disturbing item on the news in which a man planned to kidnap a child and had all sorts of stomach-churning plans for him. He had built a special sound-proof room in his basement with an operating table equipped with all sorts of straps and restraints, and this person – this abomination – planned to castrate the terrified child as he lay strapped onto the table and eat him alive. There was also a recent news item about a group of youths in Russia who videoed their sickening attack on a man they had kidnapped. The video was distributed via some underground network under the title Three Guys 1 Hammer and it graphically depicts these fiends stabbing the man, bashing his head in with a hammer as he pleads for mercy, and even prising out his eyeballs with a screwdriver. We may have finally reached the times foretold in the Vatican Letter. Be on guard.

Tom Slemen

# THE JOKER

**Life can be fun**, but more times than not, the joke's on us. Do you ever have the sneaking suspicion that some mischievous metaphysical prankster is at work somewhere, and that he plays with our minds in a very sinister way? The more I delve into the occult, and the more I investigate the shadowy world of the supernatural, the more convinced I become of an eerie "Cosmic Joker" who seems to be at large in our poorly-understood universe. A word of warning though before you read on: once you realise that some dark-humoured force is at work in the lives of the people around you, you may start to experience the Joker's influence in your own life, and realise that you weren't simply "unlucky" and that certain incidents which you find yourself implicated in are not merely "coincidences"; you will then most likely come to realise that the Universal Trickster has messed with you as well. What follows are just a few case studies which hint that some form of intelligence with a warped sense of humour seems to be perpetrating some far-out pranks on us terrestrials. In several of the cases, we even seem to catch a glimpse of the Joker...

One morning in August 1980, a 52-year-old taxi driver named Ray was driving down Lime Street in his Hackney when a tall man with a mop of black curly hair whistled to him. This man had just come out of Lime Street Station and looked to be in his early-to-mid-twenties. He got in the cab and said to Ray, 'Queen's Drive Walton, please mate – the Breeze Hill end.'

'Alright mate,' said Ray in reply and drove off, and as the taxi reached the Vines (where he planned to turn the taxi around), the passenger leaned forward and gave the house number of the address on Queen's Drive Walton – and Ray couldn't believe his ears, because it was his own address. Ray said nothing, and naturally became very suspicious. His 40-year-old wife Marie was at home. Was she expecting this young man or had the fare given the wrong house number? Ray asked the passenger to repeat the address, and then the young man asked, 'Don't you know that part of the city?'

'Oh yeah, I know it well, was just checking I heard you right,' said Ray, eyeing the stranger in the rear view mirror. 'Visiting family are you mate?'

The passenger grinned, then leaned forward, pulled down the seat near the window and told Ray: 'Well actually, I'm going to visit a bit of crumpet.'

Ray's heart pounded and he gritted his teeth. He kept an iron bar under his seat for troublemakers and felt like using it to clobber this slimy bastard who was grinning like a Cheshire Cat. 'You lucky sod,' Ray said with a flat voice, 'she as young as you? How old are you lad?'

'I'm twenty-four. She's forty, or so she says, but she

looks a bit older. I'm a bit worried though because she's married.'

'Oh, you wanna be careful lad, he might be a boxer or something?' Ray was so enraged he braked hard because he had not seen the oncoming bus as he swerved the Hackney into a 180-degree turn. The bus driver beeped his horn and Ray gave him the two-finger salute.

'Nah, he works on the cabs,' the passenger said, and gave what sounded like a phoney laugh.

'How did you meet her?' Ray wanted to know.

'Well, she works in the canteen at the university – I'm at Liverpool Uni – and we just clicked. I've just come back from London, had a job interview –' And then the student's voice suddenly ceased in mid-sentence.

'Student eh?' Ray was still recoiling from the shock of discovering the affair his wife had been having behind his back. Should he belt the student or should he do it all legally and take Marie and her co-respondent to the divorce court?

'Erm, excuse me,' said the student, 'could you possibly pull over a second by that chemist over there?' and he pointed to the pharmacy on London Road as the taxi turned the corner by the Legs of Man public house.

Ray thought to himself: If this bastard's going to get some condoms I don't think I'll be able to keep this act up – I'll have to give him a smack. The enraged cabby with a calm face pulled up at the said chemist and the student got out – and suddenly ran off down Pudsey Street! Had he realised somehow that he had been talking to Marie's husband? Ray wondered about this as he tore off after the debauchee. Ray was so furious as he drove after the student, the back right wheel of the Hackney went over the corner of the kerbstone and pedestrians dived out of his way. Somehow the lanky libertine vanished into the crowds going into Lime Street Station and Ray even left his cab and went in search of him on foot. He asked other cabbies if they had seen the student but they hadn't.

Ray drove home, and instead of letting himself in, he knocked on the door – and Marie answered in full make-up – and she wore a low-cut top and a tight little black leather skirt above her knees.

'Expecting your student was you eh?' Ray said with a toothy smile, and his eyes were full of unbridled hatred.

Marie shot a perplexed look, then said, 'What are you on about? Why are you home early?'

'Talk about mutton dressed up as lamb,'Ray remarked as he looked her up and down, and then he told her what had happened; the amazing coincidence on Lime Street, and how the student had asked him to go to his own address to see a woman who, Ray added with great delight, actually looked older than she said she was.

Marie sat on the sofa with her face in her hands. She started to cry. She admitted to the affair. She believed that Ray had known about the affair for some time and had probably been playing private detective, following Clive (the name of her student lover) around the city after seeing him leave the house one Saturday night when he was supposed to be at work on the cabs. Ray swore on his 7-year-old son David's life that he had done no such thing. He had only discovered the affair through the force of coincidence.

Clive later wrote to Marie, saying he had decided to call it a day after he had realised he had hailed her very husband's cab that day on Lime Street. He had only realised who Ray was when he saw the tiny picture of his son David hanging up in the cab – the same photograph that Clive had seen standing on the mantelpiece of Marie's home when he had enjoyed his illicit affair with her. Clive had then pretended he wanted to go to the chemist and had made a break for it.

Ray forgave his wife, for David's sake. He didn't want his lad to go through all of the heartache of seeing his mum and dad split up, and Marie was never untrue again.

The devious demon of coincidence can also have a very black sense of 'humour'. On 21 July 1975 the *Liverpool Echo* published an article about two Liverpudlian brothers who both died in tragic road accidents in Bermuda a year apart, and in each case, the same taxi driver was responsible and was carrying the same passenger when he crashed into the same moped each brother was riding upon at the same location.

In the 1950s, a man named George, who was regarded as the king of the pickpockets in Liverpool, was released from Walton Jail after serving a three-month prison stretch for theft. Within a week of his release he decided to go to Lewis's for a spot of pick-pocketing one afternoon, but unfortunately, on the one day he chose to revert to his illicit occupation, there was a store-detectives' convention at the Adelphi Hotel just across the road, and just before the convention got underway, some thirty-odd store detectives had gone over to Lewis's to present a gift to a detective who had worked at the famous store for years – and of course, George's suspicious behaviour was quickly noticed by the expert eyes of the professional pickpocket-hunters gathered in Lewis's – and he was caught red-handed, then subsequently charged. He was back in jail within weeks. George never set foot in Lewis's again.

One of the strangest coincidences I heard of came from a reader named Maude, a retired midwife in her seventies. Maude told me how, one day many years ago when she was in her thirties, she was going to her flat on Rodney Street from the Mount Pleasant end, and as she passed a red telephone call box she heard it ring. Normally, Maude wouldn't have answered a call to a public telephone box, but found herself walking towards it, as she actually felt the call was for her for some unfathomable reason. She picked up the receiver and said, 'Hello?'

And a female voice said, 'Hello, is that Maude? It's Joan.'

The caller's voice was instantly recognisable as belonging to Maude's friend Joan Hexley, who lived in Wirral. The two ladies had not seen one another for five years and Joan – who had terrible eyesight – had meant to dial the telephone number for Maude's old address (in the Old Swan area) and had somehow dialled the number to the Rodney Street telephone box that Maude just happened to be passing at that exact moment. Was this just an incredible coincidence, or was some higher force acting as a the 'operator'? Maude could not accept the incident being down to coincidence, because she had felt the strange need to answer the call in that street phone box that day.

Some people seem to attract coincidences of a fatal nature, and in my experience over the years I have collected quite a few accounts of plain unlucky people – walking jinxes – and a surprising amount of them have been clowns. When I was a child I recall going to a funfair at Newsham Park, and in the midst of eating some candy floss with my mates, a tall thin clown in a harlequin-patterned suit approached us juggling a rainbow of balls. His hair was green and combed into three points to look like a jester's cap and of course, his face was a deathly white with two black X's over his eyes, a wide painted frown upon his mouth, and the customary big red nose. Before he could even reach us, a rather corpulent woman in her fifties came bounding over to the clown and used language that would make a docker blush. She began to hit the clown with her handbag as she called him everything under the sun, and two burly fairground workers had a hard time restraining the aggressive woman. The clown turned and ran off and was soon lost among the crowds. I later heard from my mother that the belligerent woman had lost her child at the fairground a few years before. Her son had choked to death on a boiled sweet as the clown was playing tricks on him and – allegedly – as the boy's face turned blue, the clown performed a sinister mime where he fell onto his back, kicking his legs in the air as he laughed – instead of attempting to clear the obstruction from the boy's throat or attracting help from any first-aiders who might have been present. Then it transpired that this clown had been present when three other children had choked to death at various fairgrounds and circuses in the Liverpool area. This was naturally seen as very sinister indeed, especially the way the clown went through his mime act as the boy was gasping his last breath.

Another unlucky buffoon with a painted face who visited Liverpool on several occasions was Nelson the Clown. His real name was Arthur Nelson and he was a fairly famous performer who travelled the country with William Cooke's Circus in Victorian times. Wherever Nelson went, children died in some bizarre circumstances, but rational people said it was all down to the funny man's unlucky share of dark coincidences, until Nelson the Clown visited Great Yarmouth on 2 May 1845 to perform an audacious stunt. Nelson announced that he would sail through the waters in a bathtub pulled by four geese from Haven Bridge (at Hall Quay) to the Suspension Bridge at North Quay. People said Nelson the Clown was mad to even consider this bizarre feat, but true to his word, the odd-looking clown duly appeared on the River Bure in his washtub (which, on closer inspection, was wooden), and he was indeed being (partially) drawn by four geese. Four hundred spectators – most of them children – watched the funny spectacle from the old suspension bridge over the river, and when Nelson and the geese passed under it, the four hundred rushed to the other side of the bridge to see him emerge – and tragedy struck. A link in one of the chains of the bridge gave way, then toppled, throwing the four hundred spectators into the waters. Seventy-nine people drowned – and most of them were children. The curse of Nelson the Clown had struck again.

When I think of the Cosmic Joker who may be behind all of the weird aforementioned "coincidences" I tend to visualise the Joker found on our playing cards. No one knows who he is or what he is supposed to represent. It was once conjectured that the Joker was an imitation of The Fool found in the Tarot deck but this has never been vindicated, and it is my own belief that the Joker represents the Great Trickster – yes, *him* – Old Nick himself, who is said to use so many cunning deceptions to lead humans astray. Whoever the Joker is, he has a weird sense of humour. For example, on the Thursday evening of 8 November 1984, a 17-year-old Liverpool lad named Trevor went to stay with his Uncle Colin and Auntie Daphne at their house in Accrington. The boy was into computers, and owned a Dragon 32 computer, but told his uncle how he wished he could have an Apple Mackintosh computer for Christmas (which wasn't that far away). At that moment, the boy's Uncle Colin laughed and said 'The only apples I know about are the ones you make pies with,' and at that moment, a trailer came on the television screen, telling viewers that *Gardener's Calendar* would be on at 8.30pm on the following evening, and, coincidentally, the host of the gardening programme, Hannah Gordon, said she would be asking advice from experts of the Royal Horticultural Society on planting Cordon Apple trees. 'Isn't that a funny coincidence?' Aunt Daphne remarked, because of the talk of Apple computers and Apple trees, and Daphne then settled down to watch a documentary about the alleged medium Doris Stokes, and throughout the programme, Uncle Colin kept saying, 'Ha! It's all rubbish. Mumbo jumbo!'

And then, around midnight, an incident took place over Accrington which has never been explained to this day. Over 300 apples, all said to be of the Bramley and Cox variety, rained down on the rooftops of Accrington, and they created a terrifying thundering sound which startled residents from their beds. The 'downpour' went on for about an hour, and the apples smashed car windscreens and cracked windows, as well as dislodging slates from roofs. No planes were flying over at the time, and had there been any in the sky they would have had to circle for over an hour to drop their surreal cargo. Trevor, and his aunt and uncle immediately recalled the talk of apples earlier in the evening, and shuddered. Two listeners who witnessed the downpour later called me at BBC Radio Merseyside and said they had not only seen the apples fall in a completely straight trajectory from an odd-looking cloud, they had later heard what sounded like deep laughter in that cloud. As soon as the cloud dissipated the fall of apples ceased. When Uncle Colin watched *Gardener's Calendar* on the Friday evening he kept expecting his house to be bombarded by apples from the sky. His wife Daphne was of the smug opinion that the apples had been some warning to her husband for being so critical of the medium Doris Stokes and the supernatural in general.

On 25 June 1884, a man named Peter Cassidy murdered his 49-year-old wife, Mary Jane, at their Bootle home at 9 Howe Street. Mary Jane had been staying out all night, and after staying out one night after going to see her daughter Ann in Manchester, her husband finally flipped, and battered Mary Jane's head in with a mallet and also struck her with a meat cleaver. He said he had tried to forgive Mary Jane so many times for staying out (possibly with other men who plied her with drinks) but she had always gone back to her ways. Before he was arrested he told neighbours that he had loved his wife and rambled on about time standing still when he first set eyes on her. Two eerie coincidences were observed when Peter Cassidy was sentenced to hang for his wife's murder. On the Tuesday morning of 19 August, 1884, Father Brontë, the Roman Catholic Chaplain at Kirkdale Gaol, walked with the condemned Cassidy from his cell, across the prison yard to the gallows. Inside the prison, a warder waited to hoist the infamous black flag that acts as a signal to the morbid idlers congregating outside that the Law has been carried into effect. As Cassidy was walking up the steps to the gallows, he turned to the chaplain and in a broken voice, he said he wished time would stop, and that he could go back to that summer night when he had killed the only woman he had ever loved on this Earth.

At that moment, the clock of Kirkdale Gaol stopped dead for no apparent reason, throwing proceedings into confusion, for hangings were dictated by the clock, and Cassidy was due to be executed at a given time logged in the grim registers of the prison. The clock was promptly restarted by one of the prison staff and its audible click-clack signalled a resumption of the nightmare. It was now officially eight o'clock, and a heavy rain began to fall, soaking the people outside the prison gates who were looking up at the roof of the stronghold, awaiting the appearance of the black flag. The hangman James Berry, a legendary executioner I have written about before in my books, pinioned Cassidy with his expert hands, then positioned him on the trap door. Berry adjusted the noose and placed its loop over Cassidy's head as the condemned man stood straight without a trace of fear upon his face, The white cap was placed over his head by Berry and dragged down over Cassidy's face, and it was possible to see the inhalations and exhalations of the condemned murderer as the cloth over his mouth went in and out. Based on the height of Cassidy, Berry had calculated a drop of 9 feet. As Father Bronté prayed, Cassidy plunged and although he died instantly, according to the prison physician, his heart was found to be beating five minutes after the hanging. Later that day, Father Bronté was talking about the way the prison clock had stopped when Cassidy had expressed a wish for time to stop, when a prison official took him to the mortuary to show him something very strange. An effusion of blood was discovered on the neck and back of Cassidy after he was cut down at 9 o'clock that morning, and the two trails of sticky blood from the wound (where the rope had ripped the skin on the nape of the neck) had formed the most perfect shape of a heart. Father Bronté thought of how Cassidy had told him in the last minutes of his life that Mary Jane Cassidy had been the one woman he had loved on this Earth.

On the Christmas morning of 1840, a 20-year-old Liverpool woman named Mary Higgins was attending Mass at the packed Roman Catholic Chapel of St. Francis in Dublin with a cousin. A strange-looking man with a very pallid face – as if he was wearing some kind of thick "pan stick" clown make-up – came into the church. He wore a bowler – even though it was customary to remove a hat in church – and the stranger's eyes looked very dark and unnaturally pointed at the tails of their eyelashes, which gave Mary the creeps. He wore a fine brown suit and orange chequered trousers with ankle length boots. This man suddenly pretended to be drunk, and staggered towards the pews, shouting, 'Oh be quiet!' to the priest up in the pulpit. An elderly member of the congregation seemed to know the mischievous drunkard-impersonator, and the old man shouted to him: 'You! Get thee away from this House of the Lord!'

The strange dandy suddenly cupped his hands around his mouth and yelled: 'The gallery is falling!'

And sure enough, the sound of something breaking and giving way echoed about the church. The people seated in the gallery were gripped with panic, imagining they were all about to fall to their deaths, and the hundreds of other worshippers below them also got to their feet and tried to run out of the church. An unstoppable tidal wave of people swept out of the church, and they hit young Mary Higgins head-on, knocking the wind out of her and lifting her into the air, where the frantic hands of men and women pushed her along as they all poured outside into the street. Screams pierced the air and some accounts from the survivors talked of hearing the bones and ribs and skulls of those who had fallen in the stampede being cracked and crushed under hundreds of feet. Six people were trampled to death – all because of the so-called 'drunk' who raised the false alarm. Mary Higgins was hospitalised for a comminuted fracture of the leg and for the remainder of her life she suffered terrible nightmares about the crush in that Dublin church, and always, the fiendish painted face of the unknown man who had caused the tragedy haunted Mary's nightmares. Imagine if you will then, how Mary must have reacted when she saw the very same evil joker almost thirty years later, when, at the age of forty-nine, she was attending a packed church in Liverpool on Sunday, 23 January 1870. This time the venue was St. Joseph's Roman Catholic Chapel on Grosvenor Street, near Scotland Road, and the place was so packed with worshippers, they even sat in the aisles and on staircases to hear the highly popular priest Father Raphael deliver a lecture. A schoolroom located beneath the chapel was opened to accommodate the massive influx of worshippers who wanted to hear Father Raphael. Mary Higgins was once again situated near to the entrance of the church when she saw the sinister man she had last set eyes upon back in 1841; this evil character seemed to recognise her, and he had not changed in appearance at all since their last encounter. Just as Mary was about to tell a young priest about the menacing figure, the bowler-hatted man shouted to Father Raphael: 'I have heard you long enough! Be quiet!'

Several people, including Mary Higgins, went to tackle the hideous alarmist, when he suddenly screeched: 'Fire! Fire!' in an unearthly loud voice. Pandemonium broke out as the false cries reverberated throughout the church. A scene of indescribable fear and alarm ensued as the wicked stranger ran from the church. The devout worshippers in the schoolroom below believed that the chapel above was on fire and some survivors even spoke of seeing flames that turned out to be nothing more than the flickering light from candles, but these lights from the candles were magnified in the scared minds of the worshippers, and within a few minutes, hundreds of people were heading towards the entrance of the church, and the seething multitudes became sickeningly blocked in the narrow doorway of the church, and they piled upon one another. A thin frail old man who had attempted to calm down the panicking hordes was crushed to pulp against the sandstone walls of the church, and although his eyes literally popped out of his skull and his head was compressed to just four inches by the jammed living mass, his mouth was seen to still move, and this gruesome image was imprinted on the mental retina of many of the survivors till their dying day. The bodies of men, women and children were stacking up to a height of twelve feet, so that there was only a small arc of the upper arched doorway visible, and some poor desperate souls tried to climb through this gap to escape this ghastly harvest of the Reaper. Mary Higgins awoke in hospital, and when she told a doctor about the evil man with the pale face and malevolent dark eyes, he must have thought her brush with death had turned her brain.

Mary learned that fifteen people had been trampled and crushed to death, with many of the bodies of the victims resembling nothing but blood and pulp. Thirty more had been maimed for life and left with all sorts of serious injuries. A week later as Mary visited one of the elders of St. Joseph's Chapel, he told her that in 1841, a man dressed exactly like the one who had shouted 'fire' had come into the chapel when it was being run by the Episcopalians and had attempted to cause a panic by announcing that the chapel's roof was ablaze, but on that occasion the clergyman, a Mr Andrew McCorkey, had jumped from the pulpit and landed in the central aisle, where he raised his hands to the panicking congregation and somehow assured them that there was no fire and that the man who had raised the alarm was a 'well-known troublemaker' who had disrupted services many times before. Some of the congregation in another part of the church still fled the building and there were a few casualties, but none as serious as the one which had occurred on Sunday. Mary then told the church elder that she had also seen the exact same man with the bowler hat in the Chapel of St. Francis in Dublin when she was 20, back in 1841, so whoever this evil person was, he apparently never aged, and had gone to enormous lengths to disturb religious services by travelling between Dublin and Liverpool. The church elder then told Mary that the man who had caused so many deaths in churches in Liverpool and Dublin was possibly an agent of the Devil, out to wreak as much havoc as possible in the Church. Was this diabolical saboteur of the church a demon, or was he the Cosmic Joker we have been speculating upon? Or, are they one and the same?

In September 2012 a 27-year-old woman named Joanne emailed me to say that, for the past two months, she had been haunted by the number 111. She kept waking up at exactly 01.11 am each morning, even when she had gone to bed exhausted around 11pm. The number was on the timer display of her microwave, and it is even on the 'long number' of her credit card. She had been talking to a friend on the telephone, wanting to arrange a meeting with her one afternoon, when her friend had said, 'What time's it now? Let's see, eleven minutes past one...' And Joanne had gone cold. Then Joanne started noticing 111 in car registrations, on her bills, and so on. She asked me what I thought and I told her that it was either a 'mental set' thing – that these numbers, like other certain groups of numbers, are always about, but that she was merely noticing them more now because she was focussing on them, or there was some metaphysical phenomenon going on, possibly part of the 11:11 occurrences which get reported to me on almost a weekly basis. People claim that they are seeing 11:11 whenever they feel a strange impulse to look at a digital watch or the time on their mobile phones. Anyway, Joanne asked me if the ubiquitous 111 was something bad, and I said I didn't think it was. I told her not to be afraid of it. Perhaps something, somewhere was trying to get some message across. Joanne then told me that her grandmother, who she had been very close to, had died on the 1 November 2011. Could this have some relevance, we both wondered. Joanne said she would ignore the numbers because she was becoming obsessed with them.

In early October she decided to have a go at the National Lottery, and as a lot of people do, she chose numbers based on people's ages and their door numbers etc. The numbers Joanne began to write down were: 27 (her own age), 42 (the age of her older brother),16 (her door number), and 18 (the door number of her neighbour and best friend Carly). Joanne then needed two more numbers, and was tempted to choose 1 and 11 – the numbers that had been haunting her for the past two months, but decided against it because it had been the date of her beloved Gran's death. Two other random numbers were chosen instead: the supposedly 'lucky' number 7 and 4 - the age of Joanne's daughter Leah.

On 6 October, the Lottery numbers were generated by the random number generator named Lancelot, and they were 1,11,16,18,27,42 and the bonus ball was 4. Had Joanne decided to go with her 111 hunch, she would have netted 3.78 million pounds. Ouch.

Since then, Joanne has not noticed 111. Perhaps her late Gran – or the cosmic Joker – had been trying to tell her something? If opportunity – metaphysical or otherwise – comes knocking at your door, it may pay to heed it.

# FUTURE RAVE?

**The following strange story** was related to me by Sandra, the lady featured in the account, at a talk I gave on the paranormal many years ago in Speke Hall.

Around September 1974, 24-year-old Sandra Williams decided to go with her best friend Jill Brixham to a discotheque called Mirandas over in Leighton Court Country Club, Neston. The plan was to leave Sandra's flat in Aigburth, get the bus to Jill's house in Garston, where the latter's brother, Andy would take the girls over to Neston in his old but reliable Vignale Vanguard Saloon. This arrangement almost went awry at first because Andy had a blazing row with his girlfriend at her house, which detained him for about forty minutes, but he was true to his word, and he took Jill and Sandra over to Mirandas in Neston and promised he'd collect them when they came out the discotheque – if they could get out before 1.30am because he had work in the morning. The three young people reached the club around 9pm.

As well as a disco, the Wirral club had three bars and a restaurant, and the DJ upon this night – which was a Sunday - was a certain Pete Price, who was then with Radio Merseyside. The floor of the discotheque was packed, and by 10pm a friend of Jill – a 22-year-old blonde from West Kirby named Shelly arrived and soon the girls were dancing to the sounds of the Osmonds, Suzi Quatro and The Sweet. At this time, Sandra had quite a crush on a TV presenter named Mike Smith, who presented a DIY programme called *Jobs Around the House* and a rugged-looking guy 'bopping about' on the dance floor was the spitting image of him. Sandra tried to dance her way over to this handsome lookalike, but found her way barred by a man in his forties nicknamed 'Clement Freud' because his hanging jowls gave him the slight resemblance of a Blood Hound (and Clement Freud was featuring in telly adverts for dog food with such a hound around this time, hence the nickname). Sandra's friend Jill saw the older man attempting to dance as he deliberately blocked Sandra's way and she shouted 'Hey, cradle-snatcher, take the hint!'

The man moved aside in a huff and Sandra walked across the floor towards the tall double of Mike Smith, when she seemed to vanish amidst the flashing multicoloured lights. Jill stopped dancing and told Shelly what had just happened, and the two girls tried to look for Sandra but found their mission hampered by every groper and womaniser in the club. Sandra was nowhere to be seen. The girls searched the toilets, the three bars and the restaurant – but there was no sign of Sandra. 'We'd better call the police, Shell,' Jill suggested, with mounting panic in her voice, but then Shelly's eyes widened and she pointed at the crowd in the discotheque. Sandra had reappeared among the dancers, and she looked very confused. Her black low-cut top also looked disarranged, as if – surely not? Had someone assaulted her? That hideous thought went through the minds of Jill and Shelly. The three girls went into the toilets so they could hear Sandra's account of where she had been for the past fifteen minutes. Sandra said that as she had walked over to that man she fancied, everything changed around her, and she was deafened by a strange futuristic-sounding music which bordered on a racket. Blinding beams of light shone everywhere, and naked men and women surrounded her, dancing in weird jerky movements to a deep thumping beat, and most of the crazed dancers were covered in some odd-looking tattoos and wore bizarre masks with long noses. A naked man with blue and gold streaked hair and yellow nail polish made very suggestive dancing movements towards Sandra and tried to remove her clothes so she slapped him. He recoiled backwards in horror, felt his face where Sandra had struck him, and seemed near to tears. Sandra threw her hands up to her ears because the rhythmic racket was making her skull vibrate. She saw three nude men holding hands float slowly upwards into the air as all sorts of coloured geometric shapes flashed over their bodies. Something then prodded

Sandra's bottom and she turned to see a heavily tattooed man on all fours, poking her behind with his long phallic false nose, and this scared her so much, she tried to run back to the club she knew, but it soon became clear she was not, by any stretch of the imagination, in Mirandas. Weird sparkling five-pointed stars and other geometric shapes floated past in mid air, apparently projected from a huge silvery globe which rotated on the ceiling. This globe was also the source of the high-powered narrow beams of rainbow light which flashed over everyone. Sandra began to panic, and she closed her eyes hard then opened them again, and the outlandish naked dancers were still there, but then all of a sudden, Sandra felt her stomach turn over, and she could only liken the sensation to that felt in the pit of her stomach when she'd descended quickly on a roller coaster at the fair. Then she found herself surrounded by music she recognised, and she saw that the people dancing around her were all thankfully clothed.

Sandra and the girls were at a complete loss to explain what had happened. They were not as acquainted with timeslips and the surreal nature of quantum physics as we are in this day and age. I think it's likely that Sandra somehow, through some localised slippage in time, visited some rave party of the future, perhaps fifty years ahead of us. Sandra described some of the dancers as apparently floating about, and this makes me think the rave she saw was taking place in a future period where some form of gravity-control technology has been achieved. As far as I know, Mirandas nightclub no longer exists, but I'd have liked to investigate the premises to see if time was flowing in the club uniformly. My test in cases of this sort usually involves leaving an array of about fifteen digital chronometers about the place and mapping any discrepancies in the timepieces to establish a type of contour map of the timeslip.

# CAN YOU SEE THEM TOO?

**On St Patrick's Day** (March 17) 2002, a 20-year-old Dovecot girl named Kirsty went to O'Neils bar on Wood Street, and drank nothing but a diet Coke, as she just couldn't get into the Celtic mood of the night. A few lads in the pub offered to buy her drinks, but Kirsty knew accepting a drink from a male usually came at an awful price. She tired of O'Neils after around twenty minutes and moved on to the Jacaranda on Slater Street. It was the same old story here too – not a good bloke to be found. Being St Patrick's Day, the streets of the city centre were chockablock with merrily-intoxicated people, and many of them were dressed in green, and quite a few wore "leprechaun" hats and pointed ears. Kirsty left the Jacaranda and jostled through these crowds and felt so alone and aimless. She wore a beautiful low-cut satin Persian-blue dress from River Island and an expensive pair of strappy Sandals from Schuh, and as she hastened down Hanover Street, a big-mouthed drunken lout in the back of a hackney shouted something very coarse at the girl, and the vulgar remark brought her to tears. 'Where's romance?' she muttered to herself, and carefully wiping the tears so as not to smudge her mascara, she took a good look around her at the men folk. They were all of Cro-Magnon lineage; one-track-minded shaven-headed morons with billowing white shirts hanging over baggy concertina-legged trousers, beer bottle in one hand, mobile in the other, each thinking his hackneyed spiel would charm the birds out the trees and into their beds.

Oomph! Kirsty walked blindly into somebody on the corner of Church Street. It was a fortunate collision because it was Francesca Burns – a beautiful red-head Kirsty had known since infant school. She looked stunning; naturally long straight mahogany-red hair, and long curled eyelashes which sprouted from heavy eggshell lids, and this girl possessed a figure as perfect as any Lewis's window mannequin. She was as tipsy as Kirsty, and the two young ladies laughed and hugged and kissed one another. 'Fancy bumping into you!' they both said amid wolf whistles from the packs of philandering throwbacks who read the hugging, kissing, giggling girls in the usual warped way. The girls went to the nearby Midland pub on Ranelagh Street, where a tearful Kirsty poured out her heart. Everyone she knew was engaged and some of her friends already had a baby. All she wanted was to find a true love – a lad who was as romantic as her.

Francesca knew how romantic her friend was. She recalled how Kirsty loved to read romantic poems in the school library and how she'd almost cry at the sentimental endings of old movies like Brief

Encounter, Ghost and Breakfast at Tiffany's. Kirsty, like most girls, wondered if real love existed in the world today or whether it was just some cruel mirage.

Amid the din of the Midland clientele, Francesca whispered a secret in her troubled friend's ear. She had "Fairy ointment" in her handbag, and this, applied to the eyes, allowed one to find true hearts and behold a world normally unseen to mortals. Francesca had always been into witchcraft, even as a child, and had now formed a coven. Kirsty recalled some of the odd things Francesca had appeared to do in her younger days; putting curses upon people, attracting boys to her with various spells and rituals. They say a good witch is born and not made, and Francesca had always seemed very different to all the other girls in school. A lot of people said she had what could only be described as an aura about her.

The two girls went into the pub loo, and Francesca duly produced a tiny bottle of blue liquid. She rubbed some of this syrupy fluid in each of Kirsty's eyes and the latter cried out, 'It stings!'

Then the burning sensation faded and Kirsty had to fix her eye make-up.

Francesca said the effects of the ointment would kick in soon, kissed Kirsty on the cheek, then left the pub. Kirsty went after her, but Francesca said she was going home, as she felt sick with all the drink. And just before she somehow attracted the attention of a taxi driver who was passing by amid a hail of whistles from a bunch of potential fares, the beautiful witch promised Kirsty she'd find a true love before the night was through. And then the Hackney came to her and she winked and left Kirsty standing there at the kerb feeling so alone again.

An hour went by and Kirsty felt no different and saw nothing. By 2am, she was trying to get a taxi home on St John's Lane. Her strappy heeled sandals hurt so she sat down on the kerb ready to take them off, but before she could she saw something moving on the floor in the gutter. It was a tiny man and woman, both a few inches tall, and each carrying a little flower (a white one and a yellow one) as they walked past her toes. She asked a passing girl if she could see the little people and received a strange look. Kirsty crouched down and saw the little man stand aside in a courteous manner as his lady walked into a gap between the kerb stones. He followed her a moment later, and then they were gone. Kirsty said to the gap in the kerb: 'Come back. Come out, please,' but the little people didn't emerge. The man had worn a sort of tall hat, a bit like the old Victorian topper, only with a rounded point to it instead of a flat top, and he had also been wearing an old fashioned grass-green coat with hammer tails and a pair of tight pale green trousers and brown boots with a jagged top to them at his shins. The lady with him wore a quaint old shawl in lime green and a long dress to her tiny feet which was also of a green shade.

Kirsty slowly stood up and began to panic, for she naturally wondered if her drink had been spiked with some hallucinogenic drug at the last club she went to, but then the more she considered this possibility, the more she realised that it was quite unlikely as she had nursed one vodka and orange and two Bacardi and cokes for most of the night as she hadn't even been in the mood for dancing, and hadn't left any of the drinks unattended. She went to the loo once but never left a drink unattended when she did; she had left the club after leaving the toilet.

Then she remembered the so-called "fairy ointment" Francesca had applied to her eyes. Surely that had been nothing but Wiccan nonsense?

Then why had she seen those two little figures a minute ago? Kirsty backed away from the roadside towards the walls of St John's Gardens, which are, of course, located at the back of St George's Hall. When Kirsty looked into these gardens, she saw a hundred glow-worm lights swimming about over the lawns and shrubbery. She squinted and shielded her eyes from the glow of a streetlamp with her hand, and looked as if she was giving a salute. Now she was seeing things that convinced her that Francesca's ointment had worked. She saw tiny silhouetted figures dancing about in the gardens, and thought she could also hear strange pipe music. Then doubt – that recurring failing of humans – began to creep in. Perhaps some spiteful spiker - one of the many desperate lotharios that had been knocked back by Kirsty - had slipped LSD into her drink, she thought, and yet she knew somehow that this wasn't the case. All the same, she couldn't come to terms with the little fairy party she was witnessing, and she hurried away from the gardens in a panic – and ran straight into the arms of a tall dark man of about 25.

His name was Sean. 'You okay?' he asked, and Kirsty noticed a very faint pinkish purple aura around his head, and his eyes had a strange greenish phosphorescence to them.

'I'm sorry,' she said, looking up at him. He looked to be about six feet five to Kirsty and she was in heels.

'It's okay, I wasn't looking where I was going too,' he told her, then asked: 'You looking for a taxi as well?'

'Yeah,' Kirsty replied, 'I am.'

'I'll get you one. I'll phone – ' Sean was saying when Kirsty interrupted him.

'Could you do me a favour?' she asked.

'Yeah, I know, I'll beat it – ' Sean said, resignedly, and his barely visible aura turned a violety blue, as if tinged by sadness.

'No! No, don't go, just do me a favour,' Kirsty grabbed his forearm, and then pulled him towards the wall of St John's Gardens. 'Can you see anything strange over there?' She pointed to the myriad lights still milling about in the park.

Sean smiled and gave a puzzled look, but then his smile straightened out into a serious gaping mouth. 'What is it?' he asked.

'Can you see them too?' Kirsty queried with great excitement in her voice.

'Yeah, what are they?' Sean thrust his head over the wall, stretching a long thin neck.

'Just so I know I'm not seeing things, can you tell me what you can see?' Kirsty added, unconsciously squeezing Sean's wrist and hand with her two hands.

'Like little lights and – looks like, well, looks sort of like – little people.' Sean was spellbound by the spectacle. And then he walked rather fast up St John's Lane, and Kirsty's heart fluttered. She asked him where he was going, then realised he was going to the steps of the entrance to St John's Gardens. The two of them walked into the park and ever so slowly they crept up on the legion of lights and little dancing people. Two people from the world of doubt and scepticism felt as if they had wandered into Oz.

'I've got to take a picture of this,' Sean said, and reached for his mobile phone, but Kirsty's hand intercepted his and she simultaneously said, 'No!'

Sean looked down at her, and somehow he understood her protestation, and he softly nodded, and then he looked back at the Little Folk.

Kirsty noticed an old man – a vagrant with a white beard – and he was laying on a bench, watching the gala of the faeries. He looked quite complacent as if he was used to seeing them. A strange stillness then descended for about thirty seconds, and during this time the little people and the lights all moved off further into the gardens, and their beautiful pipe music went with them. Kirsty and Sean had the strangest feeling at this point that the Little Folk were going back to their world, and if they were followed by humans then there would be no coming back. Sean felt drawn to the retreating figures, but Kirsty pulled him back.

Blue flashes of light broke the couple out of the spell of altered consciousness. It was a passing police car which started up its siren, bringing the couple out of the wonderful enchantment. Kirsty and Sean could not get a taxi that night, but seeing as Sean lived only a stone's throw from Kirsty's Dovecot home in Huyton, the couple walked home, and were left so energised by the strange events of the night, they could hardly remember the long walk to their homes. The ointment wore off and Sean's aura, and the 'lovelight' in his eyes faded away. Sean later said that it was like meeting an old friend that night, and Kirsty felt the same when she first encountered her true love, and within a year of meeting they married. Kirsty soon discovered why Sean had been able to see "the Fay" (the old name for the Faery race) - he had a psychic streak which he had been in denial of for many years, but Kirsty encouraged him to nurture it. For a few years they revisited St John's Gardens on St Patrick's Day in the hope of seeing the Little People again, but sadly the faeries and their kin were nowhere to be seen.

# THE WHITE TRAIN MYSTERY

**Thousands of commuters** flow in and out of Liverpool in a steady flux by road and rail. In 1977, a crowd of people – many of them commuters - assembled on a platform at Liverpool Central Station and naturally expected nothing more than a train to take them to their Wirral homes after another day of toil, but instead, something very strange arrived which has never been explained to this day. It was a humdrum midweek afternoon around 5pm in April when the train approached with a rumble and a blaze of headlights, but many of those waiting eagerly on the underground for their carriage home noticed immediately that the approaching train was the wrong colour – it was snow white instead of the usual yellow and grey-blue - and it also had a huge central headlamp of blinding intensity. People shielded their eyes from the glare as the peculiar train pulled up, and when this actinic light faded to normal intensity, some of the more observant noted the alphanumeric reference emblazoned in a military-type stencil font on the front of the vehicle: SR-71. It was a textbook case of crowd behaviour in a situation of surreal uncertainty – people stood rooted to the spot to see who was going to emerge from this clinical white train. No doors parted to allow the commuters onboard, and the driver was not visible through the tinted windows covered with bars and some form of thick plate shielding. Through the rows of side windows of the unidentified train was the alarming sight of people dressed in what looked like gas masks and white overalls, and they were armed with machine guns. They sat facing one another and did not even look sideways at the intrigued, anxious and shocked civilians gazing in at them. Mr Roberts, the white-collar employee of a well-known local insurance firm, was just one of about twenty people who telephoned me in 2002 at the studios of Radio Merseyside in response to my mention of the purported case of the unknown train on the Billy Butler Show, and he told me how he had a very clear look in at the masked armed men. He was in no doubt that they were soldiers wearing nuclear, biological and chemical warfare suits, but he could not identify the machine guns, which looked very sleek and futuristic. On the side of train, Mr Roberts was rather alarmed to see a circular black and yellow nuclear hazard sign. A woman named Penny, who was a 20-year-old audio secretary back in 1977, told me how the train moved off with an unusual quietness, leaving dozens of people speechless and dumbfounded. About ten minutes after this a normal train arrived, bound for Birkenhead. Penny got on this train and she and many of the other people who had seen the white train talked about it throughout the under-river journey. Some of the witnesses, like Brian Chappell, the financial controller with a global oil company, later phoned the rail company to enquire as to why a train with a nuclear hazard sign was sharing the tracks of a civilian rail network but no one in authority knew anything about the strange train, and one rail spokesman later said the whole thing could have been a 'belated April Fool stunt,' which was, of course, a ridiculous explanation. The hypothetical prankster would have to have gone to a lot of trouble to pull off such a gargantuan prank. So how can we explain the incident at Liverpool's Central Station?

This country came close to all-out nuclear war with the old Soviet Union on many occasions in the past, and some think such a nightmarish close-shave took place that day in 1977, and it's possible that the white train was a military vehicle carrying an Intercontinental Ballistic Missile (ICBM), similar to the MX missile-carriers rumoured to traverse secret railway tunnels under North America. The idea behind putting missiles on trains is simple; the enemy would not be able to target them in the way it targets fixed missile silos and military bases. As late as 25 January 1995, a Swedish rocket launched for a weather data-gathering programme was interpreted as an incoming nuclear missile by the Russian early-warning system – even though the Swedes had informed the Russians of their rocket test. For some reason the notification did not reach the high command of the generals in the Kremlin, and the rocket, seen on Soviet radar screens as being en route for Russian soil, was deemed as a first strike by the West. President Boris Yeltsin had 15 minutes to decide on a nuclear retaliatory strike against NATO, and activated his so-called nuclear briefcase which contains the dreaded 'button' to trigger an instant response from the Soviet missiles and to deploy the full might of the Red Army. At two minutes to Armageddon, Yeltsin said he 'felt' the rocket was not a Trident or ICBM, but some failed space probe returning to earth, and so, the Russians stepped back from the brink of a nuclear holocaust, and thank God, their missiles were not launched. It was later revealed that one of the most heavily targeted cities in the UK was Liverpool, because of its submarine base near Seaforth, and also because of its importance as a port should a state of war arise. So many missiles were trained on our city, had they reached us, the megatonnage would have turned most of Liverpool to fused glass. So, in the light of such international Cold War paranoia in the late 20th century, did some incident, kept from the public and the media, take place that April in 1977, and did it warrant the deployment of an ICBM, guarded by a cadre of armed personnel to be taken to some open space on the rail tracks of Liverpool or Birkenhead and fired at the Soviet Union in some lightning first strike? It's possible, but the talk of "futuristic" machine guns the suited and masked men carried in that white train makes me wonder if the so-called Bold Street time-warp effect extends to the railway tunnels beneath the streets; perhaps what was seen that midweek afternoon in 1977 was not a chilling covert military operation, but a glimpse of the world in the near future. The earth has become a very unstable place with up and coming nations obtaining nuclear weapons and long-distance missile technology. India, Pakistan, and North Korea possess nuclear weapons, and at the time of writing, none of them are a party to the Nuclear Non-Proliferation Treaty. Israel is widely believed to have in the region of 200 nuclear weapons. Since the collapse of the Soviet Union, some of the materials from their nuclear warheads has allegedly found its way onto the black market, and Iran and Libya are said to have obtained these radioactive materials on the black market, as well as from sources in Pakistan. It's probably only a matter of time before an extremist terrorist group such as Al-Qaeda or a belligerent foreign leader deploys a nuclear device in the West.

# THE VANISHING HIPPIES

**I first heard** of the following strange story from my mother when I was a child. She wasn't telling the story to me directly, but to a neighbour, and I was eavesdropping. Years later at a book-signing I heard an account of the same story from a retired policeman who had actually witnessed the inexplicable incident described in the story. I then decided it was time to set this peculiar tale down on paper.

One evening in April 1970, four hippies - all men aged between 22 and 35 – were moved on by the police from Calderstones Park, where they had attempted to set up a camp. The hippies went to Sefton Park, where they hid in a wooded area and lit a fire. They sat around this fire on blankets as a full moon rose in the east, smoking pipes and roll-ups, and one of them plucked at a Spanish guitar. They toasted bread on the fire and shared a flask of tea and a bottle of whiskey amongst themselves as they philosophised about life. A policeman was on his beat that morning around one o'clock when he heard faint echoing high-pitched laughter, and then he noticed the light of the fire in the woods in Sefton Park, and he could see five silhouetted figures sitting around this fire, so he went to investigate. The laughter was coming from these figures. When the constable reached the small clearing in the wood, all he found was a few tin cups on the floor around the fire, and some of them were half full of tea which smelled as if it was laced with whiskey. A few tartan blankets lay close by, and three pipes filled with tobacco and marijuana lay on the ground still smouldering. A round of toast was skewed at the end of a long twig, and still felt warm to the touch, but there was no sign of anyone. The policeman thought he had perhaps scared away the five people, and he waited for a while behind a tree, hoping to catch them when they ventured back to the warmth of the fire on such a chilly April night. Then, at one point in the vigil, the policeman noticed a figure sitting against a tree about fifty yards away in the moonlight. It turned out to be an old tramp, and he was using a large burlap sack stuffed with newspapers as his sleeping bag. He told the policeman a very strange tale. The vagrant said he had watched the hippies for a while as they sat around their fire, and then sometime later another hippy had turned up in a long RAF overcoat. He played what sounded like a penny whistle and the four 'beatniks' were very hospitable to him. They gave him a drink and cooked something in an old billycan on the fire. The tramp had been able to overhear the conversations of the five men, and the stranger in the long coat had told the four men a number of very strange tales in an almost hypnotic voice. Then at one point, the youngest hippy, a man of about 22, pointed to the stranger's feet and said there was something wrong with them. The man in the long coat threw his head back and emitted a spine-chilling high-pitched laugh, then jumped to his feet. He danced around the fire, and the tramp could see that the stranger either had incredibly tiny feet – or they were cloven hooves. The four hippies got up and tried to run away, but suddenly vanished in an instant, along with the dancing stranger. Minutes later, the policeman had turned up. The constable thought the tramp had been drinking too much meths and shook his head at the far-fetched tale, but a few days after this a member of the public reported finding a dead body in the park to the policeman, and that body turned out to be the tramp's corpse. He was sitting under the same tree in his 'slepping sack' with a look of utter terror on his face. His eyes bulged and his mouth was wide open. On the vagrant's chest, the coroner found the red imprint of a huge hand – as if it had been burned into the flesh. The fingers of the hand were all the same length and the thumb was much longer than a normal human digit. The cause of death was recorded as being due to 'natural causes' but the policeman wondered what had burnt the shape of that oversized hand into the old tramp's chest.

They say that every now and then, people have seen the vanished hippies sitting around the fire in Sefton Park, along with the mysterious stranger who joined them that morning, but if you approach them, the fire dims and the figures vanish into thin air.

The case of the vanishing hippies seems, to me, to have a strange parallel with the following strange incident, only this time the agents of abduction seem more rooted in the extraterrestrial rather than the supernatural.

One night in late November 1995, a 32-year-old Wallasey man named David stormed out of his girlfriend's home on Mosslands Drive after a row. David wandered the night-time streets and just before one in the morning he was strolling down Leasowe Road, intending to walk past Leasowe Lighthouse on his way to the Wallasey Embankment where he could reflect on the blazing argument and the way his relationship was going with his partner of two years. However, when David reached Lingham Lane, which is a rather narrow coastal road running past the old disused lighthouse, he came upon three drunken vagrants who were staggering down the road away from him. They were about two hundred yards away and David could hear them singing and shouting. One of them smashed a bottle of wine he had been swigging from on the tarmac then let out a cheer, so David slowed his pace and thought about turning around and going back to his girlfriend, but instead he decided to continue on his journey – after the three tramps had moved on. What happened next was to give David nightmares for years. In the sky above and to the left of Leasowe Lighthouse, at a height of about three hundred feet, a faint grey coloured triangular craft was hovering. A small but powerful light came on at each corner of the triangle, and then a huge circular light appeared in the middle of the unearthly craft. The three tramps stopped dead in their tracks when they noticed the huge UFO. Seconds later, David heard a humming sound, and a blazing cone of laser-like light shone down onto Lingham Road, catching the three down-and-outs in its bright spotlight. All of a sudden, the three men began to slowly float upwards through the air, and as they did their legs kicked about and their arms waved frantically as if they were trying to resist the sinister force that was pulling them upwards – towards the circular blinding light of the UFO. Screams echoed across Leasowe Common as the men shrieked and struggled to get back to terra firma – but up they went, and then they were gone. The beam from the triangle then flitted about Lingham Lane, then scanned the lighthouse, before settling on David, who stood rooted to the road in a state of shock. As the light fell on him he felt the hair on his head rise up as if it was being charged with static electricity. He turned, and ran, but felt as if he was running up a steep hill, even though the road was flat. David was so afraid of being abducted by whatever was in that triangular ship, he shouted a prayer out loud, and ran like the wind up Leasowe Road. He flagged down a car he saw coming towards him, and told the motorist not to go any further because there was some sort of huge UFO up by the lighthouse. The driver of the vehicle said he had seen the UFO from as far off as Twickenham Drive and that he was going to see it close up. Both men looked down the road, in the direction of the UFO, and saw a bright light suddenly shoot vertically into the starry sky at a phenomenal speed – faster than the human eye could follow. Then came a rumble like some sonic boom. David told his girlfriend what had happened and she said she had seen those three tramps on many occasions in the Leasowe area over the years. Those three vagrants were never seen again, and that month, there was a spate of sightings of a triangular UFO. It was seen over Stanlow Oil refinery and also high over Bidston Hill and in places as far afield as West Kirby and Southport.

# THE 3AM EFFECT

**One night at a house** on Wood Road, Hunt's Cross in 2009, two friends, a 44-year-old businessman named James and a 35-year-old electronics engineers named Mark talked about sports and politics over a few beers and a pizza, and by around two in the morning the men decided to get some sleep. Mark decided to stay over at his friend's because he didn't fancy the long taxi journey back to his home in Maghull, and he expected to be offered the sofa, but instead, James insisted that Mark should sleep in the spare bedroom. Mark was very grateful at the gesture and he climbed the stairs, went to the toilet, then straight to the spare room where he undressed, then got into the bed and fell asleep straight away. At precisely 3 o'clock that morning, Mark was awakened by a strange feeling of uneasiness in his dream, and when he opened his eyes he saw a faint glow move across the room towards the wardrobe on the right. Mark rubbed his sleepy eyes and sat up in the bed. He saw now that a woman was standing in the middle of an oval of light, and she looked as if she was partially transparent. She was aged about thirty to thirty-five, and had blonde hair scraped back into a bun. She also wore a blue dress that went to her knees. Mark realised he was looking at a ghost, something he had never believed in before this morning, and he also noticed a cat sitting on the floor of the spare bedroom next to the shoes of the woman. This cat was quite large and had a white coat, and yet its bushy tail was ginger.

'Tell James that Ruth stopped loving him today,' the phantomlike woman said in an eerie flat voice devoid of any emotion, and then she, and the cat, vanished along with the oval of light.

Mark found himself getting out of the bed and turning on the light. He left the spare bedroom, hurried along the unlit landing and rapped hard on James's bedroom door. James mumbled something inside his room and Mark went straight in, as he was afraid the ghostly woman would come after him along the dark landing.

Mark switched on the bedroom light and as James squinted with a painful expression on his face and tried to shield his eyes from the ceiling light with his hand, Mark stuttered out an account of the ghost he had just seen in the spare room and of the white cat with the ginger tail. James seemed lost in thought for a moment, and then he said: 'That sounds like Martine...'

'Who?' Mark wanted to know.

'My sister-in-law,' James told his nervous friend, 'she was the sister of my ex, Ruth, and she had a Turkish breed of cat exactly like the one you describe – but she died three years ago.'

Martine and her beloved cat had succumbed to carbon monoxide poisoning at a house in Surrey. James had been very saddened to hear of Martine's death because he had got on so well with her.

Later that morning the news reached James that Ruth, his ex-wife, had died in a car crash in Brussels, where she had been living with her partner since the divorce three years back. James later learned that Ruth had never gotten over the divorce and had kept all of his old love letters from their days when they were courting, nearly ten years back. Mark was fascinated by the ghostly visitor, but never again did he stay overnight at his friend's house in Hunt's Cross.

What interested me about the Hunt's Cross 'visitation' was the way the ghost seemingly awakened Mark at 3am. This could be an instance of the so-called "3am Effect" noted by many paranormal investigators, for it would seem that many people are awakened from their slumbers at three in the morning by something which interferes with the sleeping mind and then gives the awakened person the impression that he or she is being watched by something close to the bed. I have many cases in my files of incidents which fit the 3am Effect, and what follows is just a small selection.

A long succession of occupiers at a certain house on leafy Hunters Lane in Wavertree have found themselves mysteriously roused from sleep, always at exactly three in the morning, and each of them has seen a little girl with ink black eyes and an evil grin standing by their beds. I have records of this sinister apparition dating back to about 1950, when a 50-year-old man named Arthur was awakened in his bed at 3 am after feeling something cold on his hand, which was protruding from under the blankets out the side of his bed. Arthur opened his eyes and saw a little grinning girl of about eight standing to the left of his bed, and she was holding the fingers of Arthur's left hand in her small icy hand as she giggled. Arthur quickly withdrew his fingers from the clammy cold grasp of the phantom and dived under the blankets, but the girl then jumped onto the bed, screeching with laughter, and began to pull the blankets off Arthur. He fell out the right side of his bed in an attempt to get away from the ghost, and quickly got to his feet and switched on the bedside lamp, only to find that the entity which had frightened the life out of him had vanished. Arthur looked under the blankets in case she was still there, and he also looked under the bed, but thankfully the creepy apparition was nowhere to be seen. Arthur was so afraid of encountering the menacing minor again, he slept in another room after that, and always kept the bedside lamp on and, under advice from his aunt, he slept with a Bible tucked under his pillow. Although the little girl never visited Arthur again, he often heard her in his former bedroom next door all hours in the morning, singing and running about, and these supernatural goings-on proved to be a bit too much for poor Arthur, and his sleep was disturbed so much, he became ill and moved from the troubled house on Hunters Lane to a flat owned by a relative in Oxton, Wirral.

As late as 2009, a reader wrote to me to ask if I knew whether his home on Hunters Lane was haunted, as he and his wife had been awakened many times in their room in the two years they been living at the address. It turned out that the house concerned was the house haunted by the ghost of the little girl. On Christmas Eve 2008, the couple living at the house on Hunters Lane had both awakened at three in the morning, and each turned to the other and asked, 'What?' in a rather grumpy manner, because each had thought they had heard someone calling them. Then the couple heard a child giggling, and they looked around and, having no children, were naturally baffled by the sound of a youngster. Then, simultaneously the couple saw the silhouette of a long-haired girl crouching on the wardrobe, and this shadowy child screeched with laughter as she jumped off the top of the wardrobe onto the bed – but she must have disappeared in mid air because nothing landed on the couple's bed. On Boxing Day, the couple were downstairs watching television around 3.30pm, when they both became aware of the regular rhythmical sound that was coming from the ceiling. The TV volume was muted and it soon became apparent that the sound was that of someone bouncing a ball. Together, the couple went up onto the landing and listened by the door of their bedroom, and they could clearly hear the ball being bounced in the room. As soon as the door was opened though, the bouncing ball sound stopped.

In January 2009, the couple were fast asleep in bed one morning, when, at exactly 3am, the alarm clock went off, even though it had been set for 8am. Once again, the man and wife saw the uncanny silhouette of the spectral girl crouched on top of the wardrobe, poised to jump, and this time when she leaped, she actually landed on the bed, but vanished at that point.

The couple wrote to me to ask if I had heard of this ghost on Hunters Lane, and I told them about Arthur, and I also related the following story concerning their house, which took place in the 1970s. In 1975, a man in his seventies with the unusual first name of Hadley, moved into the haunted house on Hunters Lane. A friend had heard about the ghostly girl and warned Hadley against moving into the house, but old Hadley had no belief in the supernatural and he was known to be a stubborn individual who seemed to enjoy going against the grain of good advice. On the very first night at the house on Hunters Lane, Hadley had a hard time sleeping because an owl kept hooting (traditionally a sign of bad luck or approaching tragedy). Around two in the morning, Hadley dozed off as he read a Reader's Digest booklet, but at 3am, he felt something cold pushing down on his face, and in his dreams this sensation was interpreted as a woman with a cold face kissing Hadley. The pensioner woke up, gasping for breath, and pushed off whatever was pressing down on his face. It turned out to be the ghastly pale face of the girl with ink-black eyes. She had been laying face down on Hadley. The old man turned on his bedside lamp, and looked about. He saw the face of a girl with black holes for eyes, peeping at him from over the end of his bed-rail, and this naturally gave him quite a start. 'Go away!' Hadley cried out, picked up his old alarm clock from his bedside cabinet and hurled it at the head – but the mischievous ghost ducked with an unnatural lightning speed and re-emerged on the left side of his bed, where its face now looked positively evil. The black eye sockets seemed to glimmer with a faint red light, and the mouth of the girl turned down into a gaping frown and revealed a bottom row of irregularly-shaped yellowed teeth. Hadley swore at the demonic child, and lunged towards the door of his bedroom. He tried to get out of the room but felt the entity dragging him back by the trouser leg of his pyjamas. He somehow managed to break free and ran down the stairs in the dark. Hadley flew across the hall and as he was trying to undo the bolts of the front door, he heard the thump of feet as the ghost came down the stairs. Hadley undid the bolts as something grabbed at his right shoulder and he swung open the front door and ran into the night-time street, where he tripped and fell into the road, landing on the macadam, which was moist with dew. He got up, stunned, and looked back towards his doorway, and saw that the door was steadily closing. It banged shut, and Hadley was so afraid, he went to a neighbour's house and knocked on her door. The neighbour told Hadley she had heard stories about the ghost that was haunting his house, but she could not throw any light on whose ghost it was or why it kept coming out of the woodwork. Hadley died a few years later from a fall in his house and some said the pensioner was fleeing down the stairs from the ghost when he lost his footing and fell, later dying from head injuries sustained by the fall. I have tried to research the ghostly girl of Hunters Lane, and although I have no shortage of eyewitness reports, I have not been able to identify the ghost, and have even used several psychics with a decent track record, all to no avail.

Let us go now to another part of this haunted city, to look into another example of the 3am Effect, if such a phenomenon exists, for this may be all coincidence, but I wonder sometimes if the 3am manifestations of these night walkers are all part of some Satanic parody - some devilish mockery of the hour of the day when Christ is supposed to have given up his spirit on the cross – 3pm.

In the early 1980s, in the district of Knotty Ash, a certain house at Clayford Crescent, just a stone's throw from Alder Hey Hospital and Springfield Park, was visited by a very strange entity nicknamed "the roly-poly man" - and this chilling entity had a habit of manifesting himself each morning at three o'clock. The first person to see him was a woman named Margaret, the 32-year-old wife of Cyril, a joiner who had no belief in the supernatural and a man who refused to entertain such notions as life after death and spirits, even when his wife told him that she had seen a little fat bald man with no clothes on come out of the wall one night. This incident took place at 3am in July 1981. Margaret usually slept like a baby after doing all of the housework, but on this morning she awoke with a start because she thought she heard someone call her name. She lay in the darkened bedroom with Cyril snoring lightly beside her, and she decided she'd probably heard some late-night reveller calling for a taxi somewhere in the distance, but then, as she tried to settle down to sleep, Margaret heard what she could only describe as 'weird music'. She opened her eyes and strained her ears; where was this sound coming from? She could hear a faint echoing drumbeat, and at first she thought she was hearing her own heartbeat, but this drum started getting louder, and Margaret could now also hear what sounded like an oboe and another instrument that sounded like a church organ, and as she sat up in bed, trying to get a fix on the origin of this peculiar cacophony, she noticed a faint smudge of light on the wall facing. At first, Margaret thought it was the projection of car headlight shining through the window from the street, but then the Knotty Ash housewife got the shock of her life. The smudge of light was a little man who was walking towards her. He was visible in the dark blue floral patterned wallpaper as a pinkish illuminated figure which got nearer and nearer. As the image grew, Margaret could see that he was naked, bald, with a huge pot belly, and his arms swung to and fro as he walked with a strange lopsided gait. As this corpulent apparition grew to about 5 feet and 3 inches, he stood at the end of the bed, and Margaret could now see that his face looked artificial and almost doll-like. The eerie stranger's cheeks were very rosy, and his smile seemed fixed and reminiscent of the mechanical mouth of a ventriloquist's dummy. The eyes of the ghost were black and crescent shaped. Margaret also noticed that the entity's navel – the belly button – was protruding a few inches. 'Margaret!' came a muffled voice from the direction of this creepy phantom, and the mouth of the ghost did not move in synchronisation with the sudden utterance. Margaret screamed and ducked under the blankets, and then a few moments later, after she had shook Cyril repeatedly in a desperate effort to awaken him, the housewife dared to peep out from the covers, only to see that the little fat naked man was still there. Once again Margaret screamed and shook Cyril so hard she nearly pushed him out of the bed, and seconds before he woke up, the sinister nude man vanished from the wall. Cyril had an early start and he was so angry at being awakened in such a rough way. He told Margaret she had only had a nightmare and moaned that he needed all the sleep he could get because he had to be up at seven, and he almost went straight back to sleep. Margaret hugged him with her eyes shut tight for the remainder of that morning, and she only managed to doze off around five. When she awoke at half-past nine, she got out the bed and hurried downstairs, scared that, even with the sun pouring through the windows of the room, that the "roly-poly man" would pay another visit. At noon, Tommy, the young window-cleaner came to the house, and after cleaning the upper windows, he came down his ladder and Margaret opened the living room window and asked Tommy if he would like a cuppa. 'Ah, thanks, I'd love one, Marg,' he said, and came into the hallway towards the kitchen, where he sat at a table Margaret had just spread with a pink gingham cloth. Margaret pushed a plate of digestives towards Tommy, and he said, 'Oh, you don't half spoil me, Marg,' and then he said something else that sent a shiver up Margaret's spine.

'Hey Marg, did you hear someone playing a drum this morning about three?' Tommy asked.

'Yes,' Margaret told him, and sat down at the table. 'So you heard it too?'

'I used to be a drummer in a group a few years ago,' said Tommy, dipping a biscuit in his tea. 'My 'arl fellah taught me – anyway, whoever was playing that drum this morning was playing what's known as a flam.'

'A what?' Margaret asked, intrigued.

Tommy ate half of his digestive then explained: 'A flam. It's a drumbeat where you play two strokes at the same time – simultaneously like; the military bands play it like that. Who in their right minds would play that at three in the morning?'

'Tommy, what I'm about to tell you is the God honest truth,' Margaret said, already feeling a bit foolish, but she bravely went on. 'I heard that drumming sound you heard, only I saw something as well, and it's really worried me. It might be an omen, but, oh you'll probably think I'm going nuts.'

'No I won't Marg, go on, what did you see?' Tommy was very intrigued now.

Margaret told him about the 'roly-poly man' who seemed to come out of a point of light in the distance as she looked at her wallpaper in the dark bedroom, and the young window cleaner didn't laugh. He seemed a bit unnerved by the account in fact.

'I would have shit myself – pardon my French Marg – but I would have been out of that bedroom as fast as my legs could carry me,' Tommy told Margaret, and he seemed to be imagining the very events she was relating to him.

'I told Cyril and he said it was a nightmare,' Margaret recalled.

'But how can it be if I heard that drumming as well?' Tommy asked.

'Where about do you live, Tommy?'

'Acanthus Road,' Tommy said, and he pointed to the wall of the kitchen, 'just round the corner from here. I heard it Marg, and I'm almost certain it seemed to come from the direction of the footy ground at the back of our house. I'll have a listen out for it tonight.'

'There are some weird things aren't there?' Margaret reflected on the uncanny incident. She still felt a bit scared and didn't want Tommy to leave, but he soon left to continue on his rounds.

Cyril came home as usual around half-past five, had his tea, had a doze in his armchair for half an hour, then went to the pub with Margaret. They returned home around 10.40pm, and after watching the television for a while, the couple went up to bed. Cyril went straight to sleep, but Margaret sat up reading a book by the light of her bedside lamp, and every few paragraphs she would peer over at the wall where she had seen the roly-poly figure. Cyril woke up at half-past one and grumbled about his wife's bedside lamp still being on, and then he went to the toilet. When he returned, he asked Margaret why she was still reading, and she switched off the lamp and tried to force herself to go to sleep. She dozed off, holding onto Cyril's left arm and then, around three o'clock, she was roused from her slumbers, and this time she woke just in time to hear the dying echoes of her name. Someone had shouted her without a doubt. With a mounting sense of dread, Margaret listened, and sure enough, the very same drumming sound she had heard the night before returned to haunt her. 'Oh God,' she whispered, and shook Cyril gently, but without waking he turned to his right and tore her hand from his forearm. A faint pinkish smudge of light appeared once again in the wallpaper, and Margaret ducked under the blankets as the drumming sound gradually grew in intensity. 'Margaret!' said the roly-poly man, and Margaret began to shake Cyril. This time he woke up, swore at his wife, and yelled, 'What the hell has got into you?'

And then Cyril also saw the illuminated bald plump figure at the bottom of the bed. 'What the – ' Cyril muttered, and he seemed speechless for a moment, and then he tried to get out of the bed to give this naked intruder a good hiding, not realising that the stranger was a ghost, and Margaret clung on to her husband by his arm and screamed, 'No! Don't! It's a ghost! It's something evil!'

Cyril broke free of his wife's grip and bent down to get something from his joinery tool bag, which happened to be lying near to the wardrobe. He picked up a tack hammer, which he threw at full force at the smiling nude trespasser, but it went straight through him and smashed the mirror of the dresser in the corner, and as it shattered, Margaret let out an unholy scream, and she scrambled over the bed to pull her husband back. Only now did Cyril realise that the unclothed figure at the foot of the bed was a ghost. As he and Margaret looked on, the little fat bald man vanished, and as he did, the couple heard the echoing strains of a long drum roll.

Cyril switched on the ceiling light and looked at the spot where the apparition had stood, and then he swore and shook his head as he surveyed the dresser's smashed mirror. Margaret told her shocked husband to put his slippers on because the carpet was covered in small glinting shards of glass. The man and wife went downstairs to get their bearings and Margaret said 'I saw him last night and you thought I'd had a nightmare,' and Cyril didn't seem to take his wife's words in. 'We'll have to get a priest, and get shut of it,' Cyril said, and he found his pack of cigarettes and lit up. 'What does it want with us?' he said, and coughed after the first drag. 'Why's it coming to see us?'

A priest was contacted but he told Cyril in a rather joking manner that there were no such things as ghosts. He was of no use whatsoever, and so Cyril went to see an old friend named Des, a retired plumber. He was a man who had held an interest in the supernatural for many years, and often went on ghost hunts to York, much to the amusement of his workmates. Des told Cyril that ghosts often "walked" for no reason whatsoever sometimes, but people often surmised that they were omens of death or misfortune. He gave Cyril several ornate cards featuring an embossed image of the Sacred Heart, and told him to pin them on the wall where the figure seemed to come from. Cyril did this and when bedtime came, the nerves of the couple were tight as piano strings. They waited for the arrival of the "roly-poly man" but curiously he never came, although around 3am, the alarm clock on Cyril's bedside cabinet suddenly stopped – even though there was nothing wrong with the electronic timepiece's battery. At 3.10am that clock began to tick again. Tommy, the window cleaner said he had heard the drumming sound in the vicinity of his house on Acanthus Road that morning, but it didn't seem as loud. A week after this, Cyril began to complain of headaches which went on for days, and he kept taking paracetamol for them every four hours, but still the pain in his head would not go away. After a week of these headaches, Margaret tried to wake her husband one morning but he wouldn't open his eyes or react. He seemed to be breathing, and an ambulance was called. Cyril had suffered a cerebral aneurysm – a blood vessel in his brain had literally exploded. Such an aneurysm often results in death, but Cyril made a miraculous recovery and when he came to, he found Margaret clutching his hand in tears. Cyril said that he actually heard the vessel in his head burst, followed by a whistling sound in his ear, and then he discovered he couldn't move. He found himself in a black void and out of the blackness came the frightening figure of the roly-poly man with that horrible artificial face and sinister fixed grin. For what seemed like hours, Cyril ran away from the naked corpulent figure and he could hear a drum beating as he did. Wherever he went, the obese man followed, and Cyril had the feeling that he would die if the man touched him, and so he kept on running until he was too weak to go on. And then he had awakened.

The couple decided to move into a house with Cyril's bachelor brother, Billy. The couple were not bothered by any more supernatural night visitations after that move, and I do not know if the "roly-poly man" still haunts the house in question or why he haunts it, nor do I know just whose naked ghost he is or why a drum was heard when he appeared. It's a real baffler.

I could fill a book with these stories which feature the 3am phenomenon, but let us bring some closure to this chapter now with the final story in this selection. We must travel back in time to October 1966 to Wordsworth Street, just off Lodge Lane in Toxteth. Duck Apple night was just a week away, and Mary, a 5-year-old child living in this Toxteth street, was excited at the prospect of all the games associated with that special night which we now call Halloween. Mary's

Gran, Nellie, always put three-penny bits in the apples she hung from cotton threads in the kitchen doorway and the odd shilling or tanner in the big green apples that would be bobbed in a big old bathtub. Mary and her brothers would have to keep their hands behind their backs as they tried to seize the buoyant apples with their teeth, and then of course, there was grandmother's lovely chestnuts which she salted and roasted in the old oven, and some of the ones that weren't pricked exploded in the oven. And then came the ghost stories. So, it was just a week before Duck Apple Night, and Mary was sitting in her bedroom, looking at the picture panels in a girl's comic called *The Bunty*, when her father rapped on the door and entered. Dad worked on the bins, and sometimes – always against the wishes of his wife Sandra – he would bring something home he'd found from his bin round and give it to Mary. Not so long ago he brought home an old radiogram as big as a sideboard, full of glowing-orange filament valves, and it worked perfectly, and Mary often twiddled the tuner to pull in radio stations presented by people who spoke strange languages. On this afternoon, Dad brought home a little vintage jointed wooden doll with no clothes on. It had hands like spades, black pupil-less eyes and no hair, but Mary loved it, and she called the doll Dolly at first, because she couldn't think of a name, but her mother suggest Adelaide – so Adelaide it was. Mary's father Gerry said he had found the doll in the backyard of a derelict house in Aigburth, and his wife Sandra told him he shouldn't have given it to Mary because 'rats might have pissed on that thing' but Gerry told his wife she was 'going to extremes once again', and assured her that the doll was perfectly alright. His wife told him that Mary had dozens of modern dolls all over her bedroom that she never even bothered with, so what on earth would she see in a doll with no clothes and not a hair on its head. But the funny thing was, Mary loved Adelaide, and would take her to bed each night and talk to her and tell her stories. However, three days after she had received the doll, Mary came down from her bedroom one morning and asked what a certain word – a disgusting swear-word – meant. The girl's mother recoiled in horror and gasped, 'Mary! Where did you hear such a word?'

'Adelaide said it last night,' Mary explained, blushing because she sensed she had said something naughty. 'Why, Mam, what does it mean? Is it a bad word?'

'Yes it is a very bad word, Mary!' fumed her mother Sandra, 'And you are never to say that word again! Have you got that, eh?'

'Yes, and I'm not even to whisper it under the blankets where you and me dad can't hear it either, am I?'

'No!' barked the child's shocked mother, wondering where her little daughter had picked up such a coarse word.

'And I'm not even allowed to say it to other children am I? Because that would be very naughty wouldn't it Mam?' Mary went on, unknowingly voicing her flow of mischievous thoughts.

'No, you are not to even talk about this word any more Mary, or you'll get a belt!' the child's mother chided the little innocent-looking cherub.

'And that means you as well Adelaide! You naughty doll!' Mary yelled at the doll, 'And if you ever say a naughty word again, my Mam and dad will give you such a belt!'

'Be quiet now Mary,' Sandra told her, and then crouched and said to her daughter: 'Shall we go to the shops soon and get some eggs and we can make a ducky egg? And we'll get a few cakes too eh?'

Mary's eyes sparkled with excitement, and she replied with an ear-splitting, 'Yes!'

Mother and daughter - and Adelaide - went to the local shops on Lodge Lane, and ended up calling in to Cousins the confectioners, where Sandra bought two donuts with a swirl of cream and a glob of strawberry jam in the middle of their holes. When Sandra and little Mary got home they had ducky eggs and soldiers and then the donuts, and Mary was even treated to a glass of orange cordial as well.

That night, the child went to bed at 8pm and Sandra and Gerry smiled to one another in the hallway as they heard Mary talking to Adelaide as she lay in bed upstairs in her room.

At 2.55am, Sandra woke up in her bed with a start for some unknown reason. She felt as if someone was in the room – some presence – near to her side of the bed (which was the left side), and she looked to her left but saw nothing but a moonlit wall and the shadows cast onto the wallpaper by the lattice of the window frame. Just as Sandra was bout to go to sleep, she heard a girl's voice – a strange voice she had never heard before. It was not coming from the neighbouring house. It seemed to be coming from Mary's room. Sandra gently poked Gerry's shoulder blade and he awoke and said 'What? What is it?'

'Gerry, listen – I can hear a girl's voice and it sounds

as if it's coming from Mary's room,' Sandra whispered. Gerry turned and saw his wife was sitting up as she looked at the door with a worried look. Her beautiful face looked so pallid in the moonlight reflected off the wall.

Gerry sat up, listened, and he too could hear the girl's voice. He thought the accent sounded like a cousin of his who lived in Cheshire. He got up out the bed and carefully turned the squeaky doorknob. He crept out onto the landing with Sandra walking cautiously behind him, and he halted outside Mary's door. He listened.

'And she will rot in Hell and her arse shall be roasted like a pig, Mary! Ha! And her eyes shall burst in the flames and her breasts will surely pop...' the girl with the Cheshire accent was saying.

Who the Hell was in there with Mary? Gerry and his wife wondered, and they lost no time in finding out.

Gerry turned the doorknob and threw his shoulder into the door. It burst open and they saw Mary sitting up in bed, and before her there was a grimy-looking girl of about eight years of age with long greasy locks of hair, and she wore a dirty robe that looked as if it was made of sack-cloth.

'Who are you?' Gerry cried out, and the girl turned to face him.

Her eyeballs were jet black with something golden in them. Her face was almost grey and had not a trace of colour in it. She rose from Mary's bed on skeletal legs and hissed at the girl's stunned parents like a snake that was poised to strike.

'Mam!' Mary shouted, and burst into tears. Liquid came down the child's nose as she became hysterical and her little face was awash with tears and mucous.

The weird girl in the begrimed robe with the ash-coloured face began to cuss and swear, and then she opened her mouth so that it became this huge elongated black hole that was much too large to be the mouth of a normal person. She was obviously some demonic creature. She started to howl with laughter as her face contorted and underwent terrifying changes. Sandra bravely raced past her to grab Mary, and as she did, the unearthly girl spat something vile at her but it missed and splattered on the old rug.

'Die you bastards!' the girl shouted as the parents fled from the room with a hysterical Mary.

As Gerry and Sandra ran into the parlour, Mary broke free and hid under the table, where she wet herself with fear. The ceiling sounded as if it was about to come through; Mary's room was directly over the parlour, and that evil thing was up there, screaming and throwing objects about. The terrifying goings-on ceased abruptly about a minute later – then came the sound of a creak on the stairs. Gerry and Sandra barricaded themselves in the parlour. They pushed a sofa across the doorway and sat tight, expecting the weird girl to make an attempt to get into the parlour, but she never did. Sandra eventually calmed down Mary and asked her what had happened, and the child said the girl had appeared at the side of the bed as Mary was looking at the moon after she had awakened. The girl had told Mary that the doll she had was not named Adelaide at all, but Spitooks, and that doll had belonged to the girl a long time ago before she was hanged.

None of this made sense, and as soon as Gerry

heard the milkman's cart arrive in Wordsworth Street, he felt brave enough to leave the parlour and open the front door to collect the milk. Gerry said nothing to the milkman, and after he had continued on his rounds, Sandra and Mary waited outside on the doorstep as Gerry got the coal hatchet from the cubby hole under the stairs and went straight up to Mary's room. The bed had been turned over, which must have taken some strength because the frame was an iron one and the mattress was also quite heavy. Comics, and several dolls were strewn across the floor, and a wardrobe had been toppled.

Something crunched under Gerry's shoe, and he looked down to see that he had stood on the old doll Adelaide. As that doll's torso cracked beneath his sole, Gerry thought he heard a distant scream. He picked up the doll and saw that it was hollow and not carved from solid wood at all. He took the doll downstairs and showed it to his wife, and she looked at it and noticed something was rattling about inside. It turned out to be a huge black unidentified insect. It was dehydrated and died a long time ago from the looks of it. A little scroll of fabric was also found in the doll, and in tiny print, written in something brown – possibly old dried blood – someone had scrawled:

*Aggie Seddon, I place this f\_\_\_g spell upon you to ensure that you never eat nor sleep nor rest and I hope your f\_\_\_g flesh and bowels waste away and I hope that you will never find love or spend a penny ever again and I wish this from my whole heart you whore, so may you enter beggary and may your c\_\_t wither. May your husband be banished from this country also, Amen.*

At the bottom of this obvious curse, someone had written the name 'Aggie Seddon' back to front and underlined it with unknown symbols. Gerry burnt the scroll and the doll in the grate, and the spine-chilling girl never returned to haunt the house on Wordsworth Street. I described the doll "Spitooks" to a man who valued antiques on a certain radio station and he told me that the doll had probably dated back to the 18th century. He told me that such dolls containing curses from the bad old days of witchcraft were frequently found in Lancashire and Cheshire. Just who the ghost was that had been attached to Spitooks is unknown. Surely she wasn't hanged, for she looked to be only eight years old – but you never know, as the Witchfinders of days gone by were known to be ruthless with those suspected of practising sorcery, and they even drowned women in their eighties, so perhaps they did indeed hang a child.

That concludes our survey of the 3am effect; should *you* find yourself aroused from your sleep in the third hour after midnight, then close your eyes tightly, say the Lord's Prayer, and try, as hard as you can, to return to the dreamworld of dear sleep – just in case something is waiting for you in your room...sweet dreams.

# CAST IRON SHAW

**It's odd how** some objects – and even people for that matter – seem to bring misfortune - or luck. The psychologist would say the idea of jinxed and lucky objects and people is nothing more than association fuelling superstition, and that we form such unfounded associations, when, for example, we notice how we have a win on the horses or luck at bingo when we wear a certain colour or item of clothing. And yet, in my files there are many strange stories filed under 'Jinxes and Talismans' which hint that the psychologists are not always right and that there are inexplicable forces at work in this universe. These forces seem to be channelled by certain people and inanimate objects we term as charms, and this brings us to a case related to me by a man named Bryan Shaw a few years ago. In 1964, 20-year-old Mr Shaw stole money from a caravan in North Wales, and subsequently discovered he had stolen from gypsies.

Not long afterwards, Shaw had a terrible long run of bad luck. His girlfriend left him for another man, he crashed his motorbike into a tree in Widnes, and then his mother died of a heart attack at the age of 42. Shaw got a job on a building site but fell from scaffolding and broke both legs. He went to live with his uncle at a house in Blackpool but it burned down days after he had moved in. Bryan Shaw felt he had been cursed by the gypsies and one day, an old Chinese man came into the pub Shaw was drinking in – The Grapes, Mathew Street – and he was selling lucky charms in the form of little red monkeys with a cigarette in their mouths. The Red Monkey would ward off bad luck and make its owner incredibly lucky. The Chinese elder sold one of the monkeys to Shaw and said, from now, he'd be "Cast Iron Shaw" because he'd survive anything life could throw at him – but – the old charm-seller advised Shaw to try and give the money he had stolen back to the gypsies because Romany curses were potent.

As soon as he came into possession of the Red Monkey, Shaw's luck and love-life went stratospheric, but he was despicable and kept five girlfriends on the go. He bought a taxi, but one day its brakes failed and he hit a coal wagon head on. The taxi was reduced to scrap, but "Cast Iron Shaw" crawled unscathed from the wreckage, clutching the Red Monkey. At a hotel in London, he got into a lift which plummeted five storeys, killing one man and injuring two other passengers, but Shaw sustained only mild concussion. Shaw felt that the Romany curse was still at work, but was too proud to return to North Wales to pay the thirty pounds he had stolen from the gypsies, and he thought that the caravan would have long moved on by now anyway, but the shadow of ill-fortune remained cast over the Liverpool thief, and bad luck struck regularly with increasing severity. Shaw drove to North Wales, and there was the gypsy caravan he had stolen from. He walked to it and went to knock, but the door opened and an old man with very dark piercing eyes held out his hand – as if he had been expecting Shaw. Shaw handed over the thirty pounds and left, but when he returned to Liverpool, he discovered that the Red Monkey charm had vanished, never to be seen again. The spell of bad luck ended not long after.

# THE DOPPELGÄNGERS

**In 2007**, a very strange story came my way concerning a couple who lived in Woolton. In January of that year, a couple in their thirties, Simon and Rebecca, decided to move from a rented flat in Woolton, just a stone's throw from Calderstones Park, to a flat that was practically across the road. The flat Simon and Rebecca moved into was much more modern, but finding the décor a bit dated, they started to decorate the new flat, and one evening around 10.40pm as Simon was wallpapering the lounge, he noticed something that really creeped him out. Rebecca was standing on a stepladder in front of the window, putting up new curtains on a pole, and as Simon looked past her, he noticed a light come on in the old flat facing, where he and his partner had lived for seven years. A very familiar figure appeared in the window of the old flat across the road – the silhouetted form of someone who looked exactly like Simon.

Rebecca noticed this figure too, and she turned from the window and looked at Simon with a quizzical expression to ask, 'See that?'

Simon gave two nods, smoothed the wallpaper down with a brush, and was so fascinated by the appearance of his 'double' he didn't smooth out the paper down to the skirting board, but left it hanging as he quickly descended from the aluminium ladder. He went to the window and looked across some hundred feet of space to the yellow rectangle of what would be the kitchen window in the old flat. The man there was either simply the spitting image of Simon or – it was his doppelganger. The 'twin' seemed to be in one of the dark blue tee shirts Simon often wore, and he could even make out the Nike swipe on the front of the shirt. It was very uncanny, but the night was to get even weirder because a female form came into view in the kitchen as Simon and Rebecca looked on in astonishment – and this girl looked just like Rebecca, only she had her hair down, and Rebecca usually wore her hair up unless she was going out for a night on the town.

'Jesus,' Rebecca whispered, 'she looks like me as well. Oh my God, isn't this weird?'

'Hang on a minute,' Simon went to get his Samsung camcorder which was packed away somewhere in one of the many boxes in the spare room. He found it but its battery was flat and he could not find the power adaptor to charge it, so Rebecca used her iPhone and zoomed in on the doppelgangers, but the figures just came out as blurred silhouettes. Simon went searching again and came back with his old 8x30 binoculars that he used for bird-watching and looking at the horses at the Grand National. He quickly uncapped them and trained them on the animated silhouettes facing, and his jaw dropped. Now he knew beyond a shadow of a doubt that he was looking at himself. The girl had walked away from the kitchen window and was out of view, but Simon swore and said, 'It's me; I don't believe it.'

'Giz a look!' Rebecca said and Simon handed him the binoculars, and for a few seconds she too saw her partner's replica in a navy blue Nike shirt as he was doing something – possibly making a sandwich – in the kitchen. And then he walked away from the window and the kitchen light went out. Simon looked at the kitchen again, and he could see the blue fluorescent alphanumerical display of the microwave oven he often used over there to heat up snacks all hours of the night, and to the right he could see the red indicator lamp of the water boiler switch burning. Simon's head swam with a confused flow of thoughts, all of them making vain attempts to rationalise what he had seen. Had a couple moved into the flat, and had each of them merely bore some resemblance to himself and Rebecca? It was a hackneyed claim, but perhaps light did play strange tricks of a night. Perhaps they only looked like him and his partner. But then he recalled the glimpse he'd had before of his double and he felt a sort of cold shudder inside, because deep down, Simon knew that something eerie was going on tonight.

He scanned the lounge window with the binoculars and thought he could see the faint luminance of a floor lamp exuding through the heavy curtains, but there was no further activity that night. On the following day as Simon made breakfast, Rebecca scanned the lounge window because she had seen with her unaided eyes that the curtains in the lounge had now been thrown open. Someone was definitely in her former flat. The binocular search revealed nothing, and as Rebecca took the binoculars from her eyes, she saw an indignant old woman glaring at her from one of the windows of the flats opposite. Rebecca guiltily turned away from the window, feeling like a voyeur. The incensed old woman drew her curtains in two dramatic tugs.

When the couple had returned from their respective jobs at around half-past five, it was already dark, and a hair-thin crescent moon, accompanied by the planet Venus, hung in the western January sky at chimney-top level. Simon was intrigued to see that the kitchen was illuminated in his old flat, and he went and grabbed the binoculars and inspected the kitchen with them, but saw no one about over there. The couple ordered from the local chippy and as Simon was eating his salt and pepper ribs he happened to glance over from the sofa to see that his twin was back in view in the kitchen, only this time he had on a very distinct Nirvana tee shirt, and this was a tee shirt that Simon no longer had. It had inexplicably gone missing a year and a half back, and Rebecca had told him that he had probably accidentally thrown it out with some old shirts when he had cleared out his wardrobe. Simon seized the binoculars, turned off the light and hurried to the window to do some reconnaissance on his uncanny alter ego. This time the kitchen window began to steam up as if something was being boiled on the stove over there, and it was very infuriating having such a distorted view of the man who seemed to be his living mirror image.

'Perhaps we should just go over and knock,' Rebecca seriously suggested, but the idea left Simon cold, but he wouldn't admit that he was a bit fearful of confronting the doubles. He shook his head and said, 'Nah; what would we say to them? "Oh, we just thought we'd call because we think you're our doppelgangers" – there's probably a rational explanation…'

'We could make out we are calling in case any mail for us has gone to our old address, Simon, people do that every day,' Rebecca told him, squinting as she looked through the window.

'I don't know – ' Simon said and seemed stuck for words.

'You're scared aren't you?' his partner asked with a faint smile on her lips and a twinkle of amusement in her large eyes.

'No, I'm not scared, but I'm cautious. You don't know what these things are – '

'Oh, like you said there's probably a rational explanation,' Rebecca sighed, and she went and sat down and picked some red and green peppers from Simon's portion of the ribs.

No further activity was seen for a while, but around half-past eleven, Simon got into bed and watched TV for a while, and Rebecca followed him not long afterwards. At midnight, she got up to go the toilet and she was gone for an inordinate amount of time, so Simon went and looked for her. He found her in the living room, standing there by the window in the dark, looking over at the flat with the binoculars. The kitchen over in the flat was lit up and the condensation on the windows there had cleared. As Simon walked towards Rebecca, the light went out in the kitchen, but still Rebecca kept watch on the doppelgangers. She had a feeling, a hunch, that she should still watch even though the kitchen was in darkness.

'Ah, come to bed, love,' said Simon, and yawned.

There was a sharp intake of breath from Rebecca, and then she softly swore. 'Simon!'

'What?' he asked with an air of great impatience.

'The two of them are just standing there in the kitchen in the dark, and they're looking right at us,' Rebecca informed him, and her hand trembled slightly as she quickly handed the binoculars to him.

'Shut up,' a doubting Simon replied, and he had a look for himself. He turned the focussing wheel on the binoculars and he could see the kitchen in darkness, but something – or someone – was blocking out the light of the luminous timer display on the microwave and the boiler indicator lamp. And then he saw the two very pale faces – the faces of a man who looked exactly like himself, and the woman next to him was a carbon copy of Rebecca. They were looking directly at Simon, who know swore and turned to Rebecca with a look of fear. Rebecca had never seen her boyfriend this afraid in all of the eight years she had known him.

'See?' she said, and Simon looked at the creepy watchers again, then drew the curtains.

'You don't think they'll come over here do you?' Rebecca enquired.

That very possibility had already crossed Simon's mind but he shook his head and said, 'No, no. Maybe we should stop looking over there from now on and keep the curtains closed.'

The couple went into the hallway and for the first time since they had moved into the new flat, Simon put the bolt on the door, and it was quite a task to do so, as the bolt was stiff because someone had painted over it. Simon sat up watching a DVD in bed as Rebecca huddled against him under the duvet. She kept asking, 'Do you think they might come over?' and Simon snapped at one point and shouted: 'I don't know! Will you shut up about it?'

And then he felt terrible at losing his cool because it was obvious now that Rebecca was really afraid of the weird doppelgangers. She would doze off then awake with a spasmodic jolt and grip Simon's arm, so you can imagine how she reacted when, at four that morning, she and Simon heard a noise in the hallway.

'Listen!' Rebecca's eyes bulged and she sat bolt upright in the bed. 'What's that?'

There was a squeaking sound in the hallway.

'The wind's blowing through the letterbox, that's all, 'Simon replied, trying his utmost to reassure her, but Rebecca's head was near to his chest and she could hear his heart palpitating.

Simon got up and opened the bedroom door. He looked down the pitch-black hallway towards the front door, and he could see without a doubt that someone was standing outside because their feet had broken the line of illumination at the bottom of the door. Rebecca's head came round his right arm and she peered at the door and noticed the shadow of the feet in the narrow line of light. 'Oh God! Someone's outside!'

The letterbox opened, and someone looked in.

Simon let out a stream of coarse swear-words, and then he asked: 'Who is that?'

There was no reply. The unknown person continued to watch him and a hysterical Rebecca.

'I've called the police! They're on their way!' Simon claimed, but it was all bluff of course; he hadn't had a chance to call the police yet.

The claim gave Rebecca an idea, and she darted back into her room and made her way for her iPhone – which was charging as it rested on the window ledge. Before she reached it, it emitted its ring tone, making the girl jump. She imagined her young brother Danny was calling, but when she looked, the name of the caller on the screen of her mobile said: 'Rebecca' – which made no sense of course. Rebecca answered and said, 'Hello?' but she heard nothing at all.

'Tell Danny to get off the phone and call the police!' Simon whispered, unaware what was happening.

Rebecca listened. Someone was either breathing faintly or it was the sound of the January wind blowing at the other end of that phone. Three times she asked, 'Who's that?' but no reply came. She hung up, intending to dial the police but the phone rang again and on the mobile's home screen, Rebecca saw her own name appear again.

'Phone the police!' Simon urged his partner.

'I can't, my name keeps coming up! Someone's phoning me named Rebecca!'

Simon took the phone off her and listened. He too heard the sound of breathing now. He went and got his own phone and as he was dialling 999, his mobile started to ring. The name of the caller appeared: it read 'Simon'. Someone was breathing heavy when he answered his mobile, and Simon kept asking the caller to identify himself.

Rebecca somehow managed to dial 999 and asked for the police. She gave a rambling account of the doppelgangers at first, then realised the operator would thing she was insane or on drugs if she gave a proper account of what was happening, so she said burglars were attempting to break into her flat and the operator took her address and assured her that the police would be there soon. Simon went back into the hallway and saw that the light shining from the communal hallway through that long gap under the door was now unbroken, as if the menacing caller had left. When the police arrived, Simon had to say that his girlfriend had made the call after suffering a realistic nightmare, and this explanation was not taken too kindly by the lawmen, and they left without saying a word of reply.

On the following morning, Simon telephoned his former landlord and asked him if anyone had moved into the flat he and Rebecca had moved out of, and the landlord said no one had taken up the residency there yet. Simon assured him he had seen people in the flat but the landlord said he had not even sent the decorators to the flat yet. He planned to paint the walls of the lounge and put wooden floors into each room first before re-letting it.

Simon and Rebecca were so spooked by the doppelgangers, they went to stay in a tiny spare room at Rebecca's mum's over in Dovecot till they found a flat off Lark Lane. They have no idea why they saw the mysterious doubles and Rebecca still has nightmares about the unfathomable goings-on at the Woolton flats. Many years ago, a man named Rory would come to my booksignings and tell me that his doppelganger was stalking him, and he would claim that the ominous entity was trying to get rid of him so it could take his place. Rory was always branded as a crank when he told me about the doppelganger stalking him. One security guard at a bookstore said he was potty, but I asked: 'What if he's telling the truth?'

One sunny day in 2009, I was walking down Hanover Street, when I saw Rory approach, and I expected him to recognise me and tell me once again that he was being hunted by his double, but when I said 'Hi Rory,' to him, he thinned his eyes, looked me up and down, and walked on without saying a word, and of course, a chilling thought came to mind: was he really Rory, or was it that doppelganger he often spoke of? I haven't set eyes on Rory since…

# COMMUNICATING ACROSS TIME

**When the radio pioneer** Marconi successfully sent signals from Cornwall to Newfoundland in December 1901, scientists were perplexed at his achievement because it was known that radio waves, like light waves, could only travel in a straight line, so how had Marconi's radio waves travelled 2,100 miles across the curvature of the Atlantic Ocean? The answer was found in 1922: this planet of ours is surrounded by the ionosphere - a spherical shell of ionized air made of layers that extend from 50 km to 1000 km, and certain radio waves are reflected by these mirrors in the sky. Radio hams using short-wave transceivers often use the ionosphere to talk to people thousands of miles away, and in 1973, at a house in Crosby, a very strange incident took place via a short-wave radio set. A 69-year-old bachelor named John Matlin became ill with pneumonia, and his cousin Douglas Farr looked after his house a few hours each day while Matlin recovered. On the first day house-sitting Doug went up into the attic and found his cousin's short-wave radio station, and knowing nothing about the protocols and etiquette of amateur broadcasting, he turned on the set, picked up the hand-held trigger-buttoned microphone and began to ask, 'Is anybody there?'

A distorted American female voice responded and mentioned codes that were unintelligible to Doug. The woman was named Betty-May and she was broadcasting from Fort Worth, Texas. Doug had never heard of the place. When Betty-May asked where Doug was broadcasting from he said: 'Liverpool,' but his reply was a bit garbled by the atmospherics, and other radio interference, so Betty-May said, 'Where, sorry? Over.'

'Where the Beatles came from,' Doug answered. There was a pause. Betty-May had not heard of the Beatles, and thought Doug was talking about insects.

Doug asked her about Texas and if her husband was a cowboy, and Betty-May laughed and said she was a widow. She'd just moved from Dallas after her husband's death in an effort to make a new life.

'Ah, I know Dallas,' quipped Doug, 'where President Kennedy was assassinated.'

After a pause punctuated by hisses of white noise and howls of interference, Betty-May said: 'President Kennedy hasn't been assassinated. You did say assassinated?'

'Yes, years ago, in 1963,' Doug imagined she'd misheard him, but her reply stunned him, because Betty-May said President Kennedy was alive and well. His curiosity piqued, Doug asked Betty-May what year it was, and she laughed and said: 'Is this a trick question?' Doug said it wasn't and the reply came: 'Its 1962 isn't it?'

Doug went cold when he was told this. That explained why Betty-May had not heard of the Beatles; they hadn't conquered England, never mind America back in 1962. 'Wait there Betty! Don't go away! Please stay there!' Doug ran downstairs to his wife and told her about the strange two-way conversation across a decade, but she just shrugged and seemed non-interested. 'Stupid yank,' was all Doug's wife managed to say.

Doug went through his cousin's bookshelf and found a tome about history, and he then rushed back to the attic and read parts of this book to Betty-May, who thought it was all some April Fool hoax at first. He told her about Kennedy's assassination in Dallas on November 22, 1963, and skimmed over the Cuban Missile Crisis before that, the long war in Vietnam and the Moon Landings, and the latter made Betty-May giggle. 'We've landed on the moon? Gee, how did they keep that one quiet?' Betty-May remarked and laughed.

'No, listen, Betty-May, there's something very strange going on here. I'm here in 1973, and you're eleven years back in time. I don't know how, but you are. Hello? Betty-May? Are you there?' Doug listened for a reply but none came. He'd lost contact with Betty-May. He tried for a week to get back in touch with her, and then, one evening at 9pm, an American male voice came across the short-wave radio; it was a sombre-sounding man with a deep voice who said he was from the FBI. 'We know you're broadcasting from Liverpool, England and we want to question you about comments you made about President Kennedy and several matters relating to national defence. We have already alerted Britain's intelligence service.

Please supply us with your full name and your address, or we will triangulate and find you anyway. Do you understand?'

Doug recoiled in total panic at the officious voice, and he switched off the set and lived in mortal fear of being arrested by FBI agents. He visited his cousin John Matlin at hospital and seeing he was now on the road to recovery, he confessed to messing about with his short-wave radio set and told him everything.

John was of the opinion that "Betty-May" had been some hoaxer, but Doug believed that he had not been the victim of some elaborate prank; he believed that, perhaps because of some unusual weather conditions or sunspot activity, the radio transmissions had somehow breached the time barrier, and that he really had conversed with a widow back in 1962.

'Okay, then,' John told his cousin, 'for the sake of argument, let's say you *did* have a two-way conversation with a woman back in 1962; how would the FBI of that period come and interrogate you? They're eleven years in the past. It's frigging balmy.'

'I don't know what to think,' Doug admitted, 'it's giving me a headache.'

'If what you say is true, they will now have advanced knowledge of the Cuban Missile Crisis, the Vietnam War, and, of course, they might take extra security precautions when Kennedy goes to Dallas – if they haven't cancelled the visit.'

Doug immersed his face into his palms then slid his hands down to his chin and with a perplexed look, he reasoned: 'But Kennedy died at Dallas – if I had changed history, we'd know about it by now – wouldn't we?'

'Check the history books when you get back to my place,' John suggested with a quirky smile, 'just to make sure nothing *was* changed.'

And as bizarre as it seems, John did. He read about the assassination in Dallas, and he visited his library in Crosby and read the entry for JFK in a biographical dictionary, and this entry concurred with what is common knowledge – that the 35th President of the United States was fired upon by either a single gunman or several assassins on Dealey Plaza, Dallas on 22 November 1963, and died as a result. Seeing the picture of Kennedy in the library book, Doug felt sad and also a bit guilty, for he wondered: if he really had talked to a woman back in 1962, he should have insisted on her telling the authorities to forewarn John Fitzgerald Kennedy of his awful fate that sunny November day in 1963. Had he lived, would the Vietnam War have ended much sooner or not happened at all? So many on both sides of that conflict might not have lost their lives had Kennedy lived.

As the years went by, Doug wondered if the whole thing had been a hoax, or whether two people, through some fluke of quantum mechanics, had been allowed to talk across a gulf of eleven years. Doug asked me what I thought, and I told him many stories reported to me over the years concerning mysteries of the electromagnetic spectrum – that fascinating range of radiations that vary from gamma rays, X-rays and ultraviolet radiation, to the seven colours of visible light, infra red and all the radio frequencies. People use ultraviolet light to tan their skin, and mobile phones, satellite TV and microwave ovens wouldn't work without radio frequencies, but what do we really know about this wide-ranging family of radiations? Well we know that sometimes, under conditions that are poorly understood at the moment, signals sent via frequencies in the electromagnetic spectrum act in very strange ways. We now know as a fact that photons, for example, can influence each other across vast distances instantaneously — even if they are light years apart — which seems to violate the laws of Relativity. Even more bizarre is the phenomenon first observed by the English physician and physicist Thomas Young in 1801. Young set up an experiment that seemed to prove that light is a wave. Isaac Newton believed light was made up of corpuscles, and his corpuscular theory of light held sway for quite some time, until Young demonstrated, via a rather simple experiment, that light behaved as a wave. Young shone a light at a screen that had two vertical slits in it, and these slits were separated by a short distance. On the other side of the screen, the light emerged from the parallel slits and produced an interference pattern make up of alternate bands of dark and light, which proved that light had behaved as a wave as it passed through the slits, and that the peaks and troughs of the waves had reinforced and also cancelled each other out on their way to the screen on which they were projected after being split by the slits. But then came a mystery that remains unsolved to this day, and the greatest minds in the world cannot explain it. Light is now known to consist of tiny particles called photons, and we have devices at our disposal which can register a single photon hitting a special type of screen. When we run the Thomas Young experiment again with the technology of today, something very spooky happens:

the experimenter actually affects the outcome of the experiment by changing the way he or she takes the measurements. If you allow the photons to reach the projection screen one at a time, an interference pattern always exists when you use two slits, but, if you place a photon detector to register the photons as they travel through each slit, something bizarre happens: you suddenly get two patches of light – one behind each slit – without an interference pattern. In other words you have altered the outcome of the experiment by acting upon a decision on just how to observe the results of the experiment. How can the choice of the experimenter's method of measuring something affect its outcome? No one knows, and the same phenomenon has been observed where electrons have been used instead of photons. Electrons have mass, unlike photons, and yet the same thing happens. Scientists have even used atoms (and on several occasions 60-atom fullerene molecules) but the results of the experiment are always the same. A scientist at Liverpool University told me many years ago how this experiment seems to shake the very foundations of physics and he also told me how it converted him to consider that ghosts and parallel words might exist. He said the photons making up light in the Thomas Young experiment seem to know what slits are open or blocked before they get there, which of course, would suggest that photons were not mere particles, but things which possessed intelligence. I urge the reader to look into the Thomas Young experiment and the modern interpretations of it on the free web-based encyclopaedia Wikipedia to see how far-reaching this concept is. Radio waves belong to the family of waves called the electromagnetic spectrum, and this family includes infrared radiation, visible light, ultraviolet light, X-rays and gamma rays, and, getting back to the mystery of the short-wave radio set that seemed to penetrate the 'time barrier', it's possible that some atmospheric or electrical phenomenon (such as sunspot activity or a disturbance in the Earth's magnetic field) might have diffracted, polarized or refracted the radio waves from the short-wave radio set so they were able to transcend the fourth dimension of time.

I have so many of these types of cases on my files. In June 2009, a 35-year-old man named Raymond who lived on Waresley Crescent, in the Sparrow Hall area of Liverpool (just off the East Lancs) received a DAB (Digital Audio Broadcasting) radio for his birthday from his Nan, Mary, and when Raymond switched on the new set that summer's day around 1pm, he browsed the numerous digital channels, but finding many of them were bad quality because of some local electrical interference, he switched the DAB to analogue FM and then the archaic medium wave mode, and he heard a news bulletin that made Mary's ears prick up, for she had not heard such a bulletin since the 1970s and 1980s and she recognised it immediately. The familiar news bulletin jingle went: 'One Nine Four – Radio City!' And then a female newscaster announced the time – nine o'clock (but whether this was morning or evening was never ascertained) and then she said: 'This is Ruby Williams.' Mary instantly recalled that the news bulletin jingle was in use in the 1970s and 1980s back when Radio City broadcast on the 194 meters medium wave band, and

Raymond's grandmother recalled that one of the news presenters had indeed been one Ruby Williams. It was initially natural for Raymond's Nan to assume that her grandson had tuned in to some nostalgia programme, but it eventually became obvious that this wasn't so, and as Mary listened in, she deduced that Ruby Williams was reporting on the news events of 1981 because there were several references to the riots in Toxteth and Brixton. A third witness, Raymond's friend Brian Atkinson, also heard the backdated broadcast when he called around to the house. The broadcast continued until about 7.50pm, and then faded away into white noise, never to be heard again.

In *Haunted Liverpool 10* I related the uncanny account of Billy Wilson, an Aigburth man who once worked as a radio dispatcher for Merseycabs, a well-known taxi firm in Liverpool. At five o'clock one morning, Billy was intrigued to hear a rather familiar voice coming through the speakers of his radio transceiver – it was his own voice, and he was saying: 'Who's the next cab on the Kingsley Road stand?' and 'Who's on Penny Lane?' and so on – and an hour later, the complete list of jobs came up on his computer screen, in the exact order his phantom double voice had recited them earlier on, which naturally unnerved Billy. Like the previous cases mentioned in this chapter, it would seem that sometimes, radio waves can somehow – like the hypothetical tachyon particle – travel backwards in time. In Billy's case, he somehow broadcast to himself one hour into the past. It's possible that some so-called Electronic Voice Phenomena (known as EVP) may actually be broadcast from somewhere along the timeline – either the past or the future.

Could we one day broadcast messages into the past and future? Well, in a way we already have. All of the television and radio broadcasts and various radar signals emitted from military have, over the years, travelled light years away from earth into space, and if there are aliens technologically advanced enough within a fifty light years radius of us, they could now be picking up episodes of Coronation Street and other programmes from the dawn of the 1960s. technically then, this earth is broadcasting a shell of radio and television signals decades into the future, when they could possibly be picked up by any civilization that has evolved enough to develop electronics, and the opposite is true: radio astronomers regularly pick up signals from quasars millions of light years away that first began to be transmitted when dinosaurs ruled the earth – but what about an electronic device that could say, allow you to 'leak' the lottery numbers to your past self? Now that got your attention didn't it? Well, the answer is, such a transmitter is feasible, and without a doubt it would be used and abused, not only by greedy people wanting to know next week's lottery numbers and horseracing results, but also by the military chiefs of this world, because to be forewarned is to be forearmed – and any country that knows the future moves of its enemy will obviously be at a great advantage, especially in a theatre of war. How would one make such a cross-time transmitter? Well, what we would need is a four-dimensional crystal and a rather simple walkie-talkie type of circuit. Present quartz crystals, used in computers and various other electronic devices to act as a finely-tuned timer, are three dimensional like you and me; but to be able to broadcast through time we would need a four-dimensional one. The fourth dimension is, of course time; we use three coordinates to specify where a person or thing is in this world (and your SatNav system uses these coordinates) but we also have to know when a person or thing is, and this fourth coordinate relates to time. Just to clarify, I can specify where you are if say, you're in Liverpool City Centre by your longitude and latitude, together with your elevation (because you could be down a sewer or up in the police helicopter). To get a clearer picture, I have to know your fourth coordinate – so I know you are in the city centre at say, 10pm. We can move backwards and forwards (first dimension), and side to side (second dimension), and up and down (third dimension). All these three dimensions of space are at right angles to one another, but the other dimension is the fourth one, and that's the time dimension, and its very hard to visualise, but the mathematicians have all of the equations to deal with this dimension. Our transceiver to have a two-way conversation with people in the past would, as I have said, consist of a fairly simple device made from a walkie-talkie circuit board, a speaker and microphone, and a four-dimensional crystal. In the January 21-27 2012 edition of the much-respected *NewScientist* magazine, there is a very interesting article about Nobel laureate Frank Wilczek, a theoretical physicist at the Massachusetts Institute of Technology who is working on the construction of a four-dimensional crystal to be used in a computer which could store massive amounts of information and withstand any cataclysm – even the Heat Death of the Universe – a future time, many billions of billions of years in the future when the expanding universe will run down due to entropy – a truly pessimistic time when all energy will be lost. Wilczek believes if a four-dimensional crystal was created, all of mankind's achievements could be saved from the Heat Death of the Universe by storing all of the accumulated data of humanity's technology in a dimension that would not be affected by the catastrophic end of the universe. It's a bizarre idea but Wilczek has – perhaps unknowingly – provided us with a technological way to create a cross-time radio. We would need, according to the Nobel laureate, a superconductor material which would have a lattice of atoms whose electrons travel in the lowest energy states with a rotating charge, and this would give the superconducting crystal the same symmetry as a four-dimensional one. The electrons in our time crystal will not travel in a line as they do in a three-dimensional one, but instead they will travel in a loop – and this continual loop is the only kind of perpetual motion allowed by the Laws of Thermodynamics because the material is a superconductor. Superconductivity is an amazing increase in the electrical conductivity of a material when its frozen to almost absolute zero – the lowest temperature theoretically possible – minus 273.15 degrees Centigrade (also known as zero zelvin). The four-dimensional crystal will, in my humble opinion, open up the door to communicating across time, and although it seems a bit hypothetical at the moment, we should remember that most of the things we use today, from microwave ovens to the internet, all began as hypothetical concepts. Of course, if you could phone the mobile phone you had ten years ago to talk to your past self, what would you have to say? Would you issue a warning, give the lottery results to yourself perhaps? One day you might receive a telephone call from someone with a chillingly familiar voice…

# VISITING HOURS

**Julie McSharry clearly recalls** the following strange episode as if it occurred only yesterday. It was a Saturday, the last day of April, 1966, around 8.20pm. Her husband Richard wanted to watch the *Norman Vaughan Show* on BBC 1 and Julie wanted to watch Kenneth More in a new drama serial called *Lord Raingo* on BBC 2, and so they had a full-blown row which ended abruptly when 27-year-old Julie suddenly doubled up with sharp shooting pains in her abdomen. She curled up into a foetal position on the sofa and Richard asked her if she had wind. Julie swore and told him to get an ambulance. She thought she had appendicitis – and she was right. Richard used the neighbour's telephone and in no time, Julie found herself in the Royal Infirmary on Pembroke Place, where her condition worsened and she fainted from the agonising pain. When she awoke, some time after the operation, she found herself in a darkened hospital ward. She asked for Richard and the night nurse appeared at the bedside and assured Julie she'd see him first thing in the morning, and advised her to rest. The general anaesthetic use for the appendectomy had disoriented Julie, and she asked the nurse what time it was. 'Three in the morning,' said the nurse softly, so as not to wake the other patients, 'Now try and sleep Julie.'

Julie dozed off, feeling quite poorly, but was awakened some time later by a hand which grabbed hers. It was Julie's grandmother, Esther.

'Gran, what are you doing here? Its night-time,' Julie gasped, confused but overjoyed at seeing her beloved grandmother.

Esther smiled and said, 'Well this is my visiting hours love; are you alright? It came on all of a sudden, didn't it?'

'Yes, Gran, I was in agony, and I still feel ill. Have you seen Richard?' Julie asked, and Esther smiled faintly and nodded as she gripped her grand-daughter's hand. Then, as her mind slowly cleared, Julie realised something – her grandmother had died three years ago. She quickly withdrew her hand from what could only be a ghost.

'Don't be scared love, it's only me,' said Esther's apparition, and suddenly, a crowd of people gathered around the bed. One was a tall military man in a green uniform, and the others were a young man with a Beatles hairstyle, a lady with a bandaged head, a blonde girl in her twenties with a heavily bruised face, a schoolgirl with bandaged wrists, and a man in a trilby, just visible over the military man's shoulder. 'Don't look at them, Julie,' said Esther, but Julie looked at her night-time visitors in shock because they all had the same ink-black staring eyes and pallid complexion – as if they were all dead. 'You'll be coming with us soon, missus,' said the youth with the Beatles haircut, and the schoolgirl with the bandaged wrists threw her hands up to her face and exclaimed: 'Oh! Is she joining us soon? Oh, I can't wait!'

The military man leaned forward, looked into Julie's terrified eyes and in a monotone voice, said: 'I'm Captain Johnson. Pleased to meet you Mrs McSharry. We'll have you out of this bed soon.'

'Leave her alone!' Julie's grandmother screamed, and she swung her hand at the ghastly-looking entities - and the figures hovered away from the bed, back into the darkness, but they returned several times, repeatedly asking Julie to come into their world - until the light of dawn crept through the windows. As dawn broke, Julie's grandmother kissed her, then vanished with the six menacing visitors. Julie told the doctors and the nurses what happened, but they told her she'd dreamt the scenario because of the effects of the anaesthetic. However, one elderly patient in the next bed said he had also seen the ghosts several nights before while he was recovering from a serious operation, and he distinctly remembered the girl with the bandaged wrists and the military captain.

Julie was discharged a day later, and she got her husband to buy some flowers and put them on her Gran's grave in Yewtree Cemetery, as she felt Esther had prevented the sinister 'visitors' from taking her before her time. Julie also said a number of prayers each night for her grandmother. Perhaps the night visitors were the ghosts of the various people who had died in that hospital, and maybe they wanted Julie - who was quite ill at the time as she recovered from an operation – to join their ranks.

# MORE WEREWOLF REPORTS

**Over and over again** I have heard of the same alleged incidents which the modern sociologist would no doubt brand as an "urban legend" – but in my own experience I have often found that the stories told to me by readers which seem the most far-fetched are often the ones that have the most truth in them, even when the truth cannot be explained by present science. I have in my files, nine accounts of a werewolf-like creature seen in the Edge Hill and Speke areas of Liverpool in the 1970s and 1980s, and in some of the accounts the animal – or whatever it is – has attacked young people, and even injured them. I was at a book-signing many years ago at the old branch of WH Smith which stood on Church Street, when Dawn, a woman in her thirties, asked me if I had ever heard of any reports of a creature resembling a werewolf near Crown Street, which I know well because I am from the Myrtle Street area. I told Dawn I had (at the time) about three accounts, all in letter form, from readers and listeners to my slot on the radio, and the letters all mentioned a weird hairy creature which walked on all fours and sometimes on its hind legs as it prowled the old coal yards of Crown Street. A priest waiting to have his book signed chortled when he overheard the mention of the werewolf, but I told Dawn to continue. The priest stepped forward, interrupting Dawn, and enthusiastically said that he knew Crown Street well, and that the so-called werewolf was probably a huge Alsatian dog that had guarded a scrap-metal yard which once adjoined the coal yards. Dawn shook her head and said, 'No, this was no dog, this thing was huge, and I actually saw it walk on two legs – just like a man – and my best friend Marie actually saw a man turn into this thing.'

'Oh come on,' said the priest, and he beamed such a grin and shook his head. 'There's no such thing as werewolves,' and he looked at me and said, 'but no doubt you'll say there was one.'

To the holy sceptic I replied: 'I personally haven't seen a werewolf on Crown Street but I have researched these creatures and there has to be something behind the reports, because I have even heard from such trained observers as policemen – and even a pilot at Speke Airport [nowadays John Lennon Airport] saying they have encountered them.'

'Yes, but you've got to admit it's a bit far-fetched – ' the priest continued.

'Perhaps to some, but then couldn't people say the same about the stories of the Bible?' I asked. 'Some may find the idea of Jonah living in the belly of a whale, or of forty-two young people torn apart by two she-bears because they insulted Elisha, or a pair of all of the world's creatures being carried on board Noah's Ark – '

The priest stopped smiling and shrugged. 'I get the point,' he said, then added, 'I'm not into all this by the way,' and he nodded to the three *Haunted Liverpool* books he was holding, 'I'm just getting these for my nephew.'

Dawn's face had turned bright red by now, but she continued with her story. She told me how, one summer night in 1974, she had been a 13-year-old girl from Myrtle House - a tenement block in Edge Hill – and that summer she had developed a crush on a boy named Stephen, who happened to be a dead-ringer of the heartthrob pop-singer David Cassidy. Stephen lived on nearby Smithdown Lane, and Dawn began to see him. Nothing serious – they just kissed now and then and mostly roamed the streets, just talking. On this particular night, around twenty minutes to twelve, Dawn had parted company with Stephen near the Matlock public house on Grinfield Street, and with her head full of the sweet nothings the boy had whispered in her ear all night, Dawn set off home, unaware that her mother and father and two brothers had gone in search for her because she was supposed to be home at ten. The girl walked up a stretch of Crown Street which was almost pitch black because a young hooligan in the area had put out the street lights with an air pistol. A car approached, coming up the long street, which was still cobbled in 1974, and slowed as it passed Dawn. Dawn was convinced someone in this car was about to kidnap her, and she walked close to the walls and gates of a scrap yard. She was too scared to even glance at the slow car, but it picked up speed and drove on into the night. Its likely that the driver was a kerb-crawler because that part of Crown Street was often frequented by prostitutes in the evenings. As Dawn walked along, she heard what she could only describe to me as a moaning sound, and it was coming from beyond the railings of a gate leading to a scrap yard. Dawn's eyes adjusted to the low light and she could see a man lying on the floor in the yard about twenty feet from the gate. He looked as if he'd collapsed, and Dawn was just about to ask him if he was okay, when something took place which still sends a shiver down her spine today whenever she thinks or talks about the weird thing she witnessed. The man was lying face down, but he suddenly threw his arms out and reached forward, and simultaneously stretched out his legs. His posture was like that of a man leaping off a diving board, only he was lying flat on the cobbles of the yard. The man's body arched as Dawn looked on in bewilderment that was turning to horror. It was as if someone above the man was tugging on some rope that had been tied around his waist. His back rose and the man was now on all fours, and by the faint light of one distant sodium lamp post on Grinfield Street that was shining over the wall of the scrap yard, Dawn saw the silhouetted profile of the man's face – his prominent forehead and long curved nose, change before her eyes. The head seemed to inflate like an elongated balloon as the head metamorphosed into a head of some animal with a long snout, and as this terrifying transformation took place, the entity made a gurgling and choking sound, and spit spurted from its mouth. Dawn turned to run, and as she did, she heard a loud growl behind her to her left – where the man had changed into some ghastly-looking animal. The gates of the yard resounded with a loud clang, as if something had struck them, and then something began to shake them violently, and Dawn knew it was the thing that had changed before her eyes. She found herself fighting to breathe as she ran along, and her legs became weaker. She had covered about forty to fifty feet when she heard the stomach-churning sounds of the man-beast following her at some speed. She could hear the snarls and the clatter of claws on the cobbles as the thing tore after her. Dawn was that scared she began to wet herself. A little mongrel dog nicknamed Sandy, which Dawn often saw in nearby Myrtle Gardens, came trotting towards her, but then the animal stopped dead and its ears dropped flat against its head with fear as it saw the thing that was chasing Dawn, and it yelped, turned around and raced off. Car headlamps came speeding around the bend from the south of Crown Street, and Dawn waved her arms madly at the approaching vehicle. The Ford Cortina screeched to a halt, and had to swerve, otherwise Dawn would have been mown down. The driver got out of the vehicle and Dawn could see he was a black man in his twenties with a huge Afro cut, and he swore at her and called her an idiot. 'What are you playing at you stupid – ' he was saying, when he heard a loud growling to his right. Dawn got behind him as he stared at the thing in disbelief. The motorist thought it was something that had escaped from a zoo. It looked like a cross between a Great Dane, except that the body was surreally much too long, and the head was like that of a wolf. The eyes seemed to be bright yellow, but this was possibly the headlamps of the Cortina reflected by the unknown animal's eyes. The black man swore and asked Dawn what the creature was as he edged back towards his car. Dawn was that afraid, she did something she normally wouldn't do: she ran into the car of the total stranger and hid in the back seat. The driver returned to his vehicle and as soon as he slammed the door, the thing bounded towards him. It jumped onto the bonnet, snapped a huge pair of jaws at him as it looked at him through the windscreen. The thing showered the windscreen with spit as it emitted a deafening bark. The driver sounded the horn, and the thing calmly urinated on the vehicle, before jumped off the Cortina – and as it did, the car rocked on its suspension. As the huge long animal sloped off back into the darkness, the Cortina went into reverse and almost hit another car coming up Myrtle Street. Throughout the journey to the driver's home in the Low Hill area, he constantly asked Dawn: 'What was that thing?' as if the schoolgirl should know. Dawn was dropped off near the Coach and Horses pub on Low Hill, and she had to go home the long way round, avoiding Crown Street in case she met the thing again. She reached home around 1.15am that morning and her parents and brothers went berserk when she returned. When they calmed down a bit, Dawn told them what she had seen and no one believed her. She fell asleep around three that morning and had several nightmares about the 'werewolf', and on the following morning, she was visited by her best friend Marie, who lived in the Paddington area. Before Dawn could even utter a word about the trauma she had experienced the night before, Marie took the wind out of her sails by saying:

'I saw a man turn into a werewolf last night.'

'Have you been talking to me mum and dad or me brothers?' Dawn naturally wanted to know.

'No, why?' Marie returned a question to answer a question.

'You sure?' Dawn muttered. 'Well I also saw – '

'Last night Dawn, around half-past ten, I swear to God – I swear on our Joey's life [and Joey was her 6-year-old brother], I saw a man change into a werewolf.'

Marie's face seemed to turn pale as gave the details of the strange incident, and Dawn had known Marie long enough to know when she was telling the truth. Moreover, a nervous tic flickered in Marie's cheek as she told her friend how she had been walking up that shadowy stretch of Mount Vernon View, which, in 1974, ran from the Mobil Service Station up an incline to the Lybro building. Marie had been hoping she'd bump into a lad she liked who lived in that area, but instead, she noticed a foreign-looking man in his early forties in a light coloured tee shirt and flared jeans, and he was sitting on the floor of an alleyway just a little past the Mobil Service Station. He was leaning against a wall as he sat there, as if he had perhaps fallen down drunk at that spot. The alleyway was badly lit but Marie could see that the man seemed to be in distress. He was groaning and held his hand over his face. As Marie slowed down and watched the man, she saw his body stretch and become deformed. His face bulged out first, his nose and mouth stretching into what looked just like the snout of a dog, and his ears became elongated and pointy a moment after this startling transformation. Just before Marie ran off, she saw the man's arms stretch and become darker. The girl's legs felt weak beneath her as she tried to run up Mount Vernon View towards a friend's house in Kensington. She heard a car horn beeping frantically behind her, and when she looked back, she saw something half-way between a man and an animal on all fours, caught in the headlamps of a slow car, as it crossed the road near the Mobil Service Station. This thing ran towards the other side of the road, near to Paddington Comprehensive School. Marie didn't look back after that – she ran all the way to her friend Carol's house on Hall Lane.

Marie expected Dawn to disbelieve the story of the man changing into an animal, but then Dawn told her about her own unexplainable experience on Crown Street, and at first, Marie thought she was just telling lies to scare her, so Dawn called for her mother and asked her what she had claimed to have seen the night before.

'Oh, the werewolf nonsense – ' Dawn's mum replied in a dismissive way, and Marie felt her blood run cold in her veins.

That day, Dawn's boyfriend Stephen went to stay with his cousin in Betws-y-Coed for a few days, and knowing how much she'd miss him, she asked Marie to stay over at hers for two days. On the first night during the sleepover, something terrifying took place. The time was around half-past two in the morning when Marie was awakened by a strange sound. She realised she was sleeping top-tail in Dawn's bed, and, getting her bearings, she looked towards the window. The curtains were drawn, and the light from a lamp post on Crown Street was shining onto them. The sound that had awakened Marie was heard again, and it was definitely coming from the street below. Marie got out the bed, bleary-eyed, and groggily crept to the curtains. She gently pushed one of the curtains aside and saw nobody in the street below. Straight ahead she could see the old coal yards and the dark arches of a railway tunnel, but not a soul was about on the pavements and not even a vehicle passed on the wide road at this ungodly hour. Marie then glanced down – and what she saw made her sick with fear. At first she thought it was a huge dog, but then she saw that its head was set on the body of a human being, and that body was covered in grey fur. The body was impossibly stretched so that the torso looked as if it was twice the length of a normal human trunk. This abomination crouched, and then bounded upwards, towards the window where the frightened girl was rooted to the spot, paralysed with fear. The thing seemed to reach within just a few feet of the window sill before it dropped down, landing on all fours. The hands of the beast were claws, and the fingers were long, and the thumbs, protruding at right angles, looked grotesque. Marie let out an ear-splitting scream that woke Dawn, her family, and several of the neighbours. Dawn sprung up in the bed, and saw Marie fly from the window towards the light switch.

'What's wrong?' Dawn cried, and hoped that her friend had just had a nightmare and nothing more, but Marie ran into the hallway, and was there met by Dawn's mother, father and two brothers.

'That werewolf's trying to get in the bedroom!' Marie screamed, and threw herself at Dawn's mother, who held the hysterical girl.

'What?' said one of Dawn's brothers with a quizzical

smile on his face, while the other brother shook his head condescendingly at their guest.

Dawn's father barged into his daughter's bedroom and spotted Dawn at the window. She was peeping through the curtains at something in the street.

'What are you two playing at, waking everyone up?' he said, but Dawn didn't even turn around, and when her father's hand landed on her shoulder, she said to him: 'Marie's telling the truth, Dad! Look for yourself!'

The girl's father almost tore the curtains down pulling them aside. He looked out the window – and there was a silhouette of a bizarre animal running across the cobbles of Crown Street, into the shadowy area just beyond the illuminated disc of light from a mercury vapour lamp. Dawn's father swore in shock, and said, 'What the hell's that?'

He gripped the handle of the window, turned it and opened it, then looked out into the night-time street, but by now the thing had gone. 'Was that a dog?' he muttered to himself, then decided: 'No, too big to have been a dog.' He turned to look at Dawn, and noticed she was trembling.

He closed the window and said to his daughter: 'Keep this window closed, and keep away from it, have you got that? Stay away from this window?'

'What did you see?' his wife asked, but never received a reply.

They all eventually went back to bed, but Dawn and Marie hardly got a wink of sleep. They hugged one another through the remainder of the morning, and not surprisingly, on the following night, Marie said she didn't want to sleep over at Dawn's, so Dawn slept at her house instead.

Weeks went by, and Dawn and her friend saw no more of the strange creature, but one afternoon, Dawn overheard her father say that he had heard from a policeman that "that thing" had been seen by prostitutes at the other end of Crown Street, close to a building site where the new Royal Hospital was being built. Dawn heard her mother say that the thing had to be a big dog, and that people were exaggerating its size, but her husband said it was like no dog that he had ever seen. A few weeks after this, a bizarre rumour circulated the neighbourhood that was like something out of a Hammer House of Horror film – several people swore they had seen a Turkish shopkeeper turn into the creature after going suspiciously into bushes on the university campus on Oxford Street. Witnesses had even found his clothes in the bushes after the occult transformation. It was said that another Turk had gone out trying to kill his countryman with a pistol because the 'werewolf' had left a trail of havoc and murder back in Turkey. The werewolf was said to go after girls, especially virgins. The scare eventually died down, and for almost a year, Dawn and Marie would not go out at night unless they were with a gang of friends, and they kept well away from Crown Street.

I told Dawn that in 1975, a woman who I will call Rita (not her real name) was just nineteen and working as a prostitute on Crown Street. At around 1.30am one cold October morning, Rita was standing at the edge of the kerb, waiting for a potential client to pass by in a car when something struck her from behind and threw her into the road. The impact left Rita winded, and she was about to attempt to get up when something seized her ankles and dragged her across the road with such ferocity, her buttocks scraped against the tarmac, causing lacerations. Unable to scream because she couldn't recover her breath, the young prostitute expected her powerful abductor to rape and kill her. As the thing pulled her onto the pavement, the back of her head caught the corner of the kerbstone and almost knocked her out. She tried to get up again but was pulled through a bush onto some wasteland, and here, what felt like razor sharp claws tore through her coat and blouse, scratching her breasts and abdomen. And then the silhouette of the violent assailant leaned over her, and at first, Rita thought it was a German shepherd belonging to the attacker. The animal's face was contorted with pure anger, and its teeth looked huge. 'Mum!' Rita yelped, ready to pass out in shock, and reflexively put her hands out to shield her face, when she heard a screech of tyres. The beast then growled and made a high-pitched sound as it ran off, and two men came to the prostitute's aid. They helped her up, and they looked as shocked as her, for neither of the men, who were middle-aged, could say a word until they got Rita into the back seat of the car, when one of the Samaritans said, 'I don't know what the hell that was that just attacked you love,'

And Rita burst into tears. She was taken to hospital and treated for her injuries and kept in for observation on account of the wound to the back of her head which needed six stitches. The medical men could not accept that some wild animal in urban Liverpool had dragged the teenager across a road, even though the two men who came to her aid vouched for the girl's story. Rita told no one about this incident for years, until she heard me on the radio, talking about the strange reports of werewolf-like creatures in Liverpool.

From around 1982 onwards, a being very similar to the Crown Street Werewolf has been seen in around Speke and the neighbouring area of Halewood. The creature seems to be a human-animal hybrid, as sometimes it walks upright and on other occasions it moves about on all fours. To complicate matters somewhat, I also have a collection of wolf reports from around Halewood that seem to be a classic out-of-place animal or OOPA's as some cryptozoologists like to name them. For example, one blustery night around 11.15pm in March 1982, a man named Frank Heaton was driving along Lower Road from Hale Bank to Halewood, and somewhere between Brook House Farm and Ireland's Farm, Mr Heaton almost collided with what he initially took to be a large dog which passed through the headlamp beams of his car. He slowed down, but saw no sign of the fleeting animal, and drove on, but upon checking his rear view mirror he was amazed to see a huge animal running at a phenomenal speed after his vehicle. It was not a dog, nor a fox, but looked just like a wolf, only much larger, even bigger than a Great Dane. Sensing there was something malevolent about the weird creature, Heaton stepped on the accelerator, but curiosity got the better of him and he decreased his speed just to get a better look at the strange animal without allowing it to catch up. As he took alternate glances at the road ahead and then into the rear-view mirror, he wondered if some dangerous animal had escaped from a zoo or even some travelling circus, but then all of a sudden, the "wolf" halted, and stood up on its hind legs. This was naturally a shock to Mr Heaton, and he decelerated the car to about 5 miles per hour to get a proper look at the unearthly animal. The creature seemed to realise he had slowed down and it suddenly fell back onto all fours and came belting after Heaton's car – and he stalled. The engine had been acting up of late, and Heaton felt his heart pound as he tried to start the car; of all the times for the engine to conk out. He put the gears into neutral and impatiently turned the ignition key again – and the animal was now about fifty feet away. Heaton didn't know whether to wind up his window or try the ignition again. He decided on the latter, swore softly as sweat broke out on his forehead, and the engine juddered, then roared, but just before the Cortina lurched forwards, Frank Heaton felt something slam into the back of his car which such a force, he was thrown back into the seat and almost suffered whiplash injuries. It was the unidentified creature; it had pounded what looked more like hands than paws on the boot of the vehicle. Heaton jammed his foot down hard on the accelerator and put as much distance as he could between himself and the powerful humanoid-like animal. Mr Heaton never again dared to drive down Lower Road and had no wish to know what the thing was that had rammed itself into the back of his car. A priest we shall call Father Reynolds once contacted me to tell me of a chilling encounter with a werewolf-like being at Speke in February 1984. Father Reynolds had just paid a visit to an elderly woman on Dam Wood Road who had lost her best friend to a long illness. He usually only stayed half an hour to an hour in such visits to comfort his parishioners, but seeing how distraught the old woman was, he stayed with her for over two hours, and left her home around 10.40pm to get into his car. He waved to the pensioner, who was silhouetted in her window, and she waved back as the priest moved off down Dam Wood Road in his car. Upon reaching the junction at Little Heath Road, Father Reynolds noticed what he initially took to be the silhouette of a tall person crossing the playing fields to his right. There was a full moon shining down from a sky devoid of any cloud upon this chilly night, and the priest could clearly see the shadow of someone walking quickly across the playing fields, but then, as the priest turned his car into Little Heath Road, he saw that the figure had inexplicably vanished. It had been there seconds ago, and now he couldn't see anyone on this cold February night. Father Reynolds drove on up the road, intending to go along Millwood Road East, and then onto Speke Boulevard, which would take him home, but all of a sudden, the car began to shake, and the priest, to his utter horror, not only felt something moving about on the roof of his vehicle, he saw a bulge in the roof of the car as if something was pressing down from outside – then three long hairy fingers slid down from the roof and came into view at the stop of the windscreen. Father Reynolds performed an emergency stop, and the thing on the roof was thrown onto his bonnet, propelled with the sheer momentum from braking so hard. It was a man – or at least it looked like a man, quite naked, covered in a coat of ash-grey hair that Father Reynolds compared to the coat of a Keeshond, a Dutch breed of dog the priest's uncle once bred. The hairy figure rolled in front of the braking car and landed on the tar macadam. It then got up and ran at an incredible speed up Little Heath Road as the priest sat in the car gazing at the creature in disbelief through the windscreen. The thing halted at one point on the moonlit road, and glanced back for a moment before continuing on its way. It vanished around the corner onto Alder Wood Avenue, and Father Reynolds slowly drove towards that corner, where he expected to see that hairy man again, but he never did. The priest estimated the figure was over six feet in height, and recalled how it seemed to move in an unnatural jerky way. Could it have been someone dressed up in some sort of 'ape man costume', playing a prank? Father Reynolds was certain beyond a shadow of a doubt that no such extreme hoax had taken place that night, for the figure looked too real, and the way it must have sprung onto the roof of the car from the playing fields – which were over thirty feet away – puts this mysterious figure in the same league as the legendary bogeyman Spring-Heeled Jack. When I mentioned this incident on the radio one afternoon during my slot discussing various local mysteries, I was contacted by several resident in Speke and one in Halewood, and all of them said they had seen the 'hairy man', but none of them were as close as Father Reynolds when they saw the figure. The sightings covered March 1984 to June 1985 and one man named Geoff, who had been an ambulance driver at the time, told me how he saw a man covered in grey hair with a face that looked like the classic werewolf creatures depicted in the old Hammer Films. Geoff was walking his dog along Hillfoot Avenue around 11.50pm one May night in 1985 when he saw the strange creature perched on the almost horizontal branch of a tree. Geoff stopped dead, and turned around and walked straight home, and throughout the return journey the ambulance man could hear growls as if the thing was following him. On the following night, Geoff and a friend went out looking for the creature with torches but never saw it again. This unidentified beast, whatever it was, seems to have been the same one that attacked two girls the previous month in the same area. In 2010 I received a letter from Jayne McCallister, a 30-year-old Melling woman who was a 5-year-old girl living in Speke back in 1985. Jayne clearly recalls a nightmarish incident from that time when she was a child living at her home on Speke's Oldbridge Road. On the night of the incident, she had been put to bed on a warm summer evening around 8.30pm, and finding the room too warm, little Jayne had somehow managed to open the bedroom window to let some cool air in. The child then sat up in her bed, and noticed the full moon through her bedroom window. All of a sudden, a huge hairy hand with unearthly long fingers reached in through the open window and groped about the window ledge. Jayne froze in absolute terror. Then another hairy hand came in through the window at the end of a long grey arm matted with hair as thick as that of Jayne's beloved dog, Max, a Cairn terrier. But then the fearsome head of the hirsute horror came through that window, and Jayne screamed. She could plainly see that this was not an animal, but a man of some sort. The eyes and face were like those of a smiling man, but the nose was like the snout of a dog, and when the mouth opened, the little girl could see long, very white and pointed teeth. As the entity tried to get into the room, Jayne ran to the door, opened it, and ran straight into her mother, who had come to see what the scream was about. Jayne bounced off her mother's legs and fell to the floor. She pointed to her bedroom door and burst into tears. The child's mother picked her daughter up, and asked what the matter was as she tried to take her back into the bedroom, but Jayne and her mum heard a loud growling noise come from inside the room, and this naturally alarmed the mother to such an extent, she ran down the stairs with Jayne in her arms and alerted her husband to what she imagined to be a large dog up in that room. Jayne's father went up into the room and saw nothing, but the window was wide open and someone – or something – had scattered the blankets and pillows from Jayne's bed. Jayne's mother also detected an unpleasant musky smell in the room that lingered all night. The parents chided their daughter about opening windows in her room, and Jayne asked what the thing was that had tried to get through the window. The parents were unable to answer; a ladder-climbing dog was obviously out of the question. That night, Jayne slept very uneasily between her mum and dad and kept having bad dreams about the horrible fanged man-beast. Eventually, Jayne's father believed that his wife and daughter had merely heard a dog growling outside in the street, and that the sound had travelled and appeared to be in the bedroom, but his wife was adamant that she had heard the thing in the bedroom, and it had evidently left that awful scent behind after it had fled from the room. When I gave a brief summary of this incident on the radio, a number of people got in touch and told me how an almost identical "werewolf" had been seen by many people on Speke Road, Hunts Cross, near Woolton Golf Course in April 1985. I am still investigating these reports and hope to have more information on this nameless lycanthropic hybrid soon.

# RENSHAW STREET'S FACELESS GHOST

**Ghosts that walk** in the light of day are fascinating and much more common than you'd imagine. Diurnal ghosts of the daytime which happen to be apparitions of people who died in fairly recent times may not always be recognised as ghosts by the living because their clothes will not seem as unfashionable as say, a Victorian or Edwardian, and you have probably passed these modern-looking ghosts in the street and not known what they were, and you might have even sat next to them on the bus or passed them in the aisle of a supermarket.

A spiral of Liverpool fog seen in certain lighting conditions at night can be perceived as a phantom by the over-imaginative, and we all know that light and shadow can play some very strange tricks on the human eye and mind at night, but I've seen self-satisfied sceptics and smug atheists left reassessing their world view when a ghost puts in an appearance in broad daylight. I've not a quark of sympathy for narrow-minded detractors of the supernatural who are left with shattered nerves in the aftermath of a poltergeist attack or some close encounter with the dark side of the paranormal, and the following story is a case in point of a terrifying daytime ghost I recall well.

It was the early 1980s, and living on Myrtle Street at the time, I had heard vague reports of the faceless ghost who had been seen, always around 9.30 am, walking along Renshaw Street towards St Luke's. The accounts of this alleged revenant became more frequent, and then died down weeks later, and I would have been none the wiser as to whose ghost had walked Renshaw Street devoid of a face. However, many years later I was invited onto a local radio station to talk about the paranormal, and happened to mention the ghost with no face, and the station's telephone switchboard went haywire. George, a retired bank manager called to tell me how, one foggy morning in 1981, he had slipped out of his office to buy flowers for a female bank employee who had returned to work after a long illness, and on his way to the Leece Street florist he literally bumped into a tall smartly suited man who had no face. This entity grabbed the bank manager by the lapels and shook him. A voice from the egg-shell smooth face cried: 'Who am I?' twice, and George, who had a blood-pressure problem, almost collapsed. He was thrown aside and people around him gasped in horror at the faceless apparition, which crossed Leece Street and faded into the fog near the entrance gate to St Luke's (the "bombed-out church"). A fortnight later, at around 8.45am, George was walking to his bank from a car park when he noticed a familiar figure in a dark suit approaching him on Renshaw Street, coming from the direction of Lewis's. This time George hid between two parked vans and watched as the faceless figure approached a man in a black woollen hat and denim jacket and trousers. The man was carrying a green canvas toolbag, and seemed to be a workman of some sort. 'Who am I, eh?' the featureless-faced apparition asked this gentleman, who calmly sucked on a rolled up cigarette and shrugged, perhaps thinking the whole thing was some hidden-camera *Game For A Laugh* TV show type of prank; it was possible the man might have been wearing a mask – but then he faded away into nothingness, leaving the workman, bank manager and several other witnesses on Renshaw Street stunned. This workman later wrote to me from Perth, Australia, which had become his home since 1992. His name was Mick Donaldson, and he told me that a friend in Liverpool had heard me mention him on the radio, and so he was writing to me to fill me in with the details. He explained that he was a glazier, on his way to fix a shop window that morning in 1981. Mick believed the faceless man had indeed been a ghost, even though he had looked solid, and when the ghost faded away that morning, Mick said he felt butterflies in his stomach. Mick's testimony and the calls from many other witnesses to the strange events backed up George's accounts, and I was told by another caller – a former shopkeeper from Bold Street - how, one morning, a brave policeman followed the faceless ghost the length of Renshaw Street to a certain house on Bold Place near St Luke's, where it walked through a front door. The policeman later discovered from locals that the ghost was that of a man who had died of a brain tumour that had wiped out his memory years before. 'Who am I?' were his last words. I have always believed that ghosts generate their own image with sheer will power, and in the case of this sad ghost, it may be the case that, in death, as in its former life, it could not recall what its face looked like, and so it never 'formed' one.

# TRAPPED BETWEEN WORLDS?

**In the sphere** of the supernatural we are currently living in the dark ages, but hopefully a Galileo, Newton or Einstein of the paranormal will arrive soon and formulate laws and theorems to throw light on accounts of the unexplained, such as the following one.

An elderly woman named Margaret once told me a thought-provoking story involving her great grandfather James Jones, who was a constable with the Liverpool police in Victorian times. In the late 1890s, PC Jones was on his beat one wintry night near Castle Street when an excited colleague of his – Bill Quilliam (and I have traced this policeman as being PC William Quilliam 57D in various archives) approached with a strange claim. 'Jim, there's a ghost down on the landing stage,' he stated, pointing towards the river. 'Come and see it man!' he then added and rushed off. PC Jones followed him, knowing Quilliam was a tough no-nonsense down-to-earth copper, and certainly not a man prone to seeing things. As the two constables hurried down Water Street, Quilliam said: 'A tramp heard him first – and then I did – it cries for help.'

The policemen reached the landing stage where several wrecks of humanity, drunks and vagrants were standing, looking at a certain spot on the boards.

Quilliam ignored the comments of the outcasts and led Jones to the spot where a man's well-spoken voice came out of mid-air. 'Help me!' said the voice, 'Can't you see me?'

PC Jones was more intrigued than scared, and he watched as Quilliam pointed with his truncheon to the floor. 'Look! Look at that!' he said, and where he indicated with the truncheon there was a pair of polished and expensive-looking shoes laying there – and they moved as everyone looked on. Ever so slowly, the rest of the ghost appeared from his ankles up to his knees, and then something even more incredible took place: in the spot where the ghost stood, a pillar of sparkling green light appeared. Standing at well over six feet in height, and within this cylinder of scintillating light, a distinguished man of about sixty or more was visible. He had silvery hair smartly combed back, and wore a fine cloak and expensive-looking attire. He looked quite afraid, and upon his appearance, several of the drunks fled from the landing stage. The man shouted something but his voice was now muffled, as if he was behind some thick yet transparent partition. Brave PC Quilliam came within a few feet of the extraordinary spectacle and heard the wide-eyed man cry for help and say he was dying of thirst. He also said he had been trapped here for a long time. Bill Quilliam tapped his truncheon on the curtain of phosphorescent light surrounding the illustrious stranger and gauged that the unearthly enclosure was as hard as iron. 'We'll have you out sir,' Quilliam told the trapped man, then said to a mesmerised PC Jones, 'Go and get help!'

Jones ran off to police headquarters at 111 Dale

Street for assistance – and no one believed him, yet four constables accompanied him out of curiosity, but when they reached the landing stage, they saw only Quilliam standing there, alone, and he had such a defeated look upon his bearded face. 'He's gone, the whole thing just disappeared – and him with it. Into thin air.'

And that is the strange story of an unknown eminent-looking man who seemed to have become trapped in something that took him from this world. The lady who related the story to me – Margaret, said the weird tale had come down to her over the generations, and I was intrigued enough by the account to undertake some research in an effort to find out more about the incident. I discovered that, in February 1895, a prominent 60-year-old former solicitor named John Pershouse had gone missing – without a trace. Pershouse had not been depressed nor had he any health or financial troubles – and was in fact described as being in high spirits by the last people to have seen him before his baffling disappearance. Originally from Manchester, confirmed bachelor John Pershouse loved to travel around his three favourite places, which were Scarborough, New Brighton and Liverpool. He was a man of independent means who had invested in real estate and did not have to work to make a living. Just before he vanished into thin air, Pershouse had been staying at the Ferry Hotel at New Brighton, and he was in the habit of going across the Mersey to Liverpool by riverboat each morning to visit numerous restaurants, clubs and public houses. He then usually returned to New Brighton in the late afternoon, but on 12 February of that year, he remained at a restaurant on Liverpool's Water Street for quite some time, and he then went to the Imperial bar, which was also in Water Street, and the manageress watched him leave her premises that evening. She saw that he walked towards the Prince's Landing Stage, and this was the last anyone saw of him. The police in three different counties launched a search for him and some wondered if Pershouse had fallen into the river in a drunken stupor but his body was never washed up on the shores of Liverpool or Wirral. Over a thousand posters were printed with the portrait of the missing man upon them, and despite being circulated widely, the mystery of John Pershouse's fate remains a mystery. Pershouse's brother, George, and sister Louisa, waited in vain to hear of some news of their missing brother, but none ever came. Some time later, John Pershouse was declared legally dead by a court, and his estate was split between his brother and sister. Is it possible that John Pershouse walked from that Water Street bar, down to the landing stage, where he intended to board a ferry back to his New Brighton hotel – but instead, walked into something we would today term as a portal – an opening in the space-time continuum? And had Pershouse become trapped – perhaps between worlds – in that opening in time? In the light of Margaret's strange story which was, as she stated, passed down by word of mouth over the generations, it seems conceivable that constables Jones and Quilliam saw not some earthbound ghost upon the old landing stage that wintry night, but a man trapped between our dimension and some higher dimensional realm. If this was the case, perhaps Pershouse is still alive in some terrible Limbo, or perhaps he was rescued by some higher intelligence from an otherwise nightmarish fate.

# ESMA DOON

**There is an old** English idiom, said to have been first put into print by the novelist and satirist Thackeray in 1845, and this expression is: 'a skeleton in the cupboard', and it refers rather vividly to a shameful, incriminating or simply embarrassing fact from a person's past that he or she wishes to keep secret. Many an ambitious person aiming for high office in the political arena - locally and nationally - has had their aspirations nipped in the bud by rivals threatening to bring certain skeletons in the figurative cupboard to light, but the following story does not concern politicians and their dark secrets – it concerns a very strange case of an old wardrobe that seems to have acted (in some weird way) as a conscience.

One sunny May morning at a terraced house on Anfield's Pendennis Street in 1974, a 68-year-old widow named Rose answered her door and saw two surprise visitors standing there – one was welcome and the other certainly wasn't. They were Rose's 9-year-old grand-daughter Kelly, and Esma Doon, a tall gangly woman of Rose's age who had been her on-and-off friend since their childhood days on Claudia Street off Goodison Road. Esma was one of those people you could never get to the bottom of, and was infamous for the elaborate lies she came out. She was forty-faced and 'with the hare and the hounds' as Rose's late mum used to say, yet she always had some sob story or some dubious reason for wanting to stay over. On this morning, Esma claimed her house on Boaler Street had been flooded by a burst water tank in the loft and with her sad cocker spaniel eyes she asked Rose if she could stay over for a few days. Rose exhaled noisily through her nose and said, 'Oh, I don't know Esma – ', but little Kelly, who'd bumped into Esma on her way to her Nan's, suddenly pleaded with Rose: 'Can Esma stay, Nanna? Can she please?'

And that was it – Esma Doon would be here for weeks. 'My son's wallpapering the spare bedroom, Esma, so you'll have to stay in the box room,' Rose sighed.

'Ah thanks Rose, you're like my rock in this world of trouble, you are,' Esma replied, and went straight to the kitchen, saying she'd make her friend a cuppa.

'Do you want the chewy out me screwball, Nan?' Kelly asked, prising the said sweet from the bottom of a plastic cone that had been filled with ice cream just a few minutes ago.

Rose shook her head. 'No thanks, Kelly, love.'

'Do you want me screwball chewy, Esma?' Kelly asked.

An instant reply came from the kitchen, 'Ah, thanks Kel, I love chewies!'

That night, Kelly asked her Nan if she could sleep with "Auntie" Esma.

'You'll have to ask her,' Rose said, feeling a bit disappointed and a little jealous because Kelly was really bonding with Esma.

Kelly asked Esma – who was doing the Spot the Ball in the *Liverpool Echo* – if she could sleep in her bed tonight, and her surrogate aunt nodded with a wide smile. 'Course you can, pet; you don't snore do you?'

Kelly laughed and shook her head.

'Did you say you were having some supper Rose?' Esma enquired with a faux concerned look, as if she was worried her friend was not eating enough.

'I don't know where you put all this food, Esma, I don't,' said Rose, wearily rising from her chair at the dining table. 'There's not a pick on you,' she added, as she went into the kitchen.

'The worries of the world keep me thin Rose,' Esma said, carefully drawing a little 'x' on the action photograph of some football match in the newspaper.

Rose smiled and shook her head at Esma's comments, then lit a gas ring on the cooker, adjusted the gas to a low setting, and placed a big pan of scouse that had thickened from the day before on the ring of blue flame. The three of them enjoyed the scouse supper, and then, after reminiscing many incidents from the good old days over a few glasses of Guinness, Esma went up to the box room singing Pal of My Cradle Days as she clutched a big jar of pickled onions. Kelly followed closely behind, yawning and fighting the onset of sleep because she wanted to show Esma how good her drawing skills were. She carried a few felt tip pens and a big Sylvine drawing book up to bed.

The box room was very claustrophobic – just over fifteen feet in length and about six feet in width, and it seemed smaller because of a towering wardrobe of dark brown wood with a foliate frieze above its doors. Esma clutched Kelly's hand in a powerful grip as she passed the wardrobe because she had a morbid phobia of the wardrobe falling on top of her, and this was because of a tallboy that had toppled onto Esma when she was six. She had been swinging on the handles of that tallboy that day when it had fallen onto Esma, and she had been knocked clean out.

As Esma sat eating pickles from a jar in bed and Kelly sketched in a drawing book next to her, they both heard scratching sounds come from the wardrobe. 'Is that a mouse, Esma?' the girl nervously asked. 'Nah, just the house settling down,' Esma opined, but then the doors of the wardrobe rattled, and one opened slightly. A faint raspy voice said, 'Esma Doon, Esma Doon, remember what you did?' And it came from the wardrobe. Kelly yelped and grabbed Esma and Esma clutched at Kelly as she stared in horror at the speaking wardrobe. 'You pushed Peggy down the stairs and killed her!' the eerie voice said, much louder now – and then came fingers of bone from inside the wardrobe and they opened the door slightly. Kelly started to cry. A skull peeped out and its jawbone clacked as it spoke: 'You pushed Peggy down the stairs Esma Doon!'

Esma screamed, pushed poor Kelly sideways, and fled from the bed, and as she flew past the wardrobe the skeleton in the wardrobe laughed. Kelly hid under the blankets and sobbed. Some time later a hand grabbed at her, but it was her Nan. She took the hysterical girl downstairs. Esma had left. Esma later admitted she had pushed Rose's cousin Peggy down the stairs when she was 10. Peggy had died and Rose had been blamed for the death. Just how that 'thing' in the wardrobe knew the truth was never explained; was it a literal case of a skeleton in the cupboard from Esma's past coming out to haunt her? I wonder where that wardrobe is now...

# THE GHOSTLY ADMIRERS

**It's sad how** some people become afraid to 'come out' after they have had an encounter with the supernatural and I know of many who say nothing about their paranormal experiences for years because they feared ridicule. Dawn Fenning is a prime example of this self-imposed suppression of the supernatural. In 1977, Dawn was 32, single, and had just moved out from the family home in West Derby to live in the house of her friend Lynette Scott in Greasby, Wirral. One Saturday afternoon in the May of that year, Dawn's grandmother Norah telephoned her from Crosby with some advice. 'You need to get yourself married; you shouldn't be an unplucked flower at your age – go out and find yourself a husband!'

Dawn put the phone down on her Gran. 'Old people are so full of bloody advice!' she fumed and then went to put on her coat. Her friend Lynette asked her where she was going, and Dawn said nothing in reply. She put the leash on Millie, Lynette's cocker spaniel, and took her out for a long walk. About fifteen minutes later, Dawn had calmed down regarding her gran's hurtful remarks, and she was strolling down Arrowe Brook Road when she decided she'd walk towards a miniature golf course near Arrowe Hall Hospital, but Millie the cocker spaniel began to act strange. She whined and refused to go further. Dawn tugged at the animal's leash but the dog barked and then howled. Dawn said, 'Oh please yourself then,' and walked another way – towards some woods across a field – and these, unknown to Dawn, were nicknamed the Devil's Woods by the locals, and not without good reason too, for many strange supernatural goings-on have been reported in and around those woods over the years. There have even been rumours of Devil worship being carried out in the woods. Seeing rain clouds gather, Dawn decided it was time to take Millie home, but as she was about to set off, she heard a gruff male voice behind her. Dawn turned and saw two men standing about thirty feet away, and they were wearing the costumes of Roman soldiers. At first, Dawn wondered if the men were actors or extras to some historical film or programme being filmed in the area, and she ignored them and began to walk away – but then the soldiers came running after her, and one of them grabbed her forearm with a hard grip and spun her to face him, and as he did, Dawn cried out and let go of Millie' leash. The cocker spaniel growled and snapped at the outdated men, but they were smiling and looking Dawn up and down, as if fascinated by her royal blue cropped jacket and matching knee-length skirt. The taller of the two men had very dark brown penetrating eyes and he spoke in a language Dawn had never heard before. Dawn pulled away from him, and fell onto her backside. Dawn grunted with anger, quickly got to her feet, swore at the two bizarre-looking strangers, and she then ran over to Millie to grab her leash. Dawn stormed off, yanking the cocker spaniel with her. She turned around once – and the costumed duo was nowhere to be seen. Only then did Dawn wonder if there had been something supernatural about the 'Romans'. Dawn began to convince herself that the men had probably just been actors after all, and she hurried through the gathering gloom.

When Dawn got back to Lynette's house she told her about the actors she had met in their costumes, and how one of them had roughly handled her, and her friend went deadly pale. 'They weren't any actors, Dawn,' Lynette said sombrely, 'they were ghosts. My dad saw them years ago. There's supposed to be a Roman burial ground near those woods.'

Dawn had a bruise on her arm for days, made by the figure that grabbed her, and that bruise was real enough, so how could a spirit have inflicted it? 'How would a ghost leave me with a bruise like this, Lynette?' Dawn showed the yellow and purplish coloured marking on her forearm. She seemed spooked by the mention of ghosts.

'Dawn, I swear I am not trying to scare you,' Lynette assured her friend, 'but ghosts of Roman soldiers have been seen by those woods. You can ask my Dad if you don't believe me, because he saw them.'

Over the following month, the ghosts of the Roman soldiers were seen on many occasions standing outside Lynette's house – as if they were stalking Dawn. One morning around 3am, Lynette looked out her bedroom window and saw the unmistakable silhouettes of the

Roman soldiers standing in the street, gazing up at her over a hedge.

All of this proved to much of a strain on the nerves of Dawn, who moved back to Liverpool, and as soon as she left the house in Greasby, the ancient ghosts stopped paying their nocturnal visits. I believe the ghosts are still active, and I am still looking for historical evidence of a Roman burial ground in the vicinity of the 'Devil's Woods'.

# OUR HAUNTED ROADS

**Elsewhere in the** *Haunted Liverpool* books I have written of the many ghosts and malevolent forces which haunt the motorways, minor roads and leafy lanes of this corner of England, and it's a chapter that can never be finished because hardly a month goes by without someone emailing or writing to me to tell of a new apparition or supernatural visitant haunting some stretch of the macadam or even a vehicle itself.

One August night in the late 1970s, a couple in their thirties – Gary and Julie – embarked on the return journey from the home of their friends in Bebington to their home on Sugar Lane, Knowsley, and this trip necessitated a route which took them through the Queensway Tunnel. Julie listened as the car radio went dead as Gary drove into the mouth of the tunnel. Before transmitters were placed inside the tunnel, such radio silence was common, because the radio waves cannot penetrate the thick bedrock of the river to get to the car radio. In this radio silence, Julie looked at her watch and saw it was exactly midnight, and she then turned to Gary and said she'd be glad to get home to bed because she was feeling so exhausted. She had been up since six because her youngest, Danielle, had developed a bad chesty cough, and after tending to Danielle all night, Julie had somehow managed to grab thirty minutes of sleep before going to work at the Bird's Eye factory. She yawned, and then noticed something which lifted her from her lethargy into an alarmed and alert state: a silhouetted figure of a woman – standing in the middle of the road, about a hundred yards ahead. 'What's she doing standing there?' Julie gasped, and turned to look at Gary, but she saw that his eyes were bulging and his mouth was open as he stared transfixed at the woman straight ahead. If he continued on this course, he'd hit the woman squarely. Julie cried out for her husband to swerve but Gary just said '"No!' and with gritted teeth he looked through the windscreen with a strange expression of sheer determination – as if he intended to smash the Ford Cortina into the woman!

Julie's right hand grabbed at the steering wheel as she tried to turn it to avoid running the woman down, but her husband held the wheel with a vice-like grip. Julie let out a scream as the car crashed into the woman, and a strange icy coldness gushed through the car at the point of impact. Julie was now in tears but Gary said, 'Look in the side mirror! She's still there! She's a ghost! Look at her!'

And Julie glanced in the side mirror as Gary slowed the car, and she saw that the woman was still standing there in the middle of the road – even though the car carrying Gary and Julie had just run straight through her. An old Ford Anglia following behind swerved to miss the shadowy woman – and it collided with another car as a result and smashed into the wall of the tunnel.

'Jesus! Oh my God!' Julie threw her hands up to her face as she saw the smash-up in the side mirror.

Gary explained how, a year before, during a trip to Birkenhead to visit his uncle, he had seen that same eerie silhouetted woman standing in almost the same spot – near a bend in the tunnel, and when he had swerved to avoid her (thinking she was a real flesh blood person), he had narrowly missed a van just around the curve in the road. Gary had the eerie impression that the ghostly lady had been trying to make him crash into another vehicle by standing in the path of his car. Unknown to Gary, that uncanny apparition of a woman had been seen many times over the years, and the ghost seems hellbent on causing accidents. She seems to date from the 1960s, and has a bob of curly hair and wears a 'sticky-out' knee-length dress. She is quite tall – about 5 feet 8 inches in her stilettos and her attire seems to date back to the late 1950s or early 1960s. The identity of the phantom is still unknown, but she is not the only ghost that haunts the Queensway Tunnel. The ghost of a girl who had a fatal fall from a motorbike in the Queensway in the 1960s has also been seen hitch-hiking in the two-mile tunnel over the years.

There are other ghosts roaming the roads of Liverpool and the suburbs, and the most durable one is known as The Thing on Higher Lane in Fazakerley. This is a shadowy, amorphous entity which has been seen sliding across Higher Lane at night like some unearthly oil slick. The entity often takes on the shape of a man who runs out in front of cars on the lane near to Sparrow Hall playing fields, and the deadly ghost has caused many fatal crashes over the years. Even patrolling policemen at night have encountered "The Thing" on Higher Lane, but to date, no one knows whose ghost is responsible for causing so many tragedies at what has become an infamous black spot. The close proximity of Everton Cemetery to the lane could have something to do with "The Thing" of course.

Just a stone's throw from the haunting ground of the Higher Lane entity, there is a stretch of the East Lancashire Road which seems to be haunted by an invisible pair of hands that seize the steering wheel of passing vehicles. In 2010 a reader named Frank Dorlin wrote to me to tell me how, one night in May 2009, he was driving along the East Lancs around 11pm, on his way to his Aunt's home in Knowsley, when the steering wheel of the car turned in his hands as if something invisible had gripped it, and this something had terrific strength, because Frank tried to turn the wheel back and found it impossible. The car veered to the left and then suddenly the 'hands' must have released their powerful grip, for Frank just managed to regain control of the vehicle, but the invisible backseat driver then turned the wheel in the other direction, sending the car into a spin. As this was going on, the temperature in Frank's car seemed to plunge to freezing point. I have had many reports of the phantom hands grabbing the steering wheel s of cars travelling on that stretch of the East Lancs, and it may be just a dark coincidence, but that section of the motorway passes by West Derby Cemetery...

In November 1979, a series of paranormal incidents began to unfold in a most sinister way at Wallasey

Central Library on Earlston Road. An unearthly silence descending on the usual quiet environment of a library might seem ironic, but that is how the 'presence' first began to manifest itself back upon those dark and gloomy November afternoons, and the entity which muted all sound could also cause dramatic drops in temperature as well as the unsettling sensation of being watched among the staff and members of the public. Some of the older visitors to the library recalled how the building had been the venue of a supernatural mischief-maker back in the 1960s, and on that occasion, the ghost's spooky shenanigans proved too much for one of the librarians who quit her job rather than be subjected to all manner of paranormal pranks. During a strike by council caretakers in 1979, the park police were temporarily entrusted with the task of locking up the Wallasey library, and one of these policeman who brought his German shepherd with him on his rounds noticed how the animal refused to pass certain spots in the library, as if it sensed something unseen to human eyes barring its way. And then came the sounds of a horse-drawn carriage trundling past outside, always after dark. At first, the rationalists said the sounds of wooden wheels and the trot of horse's hooves was all down to the way sound echoed at night, but in December 1979, this antiquated carriage suddenly revealed itself one night to two women walking their dogs down Earlston Road near the library. They were amazed to see an old-fashioned black lacquered funeral hearse parked outside the shut gate of the library. The horse harnessed to the hearse, like the carriage and its rather diminutive driver, were all glowing with a green phosphorescence. The women naturally turned on their heels and ran off down Earlston Road, dragging their yelping dogs with them. The ominous glowing funeral hearse was seen by policemen, late-night workers, taxi drivers, milk men and clubbers returning home in the wee small hours. Many of them mentioned the little coffin on display in the rear of the hearse; it looked as if it contained the body of a child. The top-hatted driver perched upon the hearse had a sinister wizened face, and he was always described as being of very small stature. As late as March 2009, Sean and Gemma, a couple in their twenties, had a very close encounter with the eerie hearse at 4.30am one windy morning as they jogged from their flat on Seaview Road. Sean had talked his girlfriend Gemma into jogging after she told him she thought she was putting on weight, and the plan was a basic lap of Earlston Road, Kirkway Road, Rake Lane, and back home to the flat on Seaview Road, but the wind was howling that morning, and Gemma clutched her knee and cried out in agony near the end of Earlston Road, close to the library. The couple then noticed a horse, and then a carriage attached to the horse, along with the little caped man in a top hat sitting atop the carriage. As they drew nearer the couple saw that the horse and carriage – which had a coffin on show in its window, was glowing. Gemma was that terrified, she ran past the uncanny apparition, even though her knee was throbbing with pain. The couple experienced a long run of bad luck afterwards, and both believe the ghostly hearse was some omen of misfortune. A taxi driver named Jack told me how, half-past two one morning in 2009, he picked up a woman on Albion Street who asked Jack to take her to her daughter's home off Liscard Crescent. The fare's teenaged daughter had telephoned her after returning from a club to find she had lost her keys and was now locked out of her flat, so Jack was told to travel as quickly as possible to Liscard Crescent. As the taxi was travelling down Earlston Road, there was a heavy downpour, and as the taxi was passing the library, Jack saw what looked like a cloud of black smoke coming down the street towards his cab. He put the headlights on high beam and saw a black horse-drawn carriage of some sort coming his way. He slowed down, naturally apprehensive as to what was coming his way, because it looked very creepy, and the passenger in the back of the hackney urged Jack to go faster because she wanted to go to her daughter's aid as quickly as possible.

'Look at this thing!' Jack shouted to his fare, and she leaned forward to the gap in the plexiglass partition and said, 'What have you slowed down for?' But then she also saw the eerie outdated carriage coming towards the taxi at quite a speed. Jack swore in shock, knowing he couldn't swerve to avoid the horse and carriage, and he remembers instinctively squeezing his eyes shut and bracing himself for a possible fatal collision. He heard the carriage smash into the taxi and he heard the woman in the back of his vehicle scream so loud, it left his ears ringing, but when Jack opened his eyes, he was still there and his hackney cab was still intact. He could clearly hear the clatter of hooves continuing down Earlston Road, and when he looked in the rear view mirror, he saw the ghostly black carriage and the rider atop of it swerve to the right, through the closed gate of Wallasey Central Library, and here it vanished. Then Jack noticed the woman in the back was nowhere to be seen. He got out the cab and went to see what had happened, and he found the lady on her back on the floor of the vehicle, out cold. When she came to she recalled something taking the wind out of her stomach as it hit her with a tremendous force, but she didn't see what the thing was that had thumped into her. Jack took her to Liscard Crescent, where her daughter was waiting patiently in the rain. The daughter and mother invited the cabby into the flat there and over hot coffee, Jack and his fare compared notes as to what had happened. The woman thought the vehicle which had somehow passed through the cab had been an old-fashioned hearse, and sometime later she learned from a neighbour that such an antiquated vehicle had been seen on Earlston Road and also on nearby Seabank Road for many years, and it was said that terrible bad luck befell those who saw the hearse, although fortunately, Jack and his fare suffered no more than the average amount of misfortune in the years following the chilling encounter.

Is the phantom hearse connected to the nearby cemetery next to Wallasey Central Library? We may know more one day.

There are many haunted lengths of motorway in the North West, and one major road that has not had much coverage in books on the paranormal is the A5300, better known as the Knowsley Expressway (a name it received from James Lobb, a pupil of Halsnead Community Primary School, when a competition was run to name the new trunk road). The Knowsley Expressway runs three miles from the Speke

Road Junction A562 to Junction 6 of the M62, where it travels northwards from then on as the M57. In the spring of 2011, a 29-year-old Huyton man named Andrew was travelling along the Knowsley Expressway; he was returning home from a visit to his friend's house in Widnes when he happened to be delayed because of an accident at the end of the trunk road by traffic lights. The delay went on for almost two hours, and during that time, Andrew sat in his vehicle with a queue of traffic in front and behind him, and he seethed. Just before the traffic began to move again, Andrew looked in his rear view mirror, and for a moment he thought someone had somehow sneaked into his car, because, for a few seconds, he distinctly saw a small person with the build of a child of about 6 or 7 years old with a very pale face, and this diminutive stranger was grinning as he sat on the backseat. There was almost something clown-like about the face, but when Andrew reflexively turned to see who or what was sitting in the back of his car, he was perplexed to see no one there. About five minutes passed and the traffic began to move, and all the way home, Andrew wondered what he had seen. He'd had the car – a Vauxhall Astra – for two years, and had never seen anything remotely supernatural in it before, so Andrew began to wonder if the whole thing had been some trick of the light, or the product of an overtired mind, as he was feeling rather fatigued in the car, waiting there in the queue for almost two hours. Andrew never mentioned the incident to his wife Ashley as he knew it would only spook her. About a month after this incident, Andrew was once again travelling up the Knowsley Expressway on the return journey from his mate's house in Widnes, and as the car travelled across the stretch of roadway that passed over Ditton Brook, the vehicle shuddered slightly, and Andrew distinctly felt something touch the back of his neck, as if someone had reached around the headrest to place cold fingertips on the nape of his neck. Andrew glanced into the rear-view mirror and this time he saw the pale faced 'midget' again, only this time the face was not grinning as it was on the last occasion – instead it wore an expression of utter hate. Andrew swore out loud in shock, and then the figure was gone. For the remainder of the journey home, he listened to the radio for company and kept looking over his shoulder, expecting the ghost to reappear, but thankfully it didn't. Two months after this, Andrew got into bed one night and found it hard to sleep, His wife Ashley, lying beside him, was also restless, and she had retired an hour earlier than Andrew but still found it hard to nod off. As the couple lay there, they talked of work and their children and then Ashley suddenly said something that sent Andrew's heart palpitating. 'I saw a ghost in the car today,' she said, all matter of fact.

Andrew, finding himself dumbfounded by this statement, muttered: 'What?'

'I forgot to tell you,' Ashley told him, and she squeezed his hand as they lay there. 'This afternoon, it was, when I was driving to Claire's,' she continued. Claire was an old friend who lived in Widnes, and before Ashley even said it, Andrew knew she'd say she saw the ghost as she was travelling down the Knowsley Expressway. Ashley said it had been in broad daylight though, and she had distinctly seen a man who looked as if he was about four-feet five inches in height, lying across the backseats of the car. He had reddish-brown hair, a very pale face with purple lips, and he was wearing a chocolate brown jacket and matching trousers. Ashley also thought the little man had been wearing dark brogues upon his feet. The figure had been there one moment and gone the next, but it had really startled Ashley. Andrew then told his wife about his two sightings of the ghost, and at first Ashley thought he was messing about, so she turned on the bedside lamp and took a good look at Andrew's face, and she saw he was deadly serious. The end result was Ashley clinging to her husband all night with the bedside lamp left on. She also refused to travel in the Vauxhall Astra on her own from then on. I mentioned this intriguing haunting on the radio and later received several calls, emails and letters from listeners who had also met the wee ghost, and most of the accounts of the entity which came my way mentioned the figure appearing after the car had crossed over Ditton Brook, which I found interesting, as Occultists and some dowsers have long claimed that streams – both on the surface and underground ones too – are capable of powering up images of ghosts with a form of energy our present science hasn't even detected yet. Could Ditton Brook be somehow responsible for 'feeding' the apparition which appears in cars which travel over it via the Knowsley Expressway? A 60-year-old lady named Maude telephoned me at the radio station after I had mentioned the carnate ghost of the little man, and she told me how she and her sister Helen had travelled up the Knowsley Expressway in her Renault Megane at around half-past eleven one night in 2003, and they had both felt hands touching the backs of their heads. Helen turned and glanced at the back seat of the car and was startled to see a man lying there across the seats with a very creepy grin on his face, which she described as being very pale. Helen said, 'Oh my God, who are you?' and the little man vanished. Maude looked around just in time to see something vanish out the corner of her eye. On this occasion, a smell, very reminiscent of cinnamon, invaded the interior of the car, and became so strong, Maude had to wind down the windows.

The identity of the ghostly dwarf of the Knowsley Expressway is unknown; perhaps it is the ghost of someone who was knocked and killed down on that road, but I have a feeling the ghost dates back to Victorian times, and may have something to do with the many farmhouses that once existed in the fields where the Knowsley Expressway now scythes through. Perhaps the pint-sized phantom is the ghost of some farmer or farmhand who died in some tragic circumstances; I will continue to examine the history of the vicinity of the trunk road in the hope of finding some possible explanation for this strange haunting.

Not all paranormal mysteries of the roads of the north concern ghosts; some strange and inexplicable goings-on seem to be the work of a higher intelligence that is possibly of an extra-terrestrial origin. The following intriguing incident allegedly took place in the Lake District, on the night of 22 September 1988, just four miles east of Kendal.

A plumber from Wrexham named Noel Harrison and his Liverpudlian girlfriend Maxine Williams were travelling up the M6 in a Transit van on their way to see Noel's cousin in Grayrigg. Noel had travelled along the route to Grayrigg many times over the previous two years and was well acquainted with the area around Kendal and Windermere. He left the M6 as usual and joined the A685, which was deserted at that time of night, 11.15 p.m. Noel left the "A"-road and took his van down a country lane which wound its way round woodland to the town where his brother worked in a dairy. As Noel turned down the lane, he saw that the road ahead was blocked by boulders. He stopped the Transit van and looked at the obstructions with puzzlement, because there were no mountains nearby that could have produced the landslide. Maxine told him he'd better turn the van around and find another route, but Noel thought there was something strange about the blocked road. He left his van and looked down the road. He thought the moonlight was playing tricks on his eyes because the boulders that were strewn across the road didn't look real; they looked flat and two-dimensional, as if they were just cardboard cut-outs. As the plumber walked towards the boulders, something curious happened. When Noel glanced down at the road again, he could no longer see the huge rocks lying about; the road looked perfectly clear. When he walked back to the van, the rocks appeared again. They were obviously some sort of illusion of rocks that appeared or disappeared depending on one's vantage point. Noel told his girlfriend about the unreality of the rocks and she too saw them vanish when she viewed them from another angle, but Maxine said the illusion was creepy and had the eerie feeling that someone was watching them, so she asked Noel to go by another route to Grayrigg.

Curiosity, however, got the better of Noel, and he

drove his Transit slowly up the rock-covered road and, as expected, the rocks seemed to have no solidity at all, since the van proceeded up the lane without encountering any physical obstruction. Noel was flabbergasted by the illusion, but upon turning the sharp bend at the end of the lane, he and Maxine witnessed a spectacle that was even more astounding than the phantom rocks. In a clearing in the woods to the left of the road Noel and his girlfriend saw something that looked straight out of a science-fiction film. A huge silvery saucer-shaped craft stood on four legs, and beneath this strange craft two figures wearing large helmets were apparently at work on some apparatus that hung from the underside of the saucer, which had an estimated diameter of a hundred feet. As the van passed, the helmeted people, who seemed to be about seven feet tall, turned and looked at the vehicle with their blank visors as if startled. A blazing beam of light shone on the van from a dome on the top of the saucer, and Noel realized what he had stumbled on. He put the van into third gear and accelerated up the lane away from the strange craft. He looked sideways at Maxine and saw she was trembling with fear at the strange encounter. Noel sped up the lane and turned the van around a bend so fast the vehicle tipped slightly. He raced non-stop to the farm at Grayrigg and told his cousin about the strange encounter, who told him that there had been an item on the local radio about a strange glowing disc that had been seen flying erratically over the nearby village of Middleshaw. One report said the disc had been seen diving into woodland near Kendal, but the astronomer Patrick Moore had said that a meteorite had probably been behind the UFO sightings.

On the following morning, Maxine, Noel and his cousin visited the woods where the strange saucer had been seen, and they saw that in a clearing there were four circular depressions, possibly left by the landing gear of the unearthly spaceship. Noel then remembered the phantom rocks, and he surmised that they had been some sort of hologram projection from the UFO to divert traffic from the area so no one would come across what seemed to have been a spaceship in need of repair. Three days later a silvery disc-shaped craft was seen flying at high speed along the shoreline at Morecambe Bay - less than ten miles from the spot where Noel and Maxine had seen the UFO.

In the early 1980s, a postman we shall called Graham was delivering mail in Hoylake one dark wintry morning, and as he was walking down Garden Hey Road, just a stone's throw from Meols Parade, he heard a car approaching, and waited at the kerb for it to pass before crossing the road – but no car passed. This baffled the postman because he had seen the car and its headlights out the corner of his eye and he had heard its engine as it came towards him, but now the road was clear – as if the vehicle had vanished into thin air. Graham crossed the road, intending to continue his deliveries in the next road (which was Wynstay Road), when he suddenly heard a car horn beep. He looked about and saw no car except for an old Vauxhall Chevette that was parked up at the end of Garden Hey Road, and the sound of the horn the postman had heard came from somewhere much nearer. The postman felt a bit unnerved by the vanishing car, and hurried towards Wynstay Road, when all of a sudden, he saw something which would perplex him for the rest of his life. Two faint discs of light appeared in the middle of Garden Hey Road, and Graham realised they were car headlights – but where was the car? Then, as he watched, he saw the car in question slowly materialise. It was a bronze Datsun Cherry, but as the postman looked on in awe, he noticed that he could see a lamp post on the other side of the car, as if it was partially transparent. He gingerly approached it and saw the car become completely solid as the headlamps became brighter. Now Graham could hear the Datsun's engine ticking over and upon this cold morning he now noticed the puff of blue smoke coming from the vehicle's exhaust pipe. A man in a flat cap was the sole occupant of the Datsun, and as Graham took a few steps towards the vehicle, the driver opened the door, got out, and then looked at the postman. He seemed to be in a daze. 'What happened?' he asked Graham, and the postman could see that the man – who looked to be in his late fifties or early sixties – seemed to be in shock.

The driver closed the door and stumbled towards the postman, who caught hold of his elbow and steadied him towards a house. The driver, whose name was George, said he had left his home on Firshaw Road (which was at the end of Garden Hey Road) to set out for a journey to his brother's house on Trinity Road, but as he came down Garden Hey Road, he felt very peculiar, and thought he might have suffered a stroke. George had seen Graham waiting at the kerb, waiting for him to drive past, but the car had suddenly stopped, and then a grey mist enveloped the vehicle on all sides. George tried to open the door of the Datsun, but it seemed locked. He looked to his right, and instead of seeing houses, he could see a beach and the sea in the distance, but there was no sign of any building. In desperation, George beeped his horn, and shortly afterwards the grey mist began to clear and the lamp post lights of Garden Hey Road became visible again. Graham then told George how he had seen his car approach out the corner of his eye and how the vehicle had vanished. He also told him how he had heard the Datsun's horn sound when the car was not even visible to the human eye. George was a bit relieved to hear this strange testimony from the postman because the man believed he had suffered some sort of stroke. Then, all of a sudden, the postman saw something coming down Garden Hey Road; it was a strange-looking cloud of grey smoke, about fifteen feet wide and about ten feet in height. At the sight of this, George panicked and got into his car, and urged the postman to get in with him, but Graham shook his head, and ran towards Wynstay Road. The Datsun peeled rubber as it sped from the road, and Graham never saw George again, even though he delivered the mail regularly in that area for a year before he left the postal service for a job down south. I have no idea what that mist was on Garden Hey Road or whether it has been seen since, but from what George has told us I would advise any motorists passing through Hoylake to give it a wide berth.

One night around 10.10pm in the summer of 1977, a group of Liverpool University students – all female and in their early twenties – were walking up Hope Street from their digs on Falkner Street. They were headed for the hip drinking establishments of Hardman Street; places like Chaucers and Kirklands, where they could let their hair down, have a drink and take a relaxing break from their studies. However, as the students reached the corner of Hope Street and Hardman Street, just opposite the Philharmonic Hall, a pale-coloured mini – possible white – came speeding down Myrtle on the wrong side of the road, narrowly missing a hackney cab. This mini swerved, mounted the kerb and hurtled towards the students who, by some miracle, managed to throw themselves out the way of the maniacal driver. The mini then drove on down the pavement, where it just missed a lamp post and a post-box. It then swerved back onto the road and made an incredible manoeuvre; it seemed to perform a right-angled turn and shot down Baltimore Street, which is a narrow backstreet off Hardman Street, leading onto Maryland Street. The mystery deepened when an off-duty policeman at the scene noticed that the mini had no driver. A few other people had noticed this sinister fact, including one of the students who had almost been mown down by the car. The students went into Kirklands wine bar, where a few male drinkers asked them if they were okay. Witnesses in Kirklands had also noticed that no one seemed to be inside the mini. This driverless car was seen on three more occasions that summer, always after 10pm and always in the vicinity of Hardman Street. Some maintained that it was a ghost car, because one motorist had seen it vanish into thin air as it sped down Pilgrim Street after missing his car by inches on the Monday evening of August 22, 1977. A motorcyclist who almost collided with the driverless mini at the junction of Hardman Street and Rodney Street also believed the vehicle was some apparition, albeit a solid-looking one – until it faded away before his eyes as it turned into Leece Street. I mentioned this phantom Mini on a local radio show and afterwards, during a booksigning on Bold Street, an elderly reader named Richard Burrowes told me a fascinating tale. Mr Burrowes, a retired financial advisor, told me how, during the phantom Mini scare, he had been a regular at Kirklands wine bar on Hardman Street, and he had seen the vehicle twice. On the second occasion when he saw the car with no driver, he noticed a very debonair man, sitting alone at a window table in the wine bar, and this man had a tiny model of a Mini – just like the Dinky or Matchbox brand of toy cars – and as most people were gazing out the window, looking at the menacing Mini, the old man was rather childishly wheeling his miniature Mini along the tabletop. This naturally struck Burrowes as very strange, and he later sat at the window table with the old man, and learned that he was from Czechoslovakia, but he never gave his name. When Burrowes mentioned the little model of the Mini, the man smiled and said, 'Ah, so you know my little game now?'

Burrowes said he didn't understand what he meant by that remark, and the man pointed to the little toy, then pointed to his forehead, and cryptically remarked: 'They think they see it.'

Burrowes went the toilet, and when he returned, the old Czech was gone, and he never saw him again. Burrowes had the impression that the elderly foreigner had somehow projected a mental image of the toy mini into the minds of the people within the locality of the wine bar, perhaps out of malice, or perhaps out of mischief. Such projections are known as thought-forms, and also tulpas. Modern physicists know that matter and energy are one and the same thing (as Einstein's famous equation states $E=MC^2$). Even the most solid, hardest object you can think of – say a diamond for example – is just fluctuating, shimmering continuum of energy manifesting as something that seems solid. Occultists have claimed for centuries that certain minds can create seemingly solid objects and even simulations of people, by manipulating energy and converting it into matter, and this talent was possibly the one the Czechoslovakian used in Kirklands that summer evening.

# THE STILT MAN

'**Mam, there's a man** with a funny mask on looking through me window upstairs!' Pippa Edwards, the 14-year-old marmalade-blonde daughter of Thelma Edwards, a 39-year-old widowed woman living on Walton's Rice Lane, seemed deadly serious, but you never could tell with this girl because she had perpetrated so many practical jokes on people in the past, and was, as we say in these parts, a 'bit of a Tom Pepper'.

'Pippa, I'll give you such a haymaker if you're having me on again girl!' Thelma warned, and she got up from the table where she had been counting a bundle of Embassy cigarette coupons and followed Pippa up the stairs.

'Hurry up mam, or he'll be gone!' Pippa urged her asthmatic mother, who wheezed: 'Pippa, how would this fellah be looking through your window, anyway? There's no drainpipe outside your window love. Has he got long legs?'

'Mam, hurry up - slowcoach!' Pippa ran from the top of the stairs, down the landing, and barged into her bedroom, and as Thelma reached the top step she heard her energetic daughter moan, 'Oh! He's gone now!'

Thelma clung to the handrail of the stairs. 'If you're acting the goat –'

'Mam, I swear on me Gran's life there was a fellah with this black thingio, like a hat, on his head, and it had eye holes in it – Mam! Stop looking at me like that! I'm telling the truth!'

This was 10.30pm on Monday, 31 July, 1978. In 2011, Pippa, now aged 47, wrote to me to tell me how, on two occasions in the summer of 1978 she had indeed seen a man wearing what looked like half of a black ski mask which came down to his nose. 'He was looking through my bedroom window, which faced onto the back yard,' Pippa told me, and her best friend Carol also saw the same weird figure a few days later, again of a night, looking through the bedroom window at the girls as they sat listening to records and chatting about boys. That bedroom window was about eighteen feet up, so Pippa and Carol had been baffled as to how he'd looked in on them. Pippa was very intrigued when I told her she might have seen the ghost of the so-called Stilt Man – a mysterious robber who used enormous stilts to gain access to unsecured windows across Walton, Everton and Kirkdale in the late 1920s and early 1930s. The stilts had padded leather bags on their ends to act as 'silent feet' on prowling missions. The Stilt Man was thought to have been a variety theatre or circus performer who donned a mask and burgled houses galore - armed with a crowbar and possibly a knife. Whilst being pursued on one occasion near Grant Gardens (on Everton Road) by three police officers, the stilt-man simply stepped over railings and a wall to facilitate an escape which embarrassed his pursuers. In an area where the locals still hadn't got over the antics of Spring-Heeled Jack, some Evertonians nicknamed the outlandish burglar Long-Legged Jack. He was said to have been most active in the severe, hungry years of the Depression, but like his contemporary, the enigmatic "Anfield Housebreaker" (another busy daredevil burglar) the Stilt Man was never brought to justice – although an elderly reader once told me that a man was found with a broken neck in a backyard in Walton in the 1930s, and a pair of stilts were lying close by, but children stole them. Not long afterwards, the ghost of a man on stilts was allegedly seen on Kirkdale's Dunluce Street, striding along through a fog. There were also sightings of the ghost on Rice Lane – where Pippa lived in the 1970s.

# THE JÜDEL

**Here's a strange** but true story from 1974 that I cannot rationally explain. One golden August afternoon in 1974, two 19-year-old girls named Jo Heaps and Sandra Thurgood came out of H Samuel the Jewellers, which was at that time on the corner of Ranelagh Street and Great Charlotte Street, where MacDonald's now stands. The girls had been dreamily looking at engagement, eternity and wedding rings, even though they were both single. The girls crossed over to Lewis's, and as they approached the famous corner entrance with its three plate-glass doors beneath Epstein's controversial statue, they got the shock of their lives. A Very familiar girl was standing in the middle of the three entrances to the store – it was a girl who was the exact double of Jo Heaps – even down to the very same clothes, shoes and hairstyle. There was a pause for a moment as shoppers swarmed past the girls and between them and the creepy double, and then Sandra turned to Jo and said, 'It's you.'

The replica of Jo Heaps had the same silky shoulder-length hair as Jo, and like her counterpart, the double had on the same red and pink tie-dye dress, black velvet Biba choker and white Dolcis sandals that Jo had on, and to make things even more sinister, the doppelgänger was sneering at the shocked girls with a curled scornful upper lip. Jo's skin crawled at this expression of contempt from her living mirror image, and she suddenly ran off up Renshaw Street with Sandra running behind her. The frightened girls kept looking back towards Lewis's until they turned the corner into Leece Street. In the 1970s not many people outside of occult circles had heard about doppelgängers, especially two teenaged girls from Toxteth, and when Jo told her parents and Nan about seeing her carbon copy, they said it was just some girl who bore a strong resemblance to her. 'But she had on the same clothes and even the same shoes,' Jo recalled, but that was put down as coincidence and nothing more. Three days later, Jo and Sandra were in Woolworths on Church Street, when all of a sudden, Sandra saw 'it' again – the unearthly "twin" of her friend Jo standing by the loose sweets section of the store, and the creepy double had obviously noticed the girls before they notice her, as the 'clone' was gazing at them with that unsettling smirk. On this occasion, as on the last, the menacing double was wearing the exact same clothes as Jo. Sandra tapped Jo's arm and then nodded at the doppelganger, and Jo's jaw dropped when she saw the uncanny spitting image of herself gazing straight at her. The girls immediately left Woolworths and dashed blindly through the crowds of Church Street – and this time, the doppelganger pursued them. The hysterical girls narrowly missed being hit by a car on Hanover Street as they raced towards Bold Street. They looked back and saw the flesh-and-blood facsimile was gaining on them, and poor Jo was near to tears. 'What is it?' she kept saying. The girls managed to lose the menacing mimic but at 6pm when Jo Heaps reached her home she saw the chilling double standing on her doorstep, so she ran off, but as she did, she heard a bang. The wall of Jo's room in her dilapidated old house had collapsed, crushing her bed. Had she been home she would have been in her room – so had the doppelganger saved her life? It was never seen again after that day...

Such a 'helpful' doppelgänger is termed a Jüdel by occultists, and I know of another local example of such a warning apparition, and this one was seen on the streets of Liverpool for three years in the 1930s. William Jones was a 22-year-old clerk in a well-known bank on Water Street, and one afternoon in 1937 he was on duty at the teller window in the bank when a customer appeared and asked him if there was an upper limit to the amount he could deposit in the bank. Jones was speechless, for the man making the enquiry was his exact double, only his face was much paler than the clerk's. Jones gave a garbled reply to the man: 'Er, no, not at all, but, er, how much were you thinking, er...'

A colleague of Jones saw the customer and did a double take. He looked at Jones and then remarked, 'Ah, I didn't know you were a twin, Jones.'

'I'm not,' Jones gasped in reply, and the man smiled, nodded, then put on a trilby and walked out of the bank.

This was to be the first of many encounters with the

doppelganger of William Jones. In a café on North John Street frequented by the bank clerks, a waitress asked Jones why he had been so rude to her on the previous Saturday. Jones said he had not been in town (meaning the city centre) on Saturday, but a male customer backed up the claims of the waitress and told Jones that he had ordered coffee and cake and had ignored the waitress and himself when they had tried to make pleasant conversation with him. William Jones brought two friends to the café who swore he was with them that Saturday, playing golf in Allerton. The waitress and the customer were adamant that Jones had been there in the café, and when Jones said he had met the 'lookalike' in question himself at the bank, the waitress and customer still didn't believe him. Grace Griffiths, the beautiful fiancée of William Jones then had an encounter with the sinister impostor on Allerton Road when she had gone to the butcher's to buy a joint of lamb. He had walked into the shop, and the butcher believed it was William, but Grace somehow knew it wasn't her fiancé because there was just something unfamiliar about his voice and mannerisms. The butcher thought Grace was playing some prank when she said the double wasn't her boyfriend, and when the butcher asked the man if he was William, he cryptically replied: 'Do I really have to answer that?' And he then walked out of the butchers. Grace watched him from the doorway and saw him cross Allerton Road and wait for a tram which would have taken him into the suburbs. When the real William Jones came to see her, Grace told him of the spinechilling meeting with his double, and with tears in her eyes she also told him that her mother had said such a double of a person being at large often meant that the original person would possibly die before the year was up. William hugged his fiancée and assured her that there was nothing supernatural about 'this damned fake' and he promised Grace he'd get to the bottom of it. He called in to the Allerton Bridewell and told a bemused sergeant about the man masquerading as himself and the policeman asked him if the impostor had actually claimed to be William Jones. Jones said he hadn't – yet. The Sergeant then posed another question at the bank clerk: 'And as he tried to abstract money from anyone whilst giving the impression he is you sir?'

'Well, not as far as I know, but say he does?' William Jones replied, 'I mean he has already been quite rude to a waitress – '

'Sir, with all due respect,' the sergeant interposed, 'can you think of anybody – a friend or perhaps an enemy – who might be simply pulling your leg? Someone who is in the habit of taking a joke a bit too far?'

William shot back a puzzled and indignant look. 'I can't think of a single soul who would go to such lengths sergeant, and you'd have to see this man to appreciate just how much he looks like me –'

'Which might mean he's a cousin, sir – or do you have an older brother – '

'Not a single relative bears any resemblance to me – and I don't have any brothers,' William told the policeman, who looked as if he was becoming a bit weary of the clerk's problem.

'Well sir, if this impersonator strikes again and if he tries to commit some fraud in your name, or some criminal act, call back and tell us about it,' was the sergeant's final word on the bizarre matter, and William Jones left the Bridewell feeling his visit to the police had been a waste of time.

Later that month, on a Sunday morning, the neighbour of William Jones, a Mrs Cowper, passed him on the street, and the clerk greeted her with the usual: 'Morning Mrs Cowper,' and the old lady gave a curious reply; she said: 'When you greeted me earlier you pronounced my name correctly for the first time.'

'Sorry?' Jones was baffled by this remark.

'You called me Mrs Cooper – and that is the correct way to pronounce my name,' Mrs Cowper told him, 'so why revert to the former incorrect pronunciation?'

Only then did the penny drop. Mrs Cowper had been greeted by the doppelganger, for this was the first time he had set eyes upon his neighbour this morning.

Then the double made its most audacious manoeuvre a few weeks later. William Jones decided to have a fancy dress party at his Mossley Hill home, and sent some thirty-five invitations out to various friends and acquaintances – including the close friends of Grace. All of the invited turned up on the day, and the party soon got into full swing. Revellers dressed as clowns, Napoleon, Henry VIII and many other colourful characters. The champagne flowed and the finest food was put on for the guests. Some had brought records to be played and a few of the guests played the piano for a marathon singalong which went an hour or so beyond midnight – when something shocking and inexplicable took place. Violet Johnson, a beautiful 18-year-old secretary from William's bank went into the back garden of William Jones during the party with a man dressed as the famous English harlequinade clown Joseph Grimaldi. With the effects of the romantic music being played on the piano, coupled with the starry skies, and, no doubt, with too much wine and champagne being consumed by the clown and Violet – who had gone to the fancy dress ball as Red Riding Hood – the couple began to make love in the secluded shade of the apple trees. Sometime later, a female scream was heard coming from the back garden during a lull in the music, and Red Riding Hood came running into the house in an hysterical state. She said the man dressed as the clown had practically raped her – and when several of the outraged guests asked who this fiend was, Violet said it had been William Jones. Grace Griffiths almost fainted when she heard this shocking claim. All of the men rushed out into the garden to confront Jones, but he could not be found. Jones was upstairs in the toilet at the time, feeling rather unwell from too much wine and rich food. He had donned the costume of a cavalier, but had removed his hat as he sat on the edge of the bath, fearing he'd be sick any second. The door of the bathroom burst open and Jones was set upon by three of his friends. They were puzzled, because Jones had not a trace of the white make up that had coated Grimaldi's face nor any of the clown's garish attire. The accusers soon apologised to William Jones and told Violet Johnson she had most certainly been mistaken, but the girl continued to accuse Jones of having his way with her, and she threatened to report the matter to the police. Jones then told his guests that he was being 'haunted' by a very strange and devious man who had gone to enormous lengths to mimic him, but most of the people present were a little too tipsy to take in the weird claims of the bank clerk. Violet said the clown had looked exactly like William, facially and in physical build as well, although he had spoken in a raspy voice, and she had thought this had been put on as some joke. Grace took Violet aside and solemnly assured the girl that she had been some victim of the impersonator who was making her fiancé's life Hell. Violet eventually decided not to press charges against the bank clerk. William Jones somehow managed to purchase a pistol, and told Grace enough was enough – and that he would kill the evil copycat who had almost disgraced him. Grace begged William not to resort to murder and eventually managed to persuade him to get rid of the gun.

Three years went by, and still the occasional sightings of the bank clerk's doppelganger were reported, but they were not as frequent as those of 1937 and 1938. In 1939, the Second World War broke out, William Jones was called up, and he willingly joined the Irish Guards as a private. In 1944 he was part of a platoon stalking retreating diehard Nazi soldiers on the outskirts of Berlin when a strange incident occurred. Jones was about to investigate an abandoned cottage, when suddenly his doppelganger appeared in the doorway, barring his access. At this time, Jones had sustained an injury to his right hand, and it was bandaged as a result. The double who stood before him, who bore the same rifle and uniform, also sported a bandaged right hand. The replica of the soldier gestured for him to go away by waving the bandaged hand, and Jones felt this was an omen of some sort. He backed away to a distance of about a hundred yards, when suddenly, the doppelganger vanished into thin air, then the door of the cottage flew open and two German soldiers rushed out, opening fire with machine guns. Jones heard the bullets whistle past his head and dived behind a water trough. When he looked up, the soldiers had run into the distance, and then came the sounds of a gun battle as British troops confronted the two Germans. Within seconds the two soldiers had been killed. Jones survived the remainder of the war, and never saw his doppelganger again. He believed that the weird twin who had previously caused him so much trouble had somehow acted as a guardian angel that day.

# THROUGH A TRAIN WINDOW

**There is an old** belief – that spirits that are not at rest are attracted to lights in the dead of night. I have investigated many hauntings which seem to suggest that this old piece of ghost lore has some truth to it. Many years ago, a certain DJ at Radio City (who has long left the station) told me how, one night, as he was waiting to go on air, he had a walk around the curved corridors of the station up in St John's Beacon when he saw something light-coloured out the corner of his eye. The DJ turned to see what it was, and there pressed against the thick plate glass was something that gives him nightmares to this day. A thin, almost skeletal old man in some sort of white flowing gown, was on the other side of the window with his hands pressed against the glass, hovering in mid air. The DJ swore at the top of his voice and backed into a news studio in shock. 'The eyes were just black with no pupils or anything to them,' the DJ told me, 'and he grinned as he floated away, backwards from the window, then vanished.' This ghost had possibly been attracted to the lights shining from the station's windows 450 feet up. The DJ was so shaken by the experience he wanted to go home but his producer talked him into presenting his show.

Around 11pm one windy night in March 1978, a 60-year-old Birkenhead postman named Ron was riding the train home from a friend's house in Port Sunlight, and as the train halted at Bebington & New Ferry Station, Ron thought he saw someone looking through the window at him, but when he looked left he saw only his own face reflected in the pane. As the train was passing Dacre Hill, Ron was startled by a rapping sound on the glass, and he turned in his window seat to see the source of the noise – and almost had a heart attack. A ghastly girl's face was looking in at him, and her eyeballs were black and shiny with red pupils. She squinted at the neon lights inside the carriage as she tapped on the window with her bony fingertips. The apparition was wearing some type of flowing pale antiquated nightdress – or possibly a burial shroud – and she also wore a huge toothless grin on her macabre face as she hovered along with the train outside the window. Ron was alone in the compartment and he had a funny turn as he fled down the train, desperately looking for someone. He saw an old woman and told her about the ghost, and this elderly lady also saw the entity looking in at her and Ron, only now its smile had turned to a spinechilling expression of utter hatred. The woman got off at the next stop – Rock Ferry, where she told her waiting daughter what she had seen. Ron went to the front of the train and sat by two drunks, just for company, until he got off at Hamilton Square. At midnight, his telephone rang. It was Ron's brother-in-law Peter. He was ringing to tell Ron that his ex-wife Claire had just died. Claire had been suffering from a serious illness for the past six months, but Ron is convinced the ghostly girl was some omen of his ex-wife's passing. The ghoulish girl of Dacre Hill has been reported to me many times over the years but her identity remains a mystery.

# THE SECRET IN THE CELLAR

**Someone once asked me** if I have ever decided not to publish a story because it seemed too far fetched, and the answer is yes – but it doesn't happen that often; I receive many accounts of very strange phenomena which even seem a bit unbelievable to even my paranormally-seasoned mind, but of course, it's not always my job to decide what is far-fetched to the reading public; people have the intelligence to make up their own minds. The following story has sat in my files for many years now, and I think it's time it was told, even though it will seem unbelievable to many people.

It all started in the December of 1962, with an anticyclone forming over Iceland. The freezing air mass larger than Ireland moved south, headed for the British Isles, bringing heavy snow showers in its wake, and sowing seeds for what would be known in the annals of meteorology as the Big Freeze of '63 for decades to come. At the end of December 62, a merciless blizzard swept south-west England and then the white menace moved northwards, leaving twenty feet snow drifts in some parts. Manchester had 6 inches of snow, and so did Liverpool, and people thought snow was to be expected in December, and the optimistic thought it would last throughout January and then the usual wintry rain would return, but January 1963 arrived – and it would go down as the coldest month in the 20th Century. It was minus two degrees at first, and some of the older folk said that was nothing compared to the winters they recalled, particularly the severe winter of December 1946 to March 1947. That winter was particularly harsh because the country had just emerged from the hardships of war, so coal supplies were low and there simply wasn't enough fuel for the power stations. The army had to be brought in to clear massive drifts of snow that had been heaped upon the roads and railway tracks, and the Minister of Fuel and Power, Emanuel "Manny" Shinwell, received so many death threats for cutting public services (including the limiting of radio and TV broadcasts and the reduction and suspension of newspapers and magazines) he was given around the clock police protection. When the thaw came in March, 1963, there was then widespread flooding, and 100,000 properties were almost ruined. Livestock had died in the big freeze, vegetables crops frozen solid into the ground, were unable to be harvested, and there were food shortages. Humanitarian aid had to be deployed and the blame went on the ruling Labour Party of the day. That Big Freeze had been a total disaster – and now another one had arrived, but hopefully it wouldn't be as bad as the post-war one. But things got worse, much worse than anyone had imagined. The temperatures plummeted to minus nineteen in some parts and the River Mersey froze over. The sea froze around the coast for a distance of one mile and then birds began to freeze to death on branches, in nests and some even fell dead out of the sky as the cold really began to bite even deeper than ever before. At a certain house on Liverpool's Marmaduke Street in-between Edge Hill and Kensington, the Harkaway family sat huddled around the coal fire in the back parlour in the middle of a snow Limbo afternoon. Fred Harkaway, the 55-year-old head of the family, was stabbing the glowing coals of the fire with the old black poker, and his 35-year-old wife Paula, sat wrapped up in blankets in her fireside chair. It was that cold, the two children, 15-year-old Alan and his 13-year-old sister Marion, would not even venture outside to play in the snow. Last winter they couldn't get out of the house fast enough when a few inches of snow fell on the town, but outside were drifts of snow three feet tall in some places, and it was hard as cast iron because of the freezing temperatures. The children sat at the table, reading comics in their coats, and Alan even had his late grandfather's old tartan scarf on. Under the table, the family dog, an old border terrier named Mack, lay curled up in his basket, and his teeth were chattering with the cold, even though Marion had put a few empty coal sacks over him. Fred Harkaway boiled a kettle on the fire, then made a strong pot of tea. Paula held her palms around her old chipped metal cup of char and enjoyed the luxuriant warmth. She thought about her cat, Corky, who had been missing now for over a week, and wondered if he was lying somewhere dead out there in the godforsaken frozen wastes of the streets. Fred went to the door of the parlour, kicked the old coats used as makeshift draught excluders from the bottom of the door, and said he was going to put some more coal on the fire. His wife asked: 'Are you sure, Fred? I'm warm enough, and they are as well,' and she asked her children: 'Are you two okay?'

'Yeah,' said Alan, and he quoted an apt fact from the comic he was reading: 'Did you know that in water content, one inch of rain is equal to ten inches of snow?'

'No, I didn't,' Paula replied, and she said to Marion: 'You alright love?'

'Yeah mam,' Marion replied, but her father left the parlour anyway and he went into the hallway where he could see his breath. He opened the door to the coal cellar, and something very strange took place. Fred Harkaway felt warm air waft out of the cellar, and at first he panicked, for he thought a fire might be raging in next door's cellar, but the warmth seemed to be coming from his coal cellar. Stranger still he could smell something sweet and refreshing – it smelt for the world like – eucalyptus. He came back and told his wife about the eerie warmth and she and the children went into the cellar to experience it for themselves. 'Oh, isn't that lovely?' Paula Harkaway said, feeling the seductive zephyr of warm air against her bare legs and her face.

'Where's it coming from Dad?' Alan wanted to know.

His father shrugged. 'I don't know son, it's funny isn't it?'

'Mam!' exclaimed Marion, making her parents and brother jump. She pointed to something on the floor; a grey shape picked out by the faint hallway light shining into the coal cellar. The shape moved.

'It's Corky!' Alan said excitedly, and he and Marion crouched down to pick him up. Marion grabbed him first and she took the cat out into the hallway. He was very docile, and looked sick, and his tongue was hanging out of his mouth, as if he was gasping for a drink. Mrs Harkaway took the tortoiseshell cat out of her daughter's arms and went straight into the kitchen. His coat felt warm and when she put him on the floor of the kitchen, he lay there, spread out straight like a fox stole, and made no effort to even move. Paula Harkaway grabbed a saucer from the crockery rack and filled it with cold tap water. She put the water by Corky's head and the cat tried to lift itself up. Where the devil had the feline been and why was he so dehydrated? Marion dipped her finger in the water and let the droplets from her digit fall into the cat's arid mouth. He lapped at her wet finger, then he dragged himself to his feet and tremblingly walked to the saucer of cold water and began to lap at it. He drank two saucers of water that afternoon, and he also ate a piece of boiled ham – and then Marion took the much-loved cat up to her room and put him under the blankets of her bed so just his head was visible, resting on the pillow. He went fast asleep and was still asleep when Marion retired to bed at 10pm wearing her pyjamas, two pairs of socks, a pair of woollen gloves, a scarf coiled about her neck and her father's old woollen hat upon her head. She snuggled into Corky as she tried to get to sleep, for in sleep she'd have some refuge from the miserable winter existence. The girl thought of the golden sands of New Brighton in the summer, of Blackpool Rock, days spent on Southport Beach, and sunbathing in Wavertree Park, but when she looked towards her window she saw huge snowflakes drifting past. It was like the feathery aftermath of a violent pillow fight out there. Where was all this snow coming from? Meanwhile, in her brother's bedroom, Alan was lying in bed with five coats over the sheets. He had an old hot water bottle he had found in the attic, tucked under his feet, which were clad in two pairs of socks. His father had told him not to use the hot water bottle in case it leaked and scalded him but the lad had taken a chance and so far, the bottle seemed intact. It was hard to sleep with a cold draught nettling Alan's nose, but he somehow managed to drift off into the pleasant world of dreams – but something awakened him at four in the morning. The dog Mack barked just once down in the hallway. He'd normally be in his kennel in the yard but in consequence of the bitter long cold spell, Fred and Paula let him stay in his basket in the hallway. Alan lay there in bed, listening but with no wish to move out of the comfort of the lovely warmth that had built up under the layers of blankets from his body heat and the hot water bottle. He thought he heard someone down in the hallway say "Shhh, be quiet.' It had been a male voice, but it did not sound like Alan's father. Then came the melodic sound in the pipes which he heard whenever anyone turned on a water tap. This sound in the pipes went on for about half a minute –

longer than it would take to fill a kettle. Mack barked once more, only this time the bark was shorter and sounded higher in pitch. 'Oh be quiet you silly hound!' said that male voice. It was not Alan's father. It was someone Alan had never heard before, and thinking it was a burglar, the boy slowly got out his bed, put on his shoes, and crept over to his bedroom door. He listened. There was movement down in the hall; a shuffling walk followed by a thud. It sounded like the door to the coal cellar being closed. Alan waited there for a few minutes until the eerie silence drove him out of his room to go to the bedroom of his parents. His father was snoring and he could hardly see his mother. He crept closer to the bed and saw the top of her head now, and the curlers in her hair.

'Mam -' he whispered in a sharp voice, and his index and middle finger tapped her shoulder. 'Mam!' he said again and shook her.

'Ooh!' Mrs Harkaway exclaimed. Her eyes shot open and she threw a startled look at her son. 'Is that you, Alan?'

'Mam, there's someone downstairs,' Alan told her.

'What?' his mother rubbed her bleary eyes.

'There's some fellah downstairs, and he sounds as if he's making himself a cup of tea or something,' Alan replied and looked at the door of the bedroom as if the intruder might enter any moment.

'You sure you haven't been dreaming?' Mrs Harkaway wondered out loud as she sat up in the bed.

'No,' Alan replied in an impatient tone, 'wake me dad up!'

Paula woke Fred up and told him what their son had said, and Fred hauled himself out from under the layers of blankets and heavy coats, and he went and got a cricket bat from a niche between the wardrobe and the adjoining wall, put on his slippers, then left the room. Alan tip-toed after his dad, and father and son sneaked down the stairs, both avoiding the infamous creaky step as they went to investigate the possible burglar. There was no one about, but tobacco smoke hung in the air in the hallway and kitchen and Mack the terrier was behaving mighty strange. The dog's tail was literally between his legs and his ears were flat against his head as if someone or something had frightened him. In the kitchen, Fred found the stub of a rolled up cigarette. Fred didn't smoke and his wife only smoked filtered cigarettes – so where did this roll-up stump come from? Alan whispered about the thud of the coal cellar door he had heard, and so his father went to see if anyone had got into the house via the manhole cover of the cellar. The manhole cover was secure but that strange unaccounted for warmth was back, and it felt even stronger than before, in fact it was stifling.

'Dad, do you think our house is haunted?' Alan suddenly asked.

'Nah, don't talk daft,' Alan's father replied with some bravado in his voice, but Alan knew it was all put on and that the strange incidents were worrying his dad.

Fred closed the door to the coal cellar and went into the kitchen to take another look at the stub of the rolled-up cigarette. 'I think that stump might be one of Mrs McKay's from next door,' Alan's father suggested, but his son had not seen any of the neighbours since the world had become virtually snowbound; everyone was too busy keeping warm in their own homes and the neighbourhood had become a ghost town with the glacial conditions. Father and son went up the stairs and went into their separate rooms. Alan tried to get back to sleep but the hot water bottle didn't even feel lukewarm now. He lay there watching the big flakes of snow spiral past the window panes until somehow, around 5.30 that morning, the teenager fell asleep. But when he awoke at half-past nine he found he had a sore throat. Alan told his sister Marion what had happened and she said he'd probably been dreaming, but Alan said he had been wide awake, and someone must have come into the house because they left the stump of a rolled-up cigarette in the kitchen on the drain board.

'Mam! Alan's trying to scare me!' Marion complained to her mother, who was twisting strips of the *Liverpool Echo* and inserting them between the coal and sticks of firewood in the grate.

'I'm not scaring her at all,' Alan moaned to his mother, and he explained to his mum how he had only described what he had heard and smelt in the early hours of that morning. 'Mack even barked at him, Mam,' Alan argued.

'Oh Alan, you do love a mystery lad,' said his mother, lighting the tapers of newspaper. 'Your dad said you dreamt it all.'

Alan sulked at this suggestion and he never spoke to his mum for about fifteen minutes – until she brought out a big tin of shortbread biscuits to have with his cup of tea. Marion still thought her brother had dreamt the intruder, but Alan looked down at Mack sitting in his cosy basket under the dining table and said to him: 'We know better don't we Mack? If only you could tell us what you saw.'

The dog's nose inched forward from under the fall of the table cloth and he ever so gently ate the half of dunked biscuit.

That night on the landing upstairs, just before Alan and Marion parted ways to go to their respective rooms, Alan told his sister to listen out for the ghost tonight. Marion looked as if she wanted to cry, and Alan cruelly said 'Goodnight,' and rushed into his bedroom. Shivering more from the prospect of a ghostly visitation than the arctic all-pervading cold, Marion hid under the blankets and coats and even clutched an old doll for company. The more she tried to sleep, the more that mysterious dozing-off mechanism of the mind alluded her.

*Crack!*

The sound echoed around the bedroom and struck terror into the heart of the 13-year-old girl. She froze below the sheets with her eyes squeezed shut, imagining the ghost had rapped hard on her window, for that was where the loud report came from. Marion opened one eye, expecting to see a face at the frosted window, but instead she saw that the bottom left pane of the four panes had cracked, probably with the cold in these record low temperatures. The faint light from a lamp somewhere outside in the hibernal streets was filtering through pretty patterns formed by the ice crystals growing on the windows. Marion watched the pattern of glinting crystalline trees and slowly her eyelids drooped. The surreal images that always heralded the onset of sleep began to appear in the mind's eye of Marion; nonsensical scenes and situations, but then something jolted the girl back into the harsh cold reality of her bedroom – and that something was the dog Mack barking downstairs. The terrier barked twice, and then Marion's bedroom door opened and the girl's heart pounded with fear – but it was only Alan.

'There's someone downstairs,' he whispered, and he held the front lamp from his bike in his hand. The light it was giving off was little better than a few candles.

'Tell me Mum and Dad then,' was Marion's straightforward reply.

'Keep your voice down,' Alan said in a low voice, the cadence of which conveyed his irritation at Marion. 'He's an old man,' Alan added.

'Tell him anyway,' Marion insisted.

Alan sighed. 'Not me Dad you idiot, the burglar – he's an old man with a big hat on – he looks harmless.'

'Alan, tell me Mum and Dad – ' Marion was saying when her brother left the doorway and went back onto the landing outside. Marion got out the bed and put on her slippers, then went to see where Alan was going. He was creeping down the stairs.

'I think he's a ghost,' Alan murmured, 'probably the ghost of the man who used to live here.'

'Alan, come back – I'm going to tell me Mum and Dad,' said Marion, standing at the top of the stairs.

All of a sudden, two figures walked past the bottom of the staircase on their way across the hall to the front door. One was a man with a large Akubra hat on – and the other was a black man with a huge head of hair – and he looked as if he was only wearing some loin cloth or oversized underpants (which is what they looked like to Marion's eyes). Both men were mostly shadow in the darkened hallway.

Alan switched off his bike lamp and stayed put on the stairs. He was naturally apprehensive about the odd intruders, and Marion wanted to scream but she couldn't speak or even utter a word because her throat had seized up with fear.

The burglars or whatever they were went to the front door, and the man with the hat on drew back the bolts and opened the door. Snowflakes whirled into the hallway, and the man in the hat said to his accomplice, 'D'yer see that Toffee? That there is snow!'

Now, by the light from a nearby lamp post on Marmaduke Street, Alan and Marion could see that the man in the hat had a grey beard, a dirty brown coat, and denim trousers and boots. The black man with him was wearing only some ragged cloth around his waist which went down to his knees – and he was barefooted. The man in the hat went out into the street and called to his comrade to do the same, saying: 'Cam on Toffee!'

"Toffee" stood his ground on the top step at the front door and eyed the snowy street suspiciously.

Marion suddenly regained the power to speak, and said to Alan: 'I'm going to get me Mum and Dad!' And she ran off to their room. They were both fast asleep, and Marion's mum was snoring. The girl shook her repeatedly, and when Mrs Harkaway awakened, she said: 'Oh, what is it now?'

Marion was so excited she could hardly get her words out in a coherent fashion. 'There's two burglars downstairs! An old man and a black man with no clothes on!'

'Oh Marion, don't talk daft!' Paula Harkaway closed

her eyes and turned towards her sleeping husband in that wonderfully cosy bed of many blankets and coats.

'I'm serious! Mum, wake up!'

Meanwhile, downstairs, Alan had descended a few cautious steps to see what was going on. A snowball hit Toffee in the head and exploded into icy powder as the man in the hat cried with laughter outside. Toffee reacted as if a swarm of bees were in his bushy head of hair, and he ran back into the hallway and frantically shook the remains of the snowball from his head. He still hadn't noticed Alan, who was eyeing him with a fearful expression. Mack the terrier went up to the black man and sniffed his feet, then went to the front door to watch the man in the hat somewhere out in the street.

Upstairs, Mr Harkaway was prodded in the ribs by his wife until he woke up. 'What? What do you want?' he groaned.

'Marion said there are two burglars downstairs! Fred? Wake up!' Mrs Harkaway shook her husband and then got out of bed.

Downstairs in the hallway, Mack ran from the front door as the old man in the hat came back in, and this time, Alan sneezed on the stairs.

The man in the hat looked up at him with an expression of pure surprise, then ran down the hallway, almost knocking Toffee over. 'Come on, Toffee! Leg it!' he shouted as he flew into the coal cellar. The hall lights went on, and then Alan's parents came down the stairs with Marion. Mr Harkaway wielded his cricket bat in readiness. 'Where are they?' he asked his son.

'They went into the coal cellar!' Alan told his dad,

and he followed him and his mum and sister to the coal cellar door, where Fred Harkaway told his wife and children to wait. He then bravely went into the coal cellar with the bat held aloft, ready to strike, but the cellar was empty. Once again Mr Harkaway felt an unaccountable intense warmness in the cellar. He had a good look around, and then returned to Paula and the kids. He shook his head then shrugged. 'There's some funny business going on in this house,' he remarked, and closed the coal cellar door. Mrs Harkaway closed the front door and then looked at the particles of snow on the hallway carpet – made by the snowball impacting upon Toffee's head.

'I'm going to the police first thing in the morning,' Mr Harkaway announced.

'Dad,' said Marion, 'where's Mack? '

'What?' Mrs Harkaway asked.

'The dog – where is he? He was in his basket in the hallway; look, the basket's empty!' Marion said, and went over to the vacant wickerwork basket.

'He must have got out,' Mr Harkaway said, and he went to the front door, opened it, and looked up and down Marmaduke Street but there was no sign of any living thing in the wintry street.

'I think he ran after the two fellahs when they went into the coal cellar Dad,' said Alan with a very foreboding look in his eyes.

'Oh no!' Marion threw her hands to her face. 'We have to go and find him.'

Mr Harkaway went and got his coat, and in his slippers, he went to the front door, unbolted it, and, despite his wife's protests, he went to look for Mack, but couldn't even see any paw prints left by him – or any other animal that should be unfortunate to be out on such a deathly cold night, and he soon hurried back home. He promised a tearful Marion he'd resume the search for Mack in the morning. Marion cried herself to sleep that morning, thinking all kinds of things had happened to her beloved dog, but that morning at half-past eight, Alan burst into her room and woke her up. 'Marion! Wake up!'

Marion awakened with a start and looked at her brother's beaming face.

'Mack's back!' Alan told her.

'Where was he?' Marion leaped out of the bed.

Alan chuckled and told her. 'Me Dad found him sitting in his basket in the hallway, and he's chewing on this great big bone!'

The two teens went down into the hallway, and there was Mack, with his front paws around a huge bone, and his backside sticking up in the air. He wagged his tail as Marion approached, but growled when he thought she was going to take his bone off him.

'No, you naughty dog,' Marion said, disappointed in the dog for a moment, 'I'm not trting to take your bone off you! Where've you been love?' And she stroked his head but he merely wagged his tail falsely to appease Marion, then tackled the marrow-laden bone again.

Mr Harkaway finished his breakfast of eggs, bacon and black pudding, then put on his two coats, his Wellingtons, his scarf and trilby, and set off for the police station. He gave his wife strict instructions to stay in the back parlour with the kids until he got back from the police station. When the desk sergeant at the police station heard about the old man in the big hat and his big black colleague in the loin cloth, he was, understandably, a bit sceptical. 'And where are these two people coming from Mr Harkaway?' he asked, and Fred Harkaway, realising how silly the matter sounded, said: 'From the coal cellar, honest.'

'The coal cellar; and are there any secret tunnels leading from this cellar?' the sergeant queried.

Fred shook his head. 'Look, I know it sounds nuts, officer, but there's something very fishy going on in our house. Did I mention the strange smells and the fierce heat that comes up out the cellar as well?'

The sergeant sipped his hot mug of cocoa, then shook his head. 'No, you didn't, Mr Harkaway. Before you do tell me, may I ask if you had been drinking before these people appeared?'

'No, I rarely drink, officer. I only have a drop of rum before bed – you know, because of this big freeze were having. On account of that, like.'

'Oh,' said the sergeant, raising his eyebrows – but the eyes beneath them regarded Fred with such suspicion.

'I know it must all sound balmy, but, well never mind. Bye officer,' Fred said to the desk sergeant, and he put on his trilby, tightened the scarf about his neck, turned up the collar of his overcoat, and left the police station. When he got home, Fred said the police were a waste of time and told his wife he'd get to the bottom of this mystery himself. For the next two nights he stayed up and kept going into the hall with his cousin's air rifle, hoping to spot the oddball intruders, but they didn't show. The cellar – which had always had faulty wiring in its lighting circuit, had a new bulb placed in the light socket in the low ceiling but when the switch was thrown the cellar remained in darkness. The cellar was therefore surveyed by the light of a brand new torch Fred had bought, and he could see that there were no secret entrances to the cellar and no one had knocked a hole in either of the walls which adjoined next door's cellars. The strange heat that had emanated from the coal cellar had also gone now. Convinced that the duo had been scared off after being spotted by the children, Fred put a simple bolt on the cellar door which would prevent anyone from coming out of that coal cellar.

However, about a week after this, it was Paula Harkaway's birthday, and a small party was held which went on till about half-past-one in the morning when the last guest – Fred's eccentric Uncle Des left – with tennis rackets tied to each of his boots to act as snow shoes. That night, Fred and his wife went to bed a little intoxicated, and Fred forgot to bolt the cellar door. Around three in the morning, Mack started to growl and yelp, and Alan heard the dog and went to investigate with his bike lamp again, and he saw the strange couple once again at the front door, looking out at the snow. This time, the bearded man in the Akubra hat turned and saw Alan on the stairs, and he reached for the arm of the black man Toffee. 'Good day lad,' the man said – even though it was the middle of the night.

'Why are you coming into our house all the time?' Alan asked, and he switched on the feeble bike lamp in an effort to dazzle the trespassers, but all they saw was a orange glimmer.

'Just exploring sonny,' said Toffee in a deep rich voice.

'Where is your house mate?' asked the man in the

hat, moving slowly towards Alan.

Alan stepped backwards – and went up a step. 'How do you mean?'

'You sound like a scouser – is this Liverpool?' the old man asked, and now, in the faint glow of the bike lamp, Alan could see he had a lined but friendly-looking face.

'Yeah, of course its Liverpool, what a daft question,' Alan said in reply.

Toffee suddenly crouched down and stroked the inquisitive head of Mack, and the dog rolled on its side then onto its back, and Toffee said: 'Aww, he loves having his belly scratched dontya?' He then playfully ran his fingers up and down the dogs pink belly.

'I suppose it does sound like a daft question – er, what's your name, son? If you don't mind me asking?' said the man in the hat.

After a thoughtful pause, Alan told him.

The bearded visitor touched the brim of his hat with his index and middle finger and said: 'Nice to meet you Al – my name's Dogey Trucker, and this big dag here's Toffee.'

'You don't sound as if you're from round here,' Alan tried to judge the accent, it sounded like some variation of the cockney twang. 'Where are you from?'

'Newcastle – ' said Dogey, and before he could say more, a familiar voice from the landing above whispered: 'Alan.' It was Marion. She was gazing, ashen faced, through the rails of the banister at the two men.

'Good day miss,' Dogey greeted the shy girl, and Toffee grunted something to her as he continued to stroke Mack, who was lapping up all the attention.

'You're from Newcastle?' Alan asked Dogey.

Dogey Trucker nodded and replied: 'Yeah, Newcastle in New South Wales - in Australia.'

'That's a long way away.' That was all Alan knew about the place. In 1963, most teens had only heard about Australia as modern teens have heard about the planet Mars.

'Stop beating round the bush Dogey, and tell him,' said Toffee, and the Aborigine stood up as Mack whined for more attention.

'Well, yeah, Oz is a long way away Al, but we seem to have found a short-cut,' said Dogey, very enigmatically. 'We only found it a few weeks back.'

Alan could read adult faces well, and he just knew the Australian was telling the truth.

'Alan! Come back up and tell mum and dad or I will!' Marion shouted down to her curious brother.

Alan glanced up, but then ignored Marion and pitched another question at the night visitors. 'What do you mean, a short-cut?'

'That's it! I'm going to tell me mum and dad!' Marion declared and she ran along the landing to her parents room.

'We'd better be going, Al!' Dogey Trucker said snappily and he and Toffee ran from the hallway to the coal cellar. Mack ran after the men.

'No! Wait!' Alan shouted after them, and then he went down the stairs and decided – against his intuition – to go into the coal cellar after them. As soon as he went in, he was hit by a wave of heat that created the impression of walking into an oven. It was so hot, compared to the icy hallway, Alan could hardly breathe. He saw a faint yellow glow in the far right corner of the cellar, coming from the brick wall, as if there was a doorway leading to a room with some massive light in it. Alan cautiously went into the light and felt a hot breeze on his face. The light was almost blinding. He stumbled over rough ground and then tripped over a rock. When he got up, he found himself in a cave. He saw shadows of two men at the mouth of the cave, and the schoolboy got to his feet and walked towards them – out of the cave. What he saw next was definitely not Marmaduke Street. He saw Dogey Trucker, Toffee the Aborigine, Mack the dog, and behind them was the vast breathtaking treeless vista of the Nullarbor Plain. As far as the human eye could see, for almost eighty thousand square miles, there was nothing but flat sandy terrain studded with bluebush. A hundred feet away down a slope was an old rust bucket of a truck, and a tent pitched out right next to it. Alan could see tiny specks of what looked like jumping men in the distance, but it was just a mob of kangaroos, their images elongated and shimmering in the searing Australian summer heat. While England froze in one of the most severe winters of all time, the nations of the antipodes were being toasted be the infernal sun. Now all of the recent supernatural events were making some sense, the strange wafts of heat and exotic scents coming from the cellar, the fascination the grown men had for the snow, and the temporary disappearances of Mack the dog and Corky the cat. When Alan had heard someone running the tap in the kitchen it had probably been Dogey or his pal filling up a can of precious water. But how could all this be so? How could one go into a damp old coal cellar in Liverpool and emerge over ten thousand miles away in this beautiful land of scorching sunshine? It was like Heaven 'down here' – but Alan's young mind – like all young minds – needed an explanation, but Dogey and Toffee couldn't supply him with one. 'I'm stumped, Al,' Dogey admitted, and he also expressed his worry at the doorway to Down Under becoming common knowledge: 'If they find out about your cellar, this place will be swarming with tourists, and then they'll build all over this place and the Nullarbor Plain will be one great concrete slab in twenty years.'

'Don't talk rot,' Toffee suddenly said, 'it'd bring commerce and business here. Who wants to look at the world's biggest piece of limestone all day anyway? Bring the big casinos like the ones in Vegas down here, and the boom towns; there's gold everywhere round here just doing nothing. That's why we are here after all, isn't it? The gold?'

'I'm so bloody disappointed with you mate,' Dogey said to his aboriginal pal, and he took out a pouch of tobacco and cigarette papers began to make a roll-up; Alan then recalled the stump of the roly his dad had found in the kitchen.

'You live in bunyipland, Dogey,' Toffee told him with a toothy grin. 'You can't stop progress; when they find out about the hole in Alan's cellar – '

Alan let out a scream. A six-foot-long tiger snake had slithered from the cover of a group of loose rocks and was closing in on the Liverpool lad.

'Keep still Alan! Stock still lad!' Dogey instructed the teen, who was shaking with fear as he watched the venomous snake flatten its body and raise its head, ready to strike. It opened its huge jaws, revealing its two long blood-orange-coloured fangs.

Mack ran towards the snake, barking furiously, and the creature turned its head towards the terrier. As Mack distracted the killer snake, Alan leaped towards Dogey and took refuge behind him, then shouted to his dog: 'Come here Mack!'

In one swift movement, Toffee picked up a pebble and threw it at the snake, hitting its head with outstanding accuracy. The snake seemed stunned for a moment, and slithered back behind the rocks. Mack went to go after it but Alan went over to the dog and grabbed him by the scruff of his neck and picked him up. 'I want to go back!' Alan told Dogey and Toffee, and the old man nodded. 'Alright lad, I don't blame you – but look, I know you'll probably blab to your parents about the secret in the cellar, but if you do – '

'Oh stop it Dogey, the game's up now; let him tell who he wants to,' said Toffee, still eyeing the rocks where the deadly snake had taken cover.

'I won't tell the grown-ups Dogey,' Alan said, and he had a solemn look in his eyes. 'Well, I'd like to tell my sister – and maybe me and her could come here because we are sick to death of all that bloody snow in Liverpool.'

Dogey smiled and nodded, and seemed to have something in his eye – but it wasn't grit or dust - it was a tear in his eye, and he wiped it away and softly, he said: 'Thanks Al.'

And Alan turned away from the hopeless prospectors and went back into the cave carrying the terrier as it struggled to get away from his hold, for that dog was probably fed up of being confined to a draughty cold hallway when there was a whole sunny world of adventure, of new sights and sounds and scents just waiting to be explored. Alan found the cold dark corner of the limestone cave and walked into it, and within seconds he was walking up the wooden steps to the coal cellar door. He opened that creaky door, stepped into the hallway and put Mack down, then turned and bolted the cellar door as Mack scratched his paw against it and whined. Marion was coming down the stairs alone. Her gaze probed the dark hallway and she asked where the strange men had gone and complained about her mum and dad being so drunk, it had been impossible to rouse them from their slumbers. Alan told Marion the secret, and he made her cross her heart and hope to die if she should tell anyone else about it. She didn't believe him at first, but he took her to that strange corner of the coal cellar and led her by the hand to the cave overlooking the Nullarbor Plain, and she was so overcome by the world of cloudless blue skies and the immense panorama of the plain, she was unable to speak for a while. The parents of the two children were so oblivious to the strange goings-on in their cellar, they thought it odd initially how Alan and Marion were so tanned in the midst of winter, but eventually thought the cold had somehow turned the colour of their skins with the harsh cold.

Then sadly one night, in the early summer of that year, as the people of the antipodes began to have their winter on the other side of this earth, the cellar's secret vanished as mysteriously as it had first arrived. Alan and Marion kept going down into the cellar though, in the hope of finding that golden opening to their new friends in a faraway untamed land – but the hole, or whatever it was, had apparently closed up. A faint scent of eucalyptus lingered for a while, then faded. Every now and then in the wee small hours, Mack would bark, and Alan and his sister would rush down into the hall, hoping Dogey Trucker and Toffee had returned, but without fail the children would be disappointed to find that Mack had merely been barking at the distant sounds of some cat-fight in an alleyway. However, who knows, perhaps the mysterious portal to the Nullarbor Plain will one day reopen in some dank and dark cellar...

# TWO MYSTERIOUS ANIMALS

**One cold dark** morning in December 2011, a woman in her thirties named Joanne entered a well-known Liverpool cemetery to pay her respects to her recently deceased father before she went to work. The time was about 8.10am. Joanne took about five minutes to reach her father's grave from the cemetery gates, and could plainly see there were no other people about, so she was very surprised to hear someone crying and whispering at a nearby grave as she knelt to put some flowers on her late Dad's grave. The eerie mourner was saying, 'Tony, come back – Tony' and a few other things which were hard to make out. Joanne stood up and scanned the cemetery nervously; unless the mourner was unusually small and hidden by the gravestones, he or she was invisible. Joanne decided to leave the cemetery, but upon hearing the uncanny lamenter again, she found curiosity getting the better of her, and decided, against common sense, to go and see who was mourning. She walked about thirty feet up a path, and heard the griever wailing, followed by the phrase: 'Tony! Where are you?'

And then Joanne noticed movement low down, almost at ground level by a tall black polished granite headstone. She froze. A head came around that stone and gazed at her. It was the head of a dog with the most unusual and expressive eyes. Joanne naturally imagined that this was the out-of-sight mourner's dog, but then that dog let out a spine-chilling wailing sound as it threw back its head, and its mouth opened, and out of it came a human sounding voice which sent Joanne running out of that cemetery. 'Tony, come back!' the canine said, and the next thing Joanne remembers is almost falling over as she bolted down the path towards the cemetery gates. She told a workmate what had happened that morning and she reassured Joanne someone had been hiding in the cemetery, playing a prank, and Joanne's sister said 'smackheads' often slept in cemeteries, and that she'd merely overheard one of them talking gibberish whilst on drugs. Joanne contacted me and I told her that she'd encountered a very extraordinary dog, a wire-haired Pointing Griffon named Ludo. The dog's owner, a man named Tony, had died after a long illness and after he was buried in the cemetery Joanne visited, Ludo broke free from the home of his new owners and somehow located the grave where its master is buried. It refused to leave the graveside, and when attempts were made to lure it away, Ludo seemed to shout out "Leave me!" – which naturally unnerved those trying to remove the devoted animal from the cemetery. When it was eventually removed, the dog merely escaped from its owners' house and returned to the grave, making a journey of over a mile to do so, and as far as I know, Ludo made quite a few visits to the cemetery, and has been seen by people night and day at the cemetery. It would seem that the common Indian starling (the Myna bird) and certain parrots are not the only animals that can mimic human speech. Most dogs keep their tongue flat in the lower jaw when they whine and bark, but certain species have been known to produce what sounds like human-like speech (and many years ago there was a dog featured on the Esther Rantzen television programme *That's Life* which featured a dog that seemed to be able to talk) – but in Ludo's case, the words were unusually clear. Could it be a case of someone who had been reincarnated as a dog? This question sits nicely as I relate another strange tale of a mysterious animal.

This story unfolds in the last century, in the early 1960s, at a time when Liverpool was taking its place centre-stage in the eyes of the world because of the Beatles phenomenon. The year was 1964, and the place was the Marlborough Pub on Slater Street in the city centre of Liverpool. It was a hot July lunchtime. A 19-year-old office worker named Jackie walked into this pub and ordered half a glass of beer, but the pumps went off through some mechanical problem, and Jackie was about to leave when an out-of-work musician of 22 years of age named Roger saw his opportunity to chat up the lovely teenager. 'You can have my pint,' he told the secretary, 'it's only just been served – my lips haven't touched it.'

'Nah, it's alright,' Jackie said, and went to leave, but Roger tapped her arm and then handed the pint to her and put on his friendliest smile. It worked. Jackie giggled, and said, 'Just a few sips then! Thanks.'

'Here, sit there,' Roger patted the bare barstool and Jackie sat there. She plonked the full pint glass on the counter and grabbed the strap of the handbag slung over her shoulder as she turned to Roger, and she opened up the handbag, searching for her purse. 'How much do I owe you?' Jackie asked.

'Oh don't talk daft,' Roger waved his hand at her to waiver the offer. 'Here, do you smoke?' he asked, producing a packet of Woodbines from the inside pocket of his black leather jacket.

'Oh, it's okay, I have my own ha!' was Jackie's reply, punctuated with a laugh.

'Would you like the shirt off my back as well?' Roger joked, reaching for the collar of his white shirt.

The young couple got chatting, and Roger learned that Jackie worked as a typist and filer for a travel agency on Bold Street. Roger told Jackie he was looking for work and wanted to form his own band (and he had even thought of their name – The Dole Drums) which would perform his own songs. Jackie told him he should go for it and chase his dream. 'Are you with someone?' Roger asked in the course of the conversation.

'Not now, now,' Jackie said, and her baby blue eyes, which had been so full of youthful sparkle, were now so sad-looking and dead. 'I was engaged, but he cheated. I broke the engagement off.'

'I'm - I'm so sorry,' Roger told the lovely typist, and then in the awful pause that followed, he added: 'He must have been mad to cheat on you; absolutely insane.'

Jackie seemed too choked up to reply for a few moments, then forced a smile. 'I'm just going the toilet,' she told Roger, and she said this in such a way, he got the impression that the girl was trying to tell him to stay put and not go away during her absence.

'Okay, Jackie,' Roger watched her go to the ladies' and then he slyly took a sip from the pint he had given to her because he was skint and unable to buy or cadge a drink.

The voice of an elderly female came over Roger's right shoulder: 'Oh, you're in for it now, lad.'

The aspiring musician turned to see the face of a woman of about sixty-something. Beneath well-shaped dark eyebrows, her eyes were of a smouldering brown and it was evident that she had been quite a looker in her heyday; the onset of accumulated time had not destroyed all the traces of her beauty. 'Sorry?' Roger said quizzically.

The elderly woman explained her remark: 'When two strangers drink from the same glass or the same cup, it means their destinies will be linked. An old superstition it is, love.'

'Oh,' Roger muttered flatly, and the woman smiled, then went to sit down at a table in the corner of the pub.

Jackie returned, and it was obvious she had been crying, but Roger asked no questions as to why this was so – he had an idea that the last boyfriend of this girl had really hurt her. Roger cheered her up with silly jokes and bar counter magic tricks involving matchsticks and beer mats, and Jackie's lunchbreak soon ended. 'Will you be here tomorrow?' she asked the hopeless young man.

'Yeah,' he said, pretending to be enthusiastic about a further meeting but secretly worrying where he'd get some money from to be able to buy her a drink. 'Same time?'

'Yeah, round half-twelve,' Jackie said, and she looked at the pint he had kindly given to her. She must have sipped a thimbleful of the beer in that glass. 'Thanks for the drink – Roger,' she said, and blushed a bit.

'It was a pleasure – Jackie,' Roger got down off his barstool, took hold of the secretary's hand, and kissed her knuckle. 'Thanks.'

Jackie then walked backwards to the door in an awkward manner, just missing an old drinker. And then she said, 'Bye,' and she was gone.

And it was as if the hand of God came down and put his hand on the pub clock on the wall, stopping time. All of the pub chit chat going on in the background faded away, and Roger found himself in love – something he had tried to avoid ever since his own heart was broken by a girl who had cheated on him three years ago. Now he wanted a full-time job, and a dream job at that – and that would be as the leader of a band, performing songs he had written and getting paid pop star's wages. Then he could afford to fall in love or he'd feel like a bummer and a gigolo – and that was definitely not his style.

The old man Jackie had almost collided with came over to the bar where Roger was agonising about his feelings. The oldster went to grab the pint Roger had given Jackie, but Roger's hand intercepted the old man's hand and he said, 'Now, now minesweeper, that's my pint.'

'That looks flat as a fluke,' said the pensioner, eyeing

the pint, which was indeed flat – but beggars can't be choosers and Roger, not having a penny in the world, wanted to drink it. He supped the flat pint and mused on his new predicament. Around 2pm that afternoon he went to his little flat off Berry Street, just a stone's throw from St Luke's Church, grabbed his guitar, then went to busk, first on Bold Street, outside a coffee bar, until a policeman moved him on. Roger then went to Mathew Street, and here he literally made a few pennies singing From Me To You by the Beatles, I Like It by Gerry and the Pacemakers, and a handful of other songs by artistes ranging from Elvis to Cliff Richard. After an hour and a half of this, Roger was sorely tempted to go and slake his thirst in the Grapes pub, but instead he went straight home to his flat, where the landlady Mrs Stenner, threatened him with immediate eviction unless he coughed up his rent arrears damn soon.

On the following day at 11pm, Roger went to see his Uncle Richie, who he hadn't seen in years, and he told Richie how skint he was. Roger's uncle loaned him five quid and Roger promised he'd pay it back soon, even though he knew this was highly unlikely. He then went to a jewellers shop on Lord Street, and bought a little charm on a necklace for Jackie, and then he went straight to the Marlborough pub at noon. Twenty-five minutes later, Jackie came in. By half-past one, the couple were sitting in a quiet corner of the pub, kissing in a loving embrace. Jackie didn't want to go back to work at the end of her lunchbreak, and Roger was surprised at wanting her to stay, as he had fought so hard against falling in love again. 'Can't you just take the afternoon off and phone in and say you're sick?' he asked Jackie, and the girl said her boss would probably fire her if she did that, even though she wanted to take the afternoon off. Just before Jackie left, Roger produced a little dark indigo case, about six inches long, and offered it to Jackie. 'For you,' he said.

Jackie blushed and put her hand to her smiling lips. 'Oh, you shouldn't have,' she whispered.

'Go on, open it, stop palavering,' Roger said, and chuckled.

Jackie opened the case. It was a gold necklace with a charm on which looked like the numeral '8'.

'It's lovely,' Jackie said, not knowing what the charm represented.

'That charm is the symbol for infinity,' Roger explained, 'it looks like a number 8 on its side. It's called a lemniscate. The jeweller said it represents eternal love, infinte love.'

Jackie hugged Roger and looked as if she was ready to cry.

Roger hugged her back then pushed her back and said, 'let me put it on you.'

The necklace was put on the secretary and they kissed, and this time, Roger walked her to her place of work – the travel agency on Bold Street. He then went home and once again racked his brains, thinking how he could get some money together so he could take Jackie out and buy her gifts. The couple became inseparable, and when Jackie realised how poor Roger was, she moved into the flat with him and began to pay the rent. Roger was dead against this, but Jackie said she knew he was no gigolo, and she encouraged him to chase his dream of becoming a pop star. For almost a year Jackie supported Roger, and during that time he solemnly promised her he'd marry her when he made it. Roger was a fairly handsome man and a few ladies had their eyes on him but his love for Jackie was so strong, the thought of even flirting with another girl never even crossed his mind. Then one day, Roger arranged for Jackie to meet him at the Cavern during her lunchbreak to see a band called The Spencer Davis Group. Roger got there a bit early, hoping to sell one of his songs to one of the many acts that played the world-famous venue, and a blonde woman named Dee, aged about twenty-two, approached Roger and asked him if he was a performer. He said he was a struggling song-writer and they got talking. Roger had hardly any money, and instead of buying Dee a drink with the few bob he had for Jackie, he gave her a Polo mint. Dee laughed and it became clear that she had a thing for Roger. It also transpired that Dee was the daughter of a successful manager who was on the lookout for a solo artist to manage. Dee borrowed a guitar off one of the members of a band rehearsing at the time, and gave Roger an audition. He sang a song he had written called Eternal Love, which he had written for Jackie. Dee thought the song was lovely and Roger's voice was unusual. She promised to tell her father about him.

Jackie came into the Cavern a few minutes after the audition and saw Roger laughing and chatting to Dee, and felt sick. She knew in those first few moments as she watched her love talking to the blonde that he was captivated by her. She felt choked up and so empty and cold inside.

When Roger saw Jackie, he hardly acknowledged

her; instead he introduced Dee to her and then told Dee, 'This is my friend Jackie.'

'Oh, nice to meet you, ' Dee said with a nod and a crooked smile.

'Your friend?' Jackie was so offended by being described as thus by Roger; 'I'm your fiancée!'

Dee said, 'Oh,' and looked the travel agency secretary up and down. She then smiled at Roger and said, 'So, you have my number Roger, give me a call in a few days and I'll let you know what my dad thinks.'

'Yeah, thanks Dee!' Roger replied excitedly, and he watched the curvaceous Dee walk to the stairs on her way out of the club. Jackie said she wanted to go somewhere more quiet than the Cavern, as she wanted to discuss a few things, and Roger had a good idea what those things were. After seeing the Spencer Davis Group perform a few numbers, Roger took Jackie out of the club and into the nearby White Star pub, where Jackie began to cry, as soon as the couple had found a few seats. 'What in Heaven's name are you crying for?' Roger asked, and instead of holding and hugging his fiancée, he seemed more embarrassed by Jackie's sobbing in front of the many drinkers present.

'You're going to leave me, Roger – ' Jackie said, and her eyes were red with crying. The tears beaded her face and she looked as if she seemed absolutely incapacitated by her imagined crisis.

'I'm not going to leave you, stop crying,' he said, and looked left and right at the regulars.

'You are,' sobbed Jackie, 'I saw the way you looked at her –'

'Looked at who? Oh, you mean Dee?' Roger said, 'Don't talk daft, I'm not interested in her. I've got you.'

Jackie suddenly clutched the front of Roger's leather jacket and squeezed her crying eyes shut. 'Please do-don't leave me! Please! Please Roger!' she stammered.

'Jackie!' this was the first time Roger had raised his voice to her, 'Stop it! You're making a spectacle of yourself!'

'I couldn't live without you, I'd rather die!' Jackie told him, with tears streaming down her face and onto his jacket now.

'Aww, come on love, he's just bleedin' said that he won't leave you hasn't he?' said a young man who had been standing at the bar, watching Jackie sobbing in the pub mirror. He smiled at the crying girl and said, 'Come on love, you'll be okay with him. I can tell just looking at him that he loves you.'

This cheered up Jackie a bit, but she started crying a few minutes later. She had become so close to Roger, and realised he really was her soulmate. She had a deep affinity with him that was almost religious, and she had never felt this intense about anyone before. The idea of losing Roger to that blonde woman in the Cavern was so unbearable to the 19-year-old, she really did think she'd be better off dead if she should lose her love.

Roger took Jackie home to the flat and had a blazing row with her. He said they should have more space, that she was too clingy and that it wasn't natural to be too close. When he threatened to walk out on Jackie for a few days unless she pulled herself together, the girl said she would kill herself rather than be without him. A week after this, Jackie was supposed to meet Roger in the Marlborough pub – the place where they had first met almost a year back. She arrived at the pub from work at exactly half-past noon but there was no sign of Roger. At one o'clock, Jackie's worrying was at fever pitch, and she left the pub and walked up Slater Street, passing the Jacaranda. A man of about thirty, who Jackie had never seen before, stopped her and said, 'You looking for your fellah?'

'Roger?' Jackie asked, wondering who the man was and what he was about to say concerning Roger's whereabouts.

'Yeah, him. He's with some blonde in the Jac,' the stranger replied, and he indicated the Jacaranda club to his left with his thumb.

Jackie felt physically and emotionally sick. The stranger walked on with a sadistic grin on his face. Jackie went into the Jacaranda and looked about. Sitting at a table in a dark corner was Roger, with his back to her, and sitting facing him at the table with a cigarette in her mouth, was Dee, the blonde manager's daughter Jackie had last seen in the Cavern.

Jackie couldn't even feel her feet as she walked to the table; she was so numb with the shock of Roger sitting with this woman.

Dee looked up and her eyes widened as she realised who was approaching. She glanced at Roger, then subtly nodded in Jackie's direction, and Roger quickly turned to face his fiancée. 'Hiya Jackie,' he said sheepishly, 'I was just going to go and get you. I got sidetracked talking to Dee; we're thinking of doing a talent contest at the Cavern with me – '

Jackie just stared at him, her eyes brimming with tears. 'How could you do this to me?' she suddenly said in a broken voice, then left the Jacaranda. Roger came running out after her and he pulled at Jackie's arm. She turned to present a face streaked with tears.

'There is nothing going on between me and Dee!' Roger bawled, 'You've got to stop this!'

'I'm not stupid Roger, I can tell you like her –' Jackie said, and she looked at the pavement and closed her eyes. 'You said you'd always love me,' she sighed and her voice trailed off as she spoke these cutting words.

At this point Roger saw the infinity charm dangling on the necklace chain and he felt a lump in his throat. 'I will always love you, and you know that,' he told Jackie, in a meagre attempt at reassurance.

'Are you coming with me or are you going back in to her then?' Jackie raised her face and looked Roger straight in the eye – soul to soul.

Roger felt as if he was balanced on the edge of a razor, and for the first time in his life he didn't know what to do; forces were pulling at his heart from both sides.

Dee appeared at the door of the Jacaranda smoking as she eyed Roger and Jackie.

Roger looked back at Dee, who raised her eyebrows as if to silently say: 'Would you really go back to that or are you coming with me?'

'I'll see you in the Marlborough in a few minutes – ' Roger told Jackie, and then he turned to go back to Dee, who gave a restrained smile.

Jackie turned without saying a word and walked off. The Marlborough pub was just twelve feet away from the Jacaranda and as Roger glanced back, he saw Jackie walk straight past the place.

When he got home that evening around half-past seven, he found Jackie sitting on a sofa watching the little black and white TV set. She said nothing and this drove Roger wild.

'Okay, this is it! It's over, Jackie!' he roared, then switched off the television and stood in front of it, glaring at her.

She burst into tears and with her face in her hands she said, 'I feel this is just a horrible dream and I want to wake up and have the love we used to have.'

'Well this is reality, Jackie, and you drove me to this, crying and carrying on, and clinging to me like Evo-Stik – all that shit is not my style!'

'I love you Roger...' she began to say and the rest of her words were lost in the sobs. At one point the girl became so upset it sounded as if she was going to be sick, and Roger patted her on the back and said: 'Jackie, please calm down – you don't deserve someone like me, you deserve someone decent.'

She wheezed and tried to catch her breath and gasped: 'But I want you Roger, that's all I want in this world.'

Roger said nothing, and he went into the bedroom for a while as Jackie lay crying on the sofa. Some time later a peculiar silence descended on the flat, and Jackie went into the bedroom to find it empty. Roger had left. That evening he moved in with Dee, and the set up with her was similar to the way things had been with Jackie, with Dee paying for everything until Roger could get his big break in the world of entertainment.

Jackie became zombie-like from that evening on, and in a daze she would wander the streets around the city centre, especially Mathew Street, where she hoped to see Roger. Just over a week after he deserted her, Jackie saw him one evening on Whitechapel, walking hand in hand with Dee, and she followed them up Stanley Street towards Dale Street, where the couple intended to go to a club. Halfway up Stanley Street, Dee happened to glance back and notice Jackie trailing about fifty yards behind in the shadows, and she told Roger. Roger had been drinking, and told Dee to run with him to the Dale Street club. They skipped along like overgrown children and thought it was so funny running off and leaving the heartbroken girl behind. As they neared the club after crossing Dale Street, Dee looked back and screamed. Roger only heard the car horn and the screech of braking tyres. Jackie had been crossing Dale Street, and because the poor girl's tormented mind had been fixed on nothing but Roger, she had not seen a car coming her way, and she was knocked down – and died at the spot. Roger found himself running to the scene of the tragic accident with Dee following close behind in tears. Roger knelt over Jackie's body lying at the side of the road. One arm looked disjointed, broken, and the other arm was lying on her chest. The girl's hand was clutching that little charm – the infinity charm – that Roger had bought her on that second day he had met up with her in the pub.

'Jackie, come on, wake up!' he said, and he attempted to pick Jackie up but a plain-clothed detective on his way to the Bridewell at Cheapside came upon the scene and told Roger not to move the girl's body. He felt her neck for a carotid pulse and said 'Nah, she's gone I'm afraid; are you related to her?'

'No,' Roger replied, and the whole world became obscured by his tears, 'I was her boyfriend. We'd just split up.'

'You'd better give me the details then sir...' the detective said, 'What's her name?'

That night, Roger cried in the arms of Dee at her flat on Falkner Street, and said he felt so guilty at Jackie's death. Dee told him it wasn't his fault, and he should stop blaming himself. 'I don't wish to sound callous, Roger, but from now on you'll have to forget her,' Dee said, and she stroked Roger's head as he lay across her lap on the sofa.

But Roger couldn't forget Jackie, and his heartache increased when he realised he still loved her. Dee was a lovely young woman but she was not as intimate as Jackie had been – there was just something lacking and Roger just couldn't put his finger on what this thing was. All the same, he decided to stay with Dee for a year, as he had no place to go and no income to provide him with any rent.

In April 1965 he was lying in bed next to Dee one morning at two, and Dee was fast asleep. Roger's thoughts were with Jackie, and he was thinking of that first afternoon when he drank from the same glass as Jackie, and how the old woman had warned him how, according to an old superstition, the destinies of two people are forever intertwined once they drink from the same vessel. He was lost in these self-tormenting thoughts when he heard something that chilled him to the bone.

*'Roger!'*

Roger sat up in the bed. He listened intently, thinking he had been hearing things. But there It was again...

*'Roger! Roger!'*

Roger went to the window and looked out. The backyard was bathed in the silvery light of the moon. There was a cat sitting atop the wall of the backyard. Roger slowly opened the window so as not to awaken Dee, and he saw that the cat had the strangest face he had ever seen; it was not feline, but resembled that of…a lady.

'Roger!' the cat said, 'I came back for you!'

'Jesus – ' Roger stepped back from the window, and then the light in the room went on. Dee had got out of bed to see what Roger was looking at.

'What are you doing?' she said, coming to his side, 'Why have you got the window open?'

And she saw the strange cat too, and now by the light from the room, Roger could plainly see whose face it was – it was Jackie's face.

'Jackie?' Roger murmured, and when Dee saw the face of the deceased girl upon that cat, she screamed, then fainted.

Roger picked Dee up and dragged her to the bed, and when he looked towards the window, he saw that the unearthly feline was now coming into the room. It stood on the window sill and now Roger could see the strange vision even more clearly than before. The cat had all the features of Jackie in its face, and even the eyes were of the same baby blue colour as Jackie's irises.

'I came back for you,' said the cat in its eerie quasi-human voice, 'I love you Roger, and I always will.'

Roger screamed at the cat to go, and it began to say: 'No! Nooo! I wooon't go! I love you!'

Roger picked up a heavy glass ashtray from the table on Dee's side of the bed and he hurled it at the cat, but the hybrid creature jumped off the window sill and out into the backyard a microsecond before the ashtray hit the spot where it had been, and shards of glass went everywhere. Roger then ran in his bare feet to the window and slammed it shut, and he was so afraid, he didn't even realise he had cut the bare sole of his left foot on a sharp fragment of the ashtray till he saw the blood on the carpet. Dee came around and stared in horror at the window. She clung on to Roger and asked him if the cat had gone, and he said, 'Yes, don't worry, it's gone – you did see it didn't you? I didn't imagine it?'

'Yes, I saw it, and heard it – what was it?' Dee asked, and her gaze remained fixed upon the window.

'Roger!' came that haunting voice again, and Dee let out a scream.

Roger swore out loud at the thing and went to the window. 'Go away! Stay away!' he yelled.

Dee was looking at him through splayed fingers as she held her face in her hands.

The couple clung on to one another in bed for the remainder of that morning with the lights on, and on the following day Dee said she thought the cat's face had somehow looked like Roger's former fiancée – and Roger agreed. He told Dee how Jackie had often told him how she would find life without him unbearable; that if he died, she'd kill herself to be with him, and if she should die before Roger did, she would somehow come back to be with him, even if It was wrong in the eyes of God.

When Dee heard this she began to have second thoughts about living with Roger, and in the days following the strange visitation of the weird cat, she told Roger she wanted him out of her flat. She was brutally honest about his chances of succeeding as a pop star too; she told him bluntly what her father had said about a demo tape Roger had made – that it showed no talent whatsoever. Roger stormed out of the flat after Dee told him that, and for a while he had to go and live with his mother. He had only been at his mother's home in Garston for a week when he heard that familiar voice coming from the back garden one night. It was that cat again. Roger's mother and father heard it too, and said it seemed to be someone calling their son's name. A neighbour's dog whimpered whenever the cat began to visit the house of Roger's parents and many people heard the animal's uncanny human-like speech. Then about a fortnight later the cat didn't show, and that was the night Roger's mother found her son laying face down in his bed. He was dead. He'd died from natural causes, even though Roger had no history of health problems. We can only surmise now as to whether he was reunited in death with the girl who was probably his soulmate – Jackie.

# WITCHES OVER STRAWBERRY FIELDS

**Over the years** I have received many letters and emails about the night a coven of witches flew over Liverpool in the early 1960s. I have also gleaned information about the alleged witch visitation from people at my talks, from readers attending booksignings and from telephone conversations when listeners have called me at various radio studios where I have been a guest talking about local reports of supernatural phenomena. When all of these reports of the witches are put together, they reconstruct a very strange event which took place over Woolton Hill in the summer of 1963. That year on the Monday night of 5 August, a full moon rose through the thickets of television aerials on Childwall Valley Road, and a gang of children playing a moonlit game of football near Jackson's Pond saw five or six silhouetted objects cross the lunar disc. A policeman on the 'graveyard beat' near All Saints Church saw the same silhouettes passing in front of the moon, and being a trained observer, noted that there was seven objects moving from left to right, headed in a southerly direction. This policeman told no one – not even his wife – about the weird figures in the sky – until he told me about them 44 years later in 2007. Unknown to the policeman, thirteen other people – as far as I know – saw the witches that night, including the six kids playing football in Childwall. A newly-married couple in their twenties, a Mr and Mrs Howard, were walking past the Abbey Cinema, Wavertree Green, around 10.10pm that Monday night, and saw what initially looked like four large birds flying across the moon's disk. Then they saw three more of these 'birds' follow the others and the Howards thought they looked like the archetypal image of the broomstick-riding witch. These silhouettes were also moving from left to right – from north to south. The most interesting sightings of the witches, however was, from a hackney cab driver named Jim Smithies, who was driving up Menlove Avenue with two elderly female passengers he had picked up at the Philharmonic Hall. As Jim was taking these ladies to their home near Clarke Gardens on Woolton Road, he saw movement in the moonlit sky. He slowed the vehicle, took a look at the group of figures seemingly flying about, then said to his passengers, 'Excuse me ladies but could you just take a look out the window on your right and tell me I'm not seeing things?'

The ladies looked out the windows with bemused expressions, but then they also saw the figures now flying at rooftop level. Jim could make out what looked like long poles that the figures – which were comprised of men and women – were gripping with both hands as they sat on them. The ladies gasped, and Jim drove after the figures out of pure curiosity – and he saw that they were circling the old gothic-looking Strawberry Field children's home. Now, in 1997, I received a letter from a woman we shall call Betty, and she told me how at the age of 8, she had been placed into care at the Strawberry Field children's home in 1962. She clearly recalled one night in 1963 when a strange girl of 7 named Violet told Betty: "The witches are coming for me soon. I have strange powers," and when she and Betty looked out the window of the home, they saw figures in black robes flying over Beaconsfield Road. Betty let out a scream and she and Violet were verbally reprimanded by two members of the administration and accordingly sent to their beds immediately. Not long afterwards, as Betty lay in her bed, she could plainly hear shrieks of laughter in the skies outside the children's home, but was too afraid to peek through the curtains – just in case the eerie visitors took her. On the following day, Betty met Violet as they played outside Strawberry Field in the play area for the children of the home, and Violet smiled smugly and said, 'I told you the witches would come for me last night, didn't I?'

Betty said she heard them as they flew around the home and asked Violet what they wanted with her.

Violet's answer was quite cryptic. 'My mother and father were witches, and I was taken from them because they did bad things. I can't say what they did because I'm not allowed to tell, but the witches will take me back to them one day.'

Betty didn't want to know anything more about the witches and the whys and wherefores of Violet being in the home, and she walked away to play with one of her friends.

In early October of that year, on the night when a huge full harvest moon was hanging over the city, Betty was looking out of the window because she found it hard to get to sleep, when she saw the witches clearly, flying over Woolton in the bright moonlight. She froze with fear as they rode on some sort of thick poles wrapped in strips of cloth. The witches were male and female, old and young and they were shouting and laughing as they headed towards the Strawberry Field orphanage. Betty ducked down and lay on the floor when she saw three of the witches come flying towards her window. She could hear them right outside the window, even though Betty was in a room two storeys up. There was a pause of some silence for about ten seconds, and Betty thought the nocturnal visitors had gone, but when the girl looked up, she saw upon a curtain, the silhouette of a man floating outside the window, and her blood ran cold. Seconds later the silhouette moved away from the window but Betty stayed flat on the floor until she was sure the eerie stalker had gone. A few days after this, Betty was adopted by a family in Wallasey, and never returned to the Woolton orphanage, but she often wondered what became of the strange little girl named Violet. Did the child really belong to the witches, and did she end up adopted – or did the witches take her back as the child told Betty they would?

# GHOSTLY WARPLANES

**Not all ghosts** are of people – in my files of local hauntings there are reports of such inanimate objects as ghostly cars, phantom buses and even spectral houses. I have also collected quite a few accounts of phantom planes in the skies of the North West over the years, and some of the most dramatic and intriguing ones have been seen over Wirral in particular. On the rainy afternoon of Wednesday 18 October, 1972, at around 3.40pm, a plumber named Roy Higgins was walking towards his home on Prenton Dell Road when he noticed a very strange plane flying low in the distance towards the village of Landican. It looked as if it had four engines and was reminiscent of a Lancaster bomber. Roy pointed out the odd low-flying plane to two passers-by, and the three men then watched in horror as the plane burst into a fireball and parts of it fell flaming onto farmland. Roy listened to the news on the radio and watched the news on the TV when he got home but he never heard a single report of the exploding plane over the Landican area of Wirral. Years later, Roy discovered – to his utter astonishment – that on Wednesday 18 October 1944, a B24 Liberator aircraft flying low over Wirral on its way from Northern

Ireland to a base in Norfolk, suddenly exploded for reasons that are still unexplained to this day. The wreckage and bodies of the twenty four souls on the bomber came down in two fields at Landican on the outskirts of Birkenhead, known as The Seven Oaks. A memorial stone today stands at the site of the air crash with the names of the 24 American servicemen inscribed above it. Roy Higgins visited the memorial and was perplexed at how he and two other men had witnessed an eerie re-enactment of the crash exactly thirty years after it had taken place, but the more Roy looked into the strange incident, the more the mystery deepened, because he subsequently learned how many people had seen that doomed Liberator bomber flying over Landican over the years, always in the month of October – the month the tragedy occurred all those years ago.

I mentioned this case and many other aerial anomalies on BBC Radio Merseyside some years ago, and a retired airline pilot contacted me with an even stranger story of our haunted skies. The pilot told me how, in 1980, he was flying a Boeing 747 over Merseyside from New York, bound for Manchester, but had to be diverted to Birmingham because of fog across the North West. As he flew south-east over the Wirral peninsula, the pilot, co-pilot and the rest of the flight crew learned that they were being followed by a light aircraft which, upon closer inspection through a pair of binoculars, turned out to be a Spitfire. As the captain and co-pilot looked on, they saw the scenery thousands of feet below bore little resemblance to the modern day flight maps, and there were vast stretches of fields where factories and towns should have been.

Less than a minute later, the Spitfire was seen to vanish into thin air, and Ellesmere Port suddenly reappeared. It was as if the Boeing had flown decades into the past for a few minutes, but understandably, the pilot and aircrew never reported the inexplicable incident to the people of air traffic control.

# THE DRUID'S CHAIR

**For many years** I sought permission to put this peculiar tale into print, and in 2010 I was finally granted approval by the wife of the man who features in the following account.

In the early 1970s, a 57-year-old Liverpool businessman named Martin felt as if he was facing the dreaded male midlife crisis. He stood in the bedroom of his Grassendale home one morning, casting a critical eye upon his reflection in the wardrobe mirror, and he saw a person who did not correspond to the young inner character he perceived himself to be. Instead he saw a man with typical male-pattern baldness, and what was left of his hair had long turned white and grey. He had a double chin, and the skin under his coarse bushy eyebrows (which used to be silky and thin) had sagged over his eyelids. He had crescents of fat hanging in bags under his eyes, and as much as he sucked in his stomach, he could still see the 'bread basket' (as his wife called it) – the pot belly that had been gaining size since his mid-thirties. On top of all that he had trouble with his prostrate which made even the simple act of urinating difficult, and he had also recently accepted that he was almost impotent. Viagra was unheard of in 1973, and Martin had no wish to experiment with Spanish Fly and other alleged 'aphrodisiacs'. His wife of twenty years, Joni – a beautiful and understanding lady of Canadian birth – was forever telling Martin not to worry about their sex life – or lack of it – because just to be cuddled by him in the night meant more to her than anything. As Martin's sex drive went into decline, he seemed to become fixated with fast cars, and sold his old Hillman Hunter saloon for a blood-red Maserati Mistral two-seater coupe, and this was the racing car he would journey around the country in, seeking out various antiques shops each weekend. Martin was something of a dabbler in the world of antiques and always had an eye out for the more unusual item. One blazing hot Saturday in July 1973, Martin drove to the little out-of-the-way antiques shop in North Wales belonging to an old Caernarvonshire man named Gareth Pepperwrack. The shop – a former sandstone cottage – had a backyard cluttered with such things as Victorian tin baths, ancient cast-iron mangles, an Edwardian rocking horse, a 1950s jukebox, an "I speak your weight" weighing machine from a Rhyl fairground, countless chairs, tables and sideboards from every era – and even the full hinged skeleton of a horse.

Martin would spend a good hour in this yard each time he visited, always returning to his Grassendale home in Liverppol with some piece of junk from

Pepperwrack's, and this day would be no different. Martin noticed what looked like a black granite boulder at the end of the yard, and went to ask Mr Pepperwrack – who was making his regular client a coffee in the shop's kitchen – what the thing was. Pepperwrack smiled and told Martin: 'That's the Druid's Chair, excavated up in Anglesey many years ago – in he 1920s I think.'

'What?' Martin shot a doubtful look at the old antique dealer – 'A genuine Druid artefact? It'd be worth a fortune.'

'You've obviously never heard of the Harborough Rocks then?' Pepperwrack queried over the top of his gold-wire spectacle frame.

Martin returned a blank stare.

'The Harborough Rocks were a Druidical circle near Matlock,' Pepperwrack explained, 'a sun-worshipping site, and they were sold by Sir Joseph Whitworth to a company for £75,000 in 1920. It was a scandal that was hushed up.'

'And what did this company want with all those stones?' Martin wondered aloud.

Mr Pepperwrack provided the answer: 'They broke them up and reworked them because those ancient stones were made of high-grade Dolomite. Imagine the outcry if the Government sold off Stonehenge to be subdivided into genuine Neolithic fire surrounds.'

The two men were sipping medium roast coffee as they stood before the ominous-looking black Druid's Chair at the end of the yard, set aside in a space cleared away from the mare's nest of junk. The chair was about five feet tall, and looked just like an armchair of black polished granite, except that the arms of this chair sloped down and outwards at angles of about forty degrees. The seat and back were remarkably smooth for something supposed to date back to a time before Caesar's invasion, but the rest of the chair was roughly hewn granite with minute traces of something that sparkled like stars the size of sand-grains. 'And how much are you asking for this?' Martin asked at last after quite a silent inspection of the unusual item.

Pepperwrack coughed, perhaps out of nerves, perhaps to clear his throat, then began his spiel: 'Well, before I tell you that, let us be mindful of the fact that this item probably dates back thousands of years to Neolithic times and seems to be a huge meteorite - '

'May I?' Martin interrupted and sat in the chair; he was surprised how comfortable it was. He felt a shudder up his spine seconds later. That was quite an odd sensation, he thought.

Pepperwrack continued: 'As I was saying, this chair may even predate Stonehenge – '

'How much? You've told me all that,' Martin asked impatiently, 'I probably can't afford it anyway. I'd love to have it though. What a talking point this would be with guests when we have a barbecue in the back garden.'

'Fifteen hundred,' said Pepperwrack, looking Martin straight in the eyes.

'Yeah, okay.'

'You sure?' Pepperwrack expected some haggling and was highly surprised at the way Martin had calmly acquiesced. This wasn't like him at all; he would normally chaffer and wrangle about the price of a thimble. 'Get off your cloud,' he'd usually say.

'What about transport?' Martin realised that the chair

weighed a ton. 'I can't put this thing on a roof rack.'

'Well, seeing how I need the space in this yard, I'll pay for the transportation costs,' Pepperwrack announced, and the two men clinked their coffee mugs together in a toast to seal the deal.

Three days later, it took four workmen, Martin, and his young neighbour Ollie to position the Druid's Chair at a spot at the bottom of the back garden in the shade of an old oak.

The kitchen table was brought out and positioned in front of the ancient granite throne, and the workmen and Ollie and Martin and his wife drank wine and enjoyed a buffet, with Martin seated at the head of the table in the chair of course while everyone else sat on the mundane dining chairs. The young keen eyes of Ollie noticed the spirals and what seemed to be Runic glyphs at the side of the Druid's Chair. 'Wonder what they signify?' Ollie asked, and Martin shrugged.

That night, Martin apologised to Joni about the cost of the chair as they lay in bed in a loving embrace, but Joni pecked his cheek and said, 'If it gives you pleasure, it's worth every penny.' And then after a pause, she asked her husband: 'What attracted you too it, anyway?'

'I don't know,' Martin realised, 'It just sort of cries antiquity – I mean, if that thing could speak, all the history it would spout – and who knows what those Druid's got up to? We know nothing of their knowledge. It took about twenty-five years to become a Druid, and they wrote nothing down, so no one really knows what they were about.'

'They sacrificed people didn't they? That's what I read somewhere,' said Joni softly as she clung on to her husband.

'I don't think so, love; I think that was all Roman propaganda. The Romans wanted their superiors back in Rome to think that the strange priests of these little islands were just bloodthirsty superstitious savages who needed to be conquered and civilised. I'm not A. J. P Taylor, but that's what I think, anyway'

About half an hour later, Joni threw the thin duvet off because of the stifling summer-night heat, and then she dozed off. When she awoke around four o'clock, she reached out for Martin and found he wasn't there. She listened, thinking she'd hear him return from the toilet, but there was just silence. Joni felt very uneasy all of a sudden, and got up from the bed and went out onto the landing. The door of the toilet was wide open and it was evident that her husband was not in there. She put on her slippers, went downstairs to the lounge, and heard early birdsong, then found the double doors which gave access to the back garden open. The diaphanous curtains draped in front of these doors were gently billowing from the mild zephyr coming in from the back garden. What was Martin doing out there at this time in the morning? She went outside and saw him standing barefoot in front of the Druid's Chair, wearing only his pyjama trousers.

'Martin? You okay?' she shouted.

He turned quickly to face her. 'You'll never believe this,' he said faintly, and Joni hurried to him in her slippers.

'What?' she asked.

'There was someone sitting in it,' he said, nodding at the chair. 'All in white he was – and then he was gone.'

'Were you dreaming or was it a ghost?' Joni asked

with a nervous smile. She stopped a few feet away from the vacant black granite chair.

'I thought I heard a voice when I was coming back from the toilet, and it seemed to come from the back garden so I went into the spare room and looked out the window, and there was a man in a long white robe and long hair, sitting in the chair. I went downstairs to look out the kitchen window and saw he had gone. He looked as if he was in his early twenties.'

The birdsong stopped, and a eerie silence fell all around.

Standing in the dark and soundless back garden at that hour, Joni felt very nervous at her husband's words, for she knew he was certainly not a man who had ever held any belief in things of a supernatural nature. 'Well, it looks like he's gone now,' she told Martin, and gently took hold of his forearm. 'Come on, let's go back inside. It's cold.'

Martin turned, almost trancelike, and let his wife lead him back indoors.

On the following morning, again around four o'clock, Joni woke and found Martin absent from the bed. She went down into the living room and once more found the double doors ajar with their curtains blowing wildly because of the strong out-of-season winds that had stirred up during the night. She went into the garden – and this time she saw Martin sitting in the Druid's Chair, and this time he was naked. His pyjama bottoms and underpants had been discarded in the centre of the back garden. Was he sleepwalking? Was he having a nervous breakdown? Could he have suffered some sort of stroke which had affected his behaviour? The questions came thick and fast and crowded Joni's thoughts as she slowly walked to her husband in the chair.

'Martin? Are you okay?' she asked, and the wind threw her long auburn hair back and then lifted it.

Martin was sitting with a blank expression, and his mouth was open as if he was yawning.

'Marty, what's the matter?' she asked, naturally full of concern for the bizarre behaviour her husband was exhibiting.

Martin never even budged. He was staring straight ahead at something with an expression of shock, and now his mouth seemed even wider than before.

Joni tried to pull her husband from the chair but it was like trying to move a statue. It was as if Martin was welded to that accursed granite seat. At one point as the winds were whistling through the branches of the oak tree behind the chair, Joni fell backwards as she lost her grip on her husband's shoulder as she tried her utmost to make him stand. She lay there on the dewy grass, near to tears. She got to her feet and tried to calm herself down. If Marty was having some breakdown or if he had suffered some stroke, she would have to call for an ambulance. She waved her hand in front of his face and there was no response. What on earth was holding his fascination? What was he staring at with that mesmerised expression? Joni turned and followed the line of Marty's sight – and saw that the full moon was in the sky, and that seemed to be the thing he was fascinated with.

'Martin!' Joni yelled over the whining wind, 'I'm going to get some blankets for you and then I'm going to call and ambulance. You're going to be okay.' She then rushed back towards the house. She went to get the duvet off the bed, rolled it up, then went downstairs to dial 999. Joni then went into the garden – and saw that the Druid's Chair was empty. She panicked and looked around, and establishing that her husband was nowhere to be seen, she went back into the house. There was no sign of Martin anywhere. Joni decided to try the bedroom, and there he was, lying naked on the bed, snoring. Joni called the emergency services again and cancelled the ambulance. She felt so foolish yet so relieved.

She put the duvet back on her sleeping husband then got into bed and held him until the dawn. He awoke around six that morning and rose to go to the toilet, and as he got out the bed, Joni asked him why he had gone to sit in the Druid's Chair. Martin had no recollection of leaving the bedroom earlier, and over breakfast he asked Joni to tell him exactly what had happened again. He began to shake when she said he seemed hypnotised by the moon.

'That's it, I'm getting rid of that thing,' Martin decided, and he began to tremble and his voice had an eerie tremolo quality to it. 'It's going back to Pepperwrack's.'

'I think that's a good idea, Marty.' Joni agreed, and clutched her husband's shaking hands across the breakfast table.

A call was made to Pepperwrack, and when Martin told him he wanted to send the chair back, the Welsh antique dealer said he couldn't refund him because they had come to a gentleman's agreement.

'No, Gareth, listen, I don't think you get the gist of what I'm saying - I don't want my money back, I just want you to get someone to come and take the blasted thing away – it's haunted!'

'Haunted?' Pepperwrack had amusement in his voice.

'Yes, take my word for it; now, when can you get those men to take it back?' Martin's hand began to tremble as he clutched the telephone handset.

'I can't afford to hire them again, Martin,' complained Pepperwrack, 'it cost me fifty quid last time.'

An impatient Martin rolled his eyes and assured the antiques dealer: 'I'll pay them for Christ's sake, just get them here this afternoon.'

After a lot of banter, Pepperwrack promised he'd have the removal men at Martin's Grassendale home by around 3pm, but 3pm came and went, and there was no sign of the men. Marty called the antique dealer again and asked where the men were.

'Their van's broken down. They'll be there tomorrow afternoon around one,' Pepperwrack explained, then he asked: 'Are you serious about all this haunted mumbo jumbo Martin?'

'Yes, I am deadly serious Gareth – that chair is haunted by something. I'm not going into it all now, I just want to be rid of the thing, pronto!'

'I never took you as a believer in all that stuff. Anyway, the men will be there tomorrow, about one.' Pepperwrack then hung up.

That night, Joni decided to lock the double doors leading from the lounge to the back garden, and she hid the key behind a row of cookery books on a shelf in the kitchen. As an extra precaution, she locked the door in the kitchen which also gave access to the back garden and hid the key to that door under a tin of Ajax in the cupboard under the sink. And yet, that morning at four, Martin went missing from the bed, and Joni went In search of him. The front door was still bolted, and when she examined the double doors to the back garden she saw that they were still locked. The door in the kitchen was also still locked, but when Joni looked out the kitchen window, she saw a figure sitting in the Druid's chair – only this time the figure had long dark hair. Joni went round the house, shouting for Martin, but couldn't find him anywhere. She finally decided to go outside into the back garden (via the door in the kitchen), and when she did she got the shock of her life. The naked man sitting in the Druid's Chair was her husband, but he was now no longer bald with those tufts of grey and white hair on either side of his head. Instead, he had a good head of long black hair, and even the grey hairs on his chest were dark.

As Joni looked on in terror, she saw the face of Martin change to that of a face she had never seen before – a much younger face with very dark penetrating eyes. The figure suddenly got up from the chair and the metamorphosed person – whoever he was, stood there, and he was obviously quite aroused by Joni. She screamed and turned to run and the strange long-haired youth followed her at a leisurely walking pace. He began to shout at Joni, but the language he spoke was unknown to her. Joni ran into the house via the door to the kitchen. Joni ran straight through the kitchen screaming, and then went through the hall to the front door of the house, where she yanked off the bolt. She then ran out of the house and didn't stop running until she reached the home of a friend named Pat, who lived half a mile away. When Joni told Pat what had happened, Pat's husband Mike drove over to Joni's house and found Martin lying unconscious in the back garden. When Martin came to, he had no recollection of even leaving his bed, and he had evidently been transformed back to his previous physical state; gone was the head of thick black long hair. The removal men turned up at the house later that day at 1.40pm and duly removed the Druid's Chair from Martin and Joni's back garden, and after this removal there were no further paranormal occurrences or instances of sleepwalking at the Grassendale house. Years later, Martin read about a murder in France where a man knifed his wife to death in a senseless murder after he had come into possession of a Druid's Chair that had been excavated at Carnac, and a Catholic priest who had known the murderer for many years stated that he had been a loyal and loving man who doted upon his wife - until something possessed him, and that something, according to the priest, was some evil spirit connected to the Druidic chair. This was no rational defence of course and the murderer was sentenced to life imprisonment. Martin went cold when he read the newspaper article detailing the strange killing, and wondered about the present whereabouts of that Druid's Chair unearthed in Anglesey – once the Druidic capital of ancient Britain.

# LADY WILLPOWER

'**I teach you the superman.** Man is something to be surpassed,' wrote the controversial German philosopher Nietzsche in the late 19th century, and his concept of the superman - that man is just a shadow of his potential self with incredible latent powers worthy of a superhero – was later seized by the thinkers of the Nazi party and twisted to justify a ruthless eugenics programme to breed an Aryan Master Race at any cost. Nietzsche was right of course: every man is a potential superman, and every woman is a latent superwoman, but it would seem that through negative psychological conditioning at an early age and severe self-limiting mental habits, most of us remain lifelong in the basement of our minds, but often, in times of crisis or in life-threatening situations, the superhuman comes through. For example, in the May Blitz of 1941, a bomb demolished a house off Scotland Road and a heavy beam fell across the beds of a woman's young children. The hysterical woman somehow drew on a normally untapped inner strength to lift that beam off the beds to free her kids – even though that beam weighed as much as a car, and the air-raid wardens who witnessed the act were left dumbfounded. There was also a case, once reported in a staid medical journal, of a Birkenhead man who, after suffering an electric shock from a faulty fridge, found he could perform phenomenal feats of mental computation and became an expert in the fields of integral calculus, non-Euclidean geometry and metamathematics. Before the electrocution, the Wirral man had been hopeless at simple addition and subtraction. There are hundreds of cases such as this, where some trauma takes place, leaving the person 'superabled', but could there be a safe way for neurologists to replicate the side effects of these traumas so that they can bring out the supermind which seems to exist in us all? There are scientists at the University of Sydney's Centre for the Mind department who have used magnetic fields to 'transcranially' switch off the front temporal lobes of volunteers, enabling them to employ what seems to be greatly boosted mental powers. This research is still in its infancy, but the day may be close when someone will create a type of superconducting helmet – a veritable "Thinking Cap" – which could turn the wearer into a genius.

The most fascinating case of a person with apparent 'superpowers' was the unknown lady who stood on one of the four stone lions of St George's Plateau on Lime Street in June 1967 and proclaimed herself a miracle worker. A crowd of bemused onlookers listened to the woman, who looked as if she was in her twenties, as she claimed to have found a technique which had unlocked incredible faculties of the human mind which would transform humans into gods. A sceptical onlooker asked the speaker to prove her claims and as a demonstration of her awesome powers she allegedly caused the statue of the lion she shared the plinth with to rise from a sitting position. Some fled at the sight of the animated leonine statue while others looked on with a mixture of fascination and fear. Whether the effect was caused by mass-hypnosis (as it often is when, say, the Indian Rope Trick is performed) is a moot point, but the intriguing speaker told the crowd that through sheer willpower and meditation they too could perform such miracles – and even raise the dead, and this latter claim sent a number of priests present in search of a policeman. The holy men called the wonder-working woman a false prophet and an agent of Satan, and stated that any attempts at raising the dead would amount to blasphemy and desecration. The woman told the priests: 'Jesus raised the dead and told you if you had faith the size of a mustard seed, you'd be able to do the same! But look at you in your old fashioned black clothes and white collars! You are mere groundlings who have no faith at all! You can save no one nor perform the smallest miracle, yet you accuse people of having no faith in God when you don't even have faith in Him yourself!'

It wasn't long before several policemen were trying to remove the incendiary speaker from the plinth. Some members of the crowd booed the police but a few cheered them on. The woman announced that she would visit a cemetery and 'raise a legion of a departed' but she was seized by the police and dragged from the statue. There were allegedly two cases of the policemen fainting when the woman pointed her index finger at them and uttered some form of curse. This could have been nothing but autosuggestion or an effective form of stage hypnotism, of course.

The intriguing woman's fate is unknown but there were rumours she had been very forcefully committed to Rainhill psychiatric hospital. I have received so many letters and emails from people who swear the stone lion *really did* stand up that summer day in 1967.

# THE LIGHT IN THE DISTANCE

**There are certain superstitions** regarding pictures – and I am referring to pictures of the framed kind that we hang on walls. There is an old Liverpudlian superstition dating back centuries which states that we must never hang pictures over doorways or on walls at the head of a bed, or we shall endure long runs of bad luck and often a death. Another grim superstition regarding pictures that is found the world over says that death will visit a household where a picture seems to fall from a wall for no obvious reason, and I have received so many letters and emails from readers about this phenomenon. In March 1983, a 52-year-old woman named Ann, of Kensington's Molyneux Road, was sitting watching television one evening around 9.10pm when the picture over her fireplace suddenly fell and crashed to the floor. The glass covering the picture was not smashed and the cord strung across the back of the picture was perfectly intact. The nail the picture had hung from remained firmly in the wall, and Ann was at a loss to say how the picture had managed to fall. Ann's grandmother, who had been dozing on the sofa when this strange incident took place, was awakened by the sound of the picture hitting the carpet, and she morbidly told her granddaughter that the unnatural falling of a picture in such a way always meant that someone in the family – or a close friend of the family, would die within a few weeks, and often within days. Ann said that was superstitious nonsense, and she hung the picture back on the nail over the fireplace. On the following day, Ann's sister was knocked down and killed in St Helens. A few years after this, the same picture fell from Ann's living room wall, again for no apparent reason, and within twenty-four hours Ann received news from the next-door neighbour (who had a telephone) that her sister-in-law had fallen down stairs at her home in Hoylake and had died instantly from a broken neck.

I have covered so many of these death omens and dark superstitions in my books over the years, and recently the following story came my way.

One overcast evening in April, 1977, Barry and Edna Callow were settling down to watch an episode of *Poldark* on BBC1, while their 13-year-old son Stuart sat at the dining table, reluctantly doing his maths homework. He was trying to tackle common fractions, but just couldn't get the hang of them, and his eyes and mind kept wandering. The lad gazed out the window of his home on Wavertree's Prince Alfred Road, and saw a faint drizzle beading on the panes as twilight gathered on this cold April night. Beyond the rain-speckled window stretched the constellation of streetlights and distant lit windows.

The doorbell sounded, and straight away, Stuart

excitedly exclaimed: 'I'll get it!' And he leaped off his chair and went into the hallway. Already he could see his grandfather's distinctive silhouette through the frosted glass of the front door. Stuart yanked open the door and in came Jimmy Callow.

'Here, don't eat them all at once or you'll have worms!' Jimmy said, taking a white crumpled paper bag of Taverner's sweets out his pocket.

'Ah, thanks, Grand-dad!' Stuart seized the bag and slammed the front door shut. He walked behind Grand-dad Jimmy into the living room where Barry and Edna grumpily received the old man. The couple had looked forward to watching *Poldark* and now they'd have to put up with Jimmy's interminable hackneyed anecdotes of his days as a bricklayer.

'What's this?' Jimmy plonked himself down in the armchair next to the TV as he squinted at the screen with a supercilious grin.

'*Poldark* Dad,' Barry replied with a sigh, without taking his eyes off the telly, and he clutched his wife's hand and told his father: 'Can we just watch this? Edna loves this show as well – '

'Yeah, go on, lad,' Jimmy nodded, 'you two watch it, go on; I'll have a cup of tea and a chat to our Stuart.'

'Do you know anything about common fractions, Grand-dad?' Stuart enquired, sitting at the table with a mouth full of toffee already.

'Never mind asking other people, Stuart,' the boy's mother told him, 'do those sums yourself or you'll never learn.'

'Does anyone want a cup or any scran or anything?' Jimmy asked, and he hauled himself off the armchair and headed for the hallway, bound for the kitchen.

'Nah, we're alright Dad, get yourself something to eat,' Barry replied, and he got up and turned the volume up on the telly.

Stuart went into the kitchen to help his Grand-dad, and as they made some cheese on toast topped with chopped onions, Jimmy Callow happened to gaze out the window – and he noticed a winking light.

'What are you looking at Grand-dad?' Stuart wanted to know.

'My vision is terrible nowadays,' Jimmy admitted, screwing up his eyes as he looked out the window. 'Is that someone shining a light at us? Right over there in the distance, across the park. Just on the left there.' He pointed a thick iced bun-size finger at the pinpoint of light that was going on and off in an irregular fashion.

Stuart looked out the kitchen window into the nightscape. Amongst the specks of light – the newly turned on red sodium lamps, the blue mercury vapour lamps, the squares of neon and tungsten-lamp light, there was indeed a tiny starlight point of luminosity flashing on and off in a strange rhythm.

Jimmy watched the light in the distance for a while in silence, and then he looked down at his grandson and said, 'I think someone's sending a message in Morse.'

Stuart's eyes widened and he smiled. This was so much more exciting than common fractions. 'Morse code?'

Jimmy nodded and turned to look back at the winking light. 'Get a pen and some paper Stu; we'll try and decode the message.'

Stuart ran into the living room, grabbed his exercise book and a cheap royal blue Bic school pen, then went back into the kitchen.

'Now, Stu, when I say "dit" I want you to write down a dot, like a full stop, and when I say "dah" you write down a dash; got that?'

'Yes Grand-dad,' Stuart opened the exercise book from the back, placed it on the formica work surface of the kitchen unit and held his pen over a blue-lined page, poised to take down the relayed message.

'Okay, let's see what he's saying,' Jimmy narrowed his eyes and watched the light in the distance. 'Dah..dit…dit…dit…got that?'

'Yeah, dash,dot dot dot!' Stuart confirmed.

'Dah…dit…dah…dah…got that Stu?'

'Yep! Dash, dot, dash, dash!'

'Definitely Morse this…' Jimmy nodded to himself, and within a few minutes, Stuart had almost filled an entire page of the maths exercise book with the dots and dashes.

The light in the distance stopped dead. Jimmy waited for a few minutes until he was sure the mysterious transmitter had definitely ceased – and then it was time to decode the message, and this was much harder than Jimmy thought. Stuart got his encyclopaedia, borrowed from Wavertree Library, off the shelf, and turned to the entry for Morse Code. There was a table of the code which covered the 26 letters of the alphabet, the numbers zero to nine, as well as the codes for punctuation and question marks. It was difficult fathoming the words at first, but Stuart persevered and he excitedly began to decode the message. 'Ah, Grand-dad! I've got it!'

'Go on, lad!'

'Shh!' Edna said to her son as she was momentarily

distracted from the 18th century Cornish TV Drama.

'It says,' Stuart whispered to his grandfather (who cupped his hand around his ear as he moved in close to the boy), 'GRANT AV, SAT NINE APRIL BYE DILLY.' And the boy pushed the exercise book with this bizarre message on its page towards Jimmy.

'Grant Avenue?' Jimmy murmured, trying to make sense of the cryptic communication. 'Grant Avenue is just near here, by the park,' he pondered. 'Saturday – well that is the ninth of April. But who's Dilly?'

'Do you think a spy is sending messages Grand-dad?' Stuart asked, and he was so serious when he posed this question.

'Nah, I don't think it's a spy, Stu,' Jimmy replied with a subdued smirk, 'I think someone is pulling our leg, and they're going to a lot of trouble whoever it is.'

*Poldark* ended at ten minutes past eight that Monday evening, and as the credits to the drama rolled, Stuart's father came over to sit at the table, and his son showed him the strange message he and grandfather had received.

Barry smiled and shook his head. 'I don't get what you mean; who would be sending Morse code in this day and age? All they'd have to do was use a telephone or a walkie talkie; you two are balmy.'

'Whoever is sending the message has the torch pointed towards our direction, so the spy he's communicating with must live near us somewhere,' Stuart reasoned, and then after a thoughtful pause, he told his grandfather: 'That old man Mr Davis next door but one could be a Russian spy. Maybe his codename is Dilly.'

'Nah, I've known him for years Stu,' Jimmy poured

cold water on his grandson's suspicions, 'he's definitely not a spy.'

Grandfather and grandson went back into the kitchen, waiting for the light in the distance to come back on but it never did come back on that night, and around 10pm, Jimmy Callow went home to his house on Thingwall Road.

On Saturday afternoon, Stuart's mother came running into the house in tears. Her husband asked what the matter was, and Edna sobbed: 'Mrs Wilkie's dog has just been run over!' Edna embraced her husband and cried her eyes out as she pressed her face into his chest.

'Did you see it, love?' Barry asked his distraught wife and felt her nodding.

When she had calmed down a bit, Edna said something which made her son's ears prick up.

'Poor little Tilly, she was only three; she never had a chance!' Edna said with a trembling bottom lip.

Stuart went ice-cold inside, for he recalled the name "Dilly" from that baffling Morse code message; that name sounded like Tilly – perhaps he and grand-dad had made a mistake decoding so that T was wrongly interpreted as D. That message had intimated that something would happen on the ninth of April – and now it had, and whoever had sent the message had known that Tilly the dog would be knocked down. Stuart suddenly had a chilling thought: had the person who had sent the Morse code been the driver of the vehicle that had knocked down the dog – on purpose?

Stuart mentioned this theory to his dad, but he just said, 'No; why would anyone do something like that, son? You wouldn't tell people what you were going to do in Morse code. Doesn't make sense.'

Later, around 8pm as darkness was falling, Stuart was in the kitchen again, ready with sheets of paper and a pencil, scanning the vista outside the window for that mysterious light, and around 8.25pm, it reappeared in the exact same spot it had the previous Monday. He tried his best to write down the dots and dashes signalled by the distant light, and after about four minutes the light went out and stayed out for that night. Before Stuart made an attempt at decoding the long message, he sneaked into the bedroom of his parents and went rooting in the wardrobe until he could find his dad's old binoculars. Stuart tiptoed back to the kitchen as his mother and father watched the TV, and he looked at the place where the light had appeared through the 20 x 50 binoculars. It was the upper window of a house on the Smithdown Road end of Grant Avenue. The window was a dark square with two threadbare curtains hanging there – but no sign of the eerie signaller in Morse.

Stuart hid the binoculars in his bedroom and then he went into the kitchen with his scribbled down Morse message, two sheets of paper, a pencil and the encyclopaedia with the Morse table in it. He set about transcribing the message after he had worked out where the gaps where between each letter. The message chillingly ran: "BYE BYE GRANDY BLOODY ENF SHUR NIGH".

Stuart ran in a panic with the message to his mum and dad, who were seated, as usual, on the sofa in front of the telly. 'Dad! There was another message, and it looks as if it says Grand-dad will die, and it mentions blood!'

'Oh, stop all this nonsense Stuart!' his father reacted angrily as his son almost shoved the message into his face. 'No one is bleeding sending you messages!'

Stuart's mother snatched the page from between her son's finger and thumb and read it with a fed-up look. 'It says "Grandy" – who the hell's Grandy? Doesn't say grandfather at all!'

'I used to call Grand-dad Grandy when I was a baby!' Stuart seemed so shocked at the contents of the message, and his mum could see a tear welling in his eye.

'It doesn't make sense!' the boy's mother bawled, and she looked back at the quiz show she'd been enjoying on the telly, then looked at the page again. 'And what does "Enf" and "shur nigh" mean?'

'I think I must have made a few mistakes,' Stuart replied with a worried look. 'I think "Shur" means "Thur" – as in Thursday, and "nigh" means "night". The "enf" probably means "End" – oh God it means Grand-dad's going to die on Thursday night!'

'Stop upsetting your mother you little idiot!' Barry growled at his son. 'Why don't you start playing out with your friends instead of sitting in each night like a hermit?'

'You two are the idiots!' Stuart suddenly hollered as he backed away with a tear dripping from his right eye. 'All you want to do is sit watching the telly!'

'You cheeky bas-' Mr Callow rose from the sofa and ground his teeth as Stuart ran out of the living room and into the hall. Next thing the boy knew he was running down Prince Alfred Road through the cold and rainy night. He heard his father calling him back but ran across the road to a gap in the railings of the park. In the centre of the park that time in the evening there wasn't a soul about, and there was only one lamp post burning a weak blood-orange sodium light on the path that bisects the greenery. Stuart looked at the stream of traffic headlamps orbiting the park beyond its perimeter railings, and then his eyes turned towards that house on Grant Avenue where some sinister person had been signalling future fatalities in Morse with that ghostly light. Stuart walked over towards the direction of the house, but fear of the unknown prevented him from going too close, and he stopped within about 150 yards of the dwelling, and suddenly had the unsettling sensation of being watched by someone in that dark window of the house. There was no traffic passing by now, and all was quiet. The rain began to pelt down, and that and the sound of Stuart's panting breath were the only noises evident now. The lad ran off, back to Grant Avenue, and back to his home. As soon as his father opened the door, Stuart mumbled an apology and went straight to his bedroom to sulk. On the following day after his tea, Stuart got on his old racer bicycle and rode it to his grandfather's house on Thingwall Road, but when he got there there was no answer, and a neighbour told him he was on the nearby allotment, so Stuart rode there and found Jimmy Callow sitting outside his hut with a blackened kettle on a fire he'd built from pieces of wood, twists of newspaper and a sprinkle of paraffin. 'Hiya lad!' Jimmy's eyes lit up when he saw his grandson, and he asked him if he wanted a cuppa.

'No thanks, Grand-dad,' Stuart replied with a half-hearted smile. And then he told him about the latest

Morse message.

'Grandy? Yeah, you used to call me that,' Jimmy recalled, reading the pencilled words on the sheet of paper. 'But you also called your other grandfather - George – that name as well. Could be him.'

Stuart forgot all about his other grandfather George Skellinge. What a horrible man he was; a drunk and a wifebeater and a thief. He lived somewhere in Stoke now. Stuart hadn't seen him since he was about five or six years old. 'I hope it is him,' Stuart said solemnly.

'You shouldn't wish death on anyone, Stu,' his grandfather reflected as he gazed into the flames of he fire under the whistling kettle, 'But I hope it's him too,' he added, and gave a little nervous laugh.

'On Thursday night you should stay in, so nothing bad can happen to you,' Stuart suggested to his grandfather.

'I always play darts down the pub on Thursday nights though,' Jimmy folded an old tea towel around his hand so he could pick up the old kettle by its hot handle.

'Well, I'm sure you can do without darts one night if your life depends on it – ' Stuart was saying, when a single magpie landed within a few feet of him and his grandfather. 'Hello Mr Magpie, how's Mrs Magpie?' Stuart asked the bird. It flew off.

'If it makes you feel any better, lad, I'll stay in,' Jimmy decided, seeing the magpie and being superstitious about the encounter with the traditionally unlucky bird.

'Yeah, I'll stay over with you and we can play cards and watch the telly!' Stuart enthused. He loved going to his grand-dad's house and listening to his funny stories about the old days. He was a natural storyteller, and he always got in decent Mr Kipling cakes and lots of lemonade whenever Stuart stayed over.

Thursday came and went, and thankfully, nothing happened to Jimmy Callow, even though his grandson expected him to drop dead every now and then. However, on the Saturday morning at eleven-thirty, Stuart's Auntie Toni paid a visit as a bearer of tragic tidings. George Skellinge had been found dead in his blood-soaked bed on Friday morning. He had died from a massive brain haemorrhage. Edna Callow burst into tears when she was told this. Her father had not been an ideal father by any means but he was still her dad, and Edna and her sister Toni held on to one another as they cried. Stuart and his father, mindful of that creepy Morse code warning, glanced at one another with flint faces. Now Stuart's father was a convert; now he believed his son was on to something. Barry angled his head in a sideways nod, gesturing for his son to follow him out of the living room. In the hallway, he told Stuart to never mention that strange light and the weird messages. He also told his son that he would look into this strange mystery with him soon, but not until after the funeral of his father-in-law.

All the same, Stuart kept a lookout for the light in the distance from that night on, and it did not show for almost three weeks, and when it did, one Monday night at 8.40pm, Stuart shouted for his father, and he saw the light too. 'Wait there, I'll go and get my binoculars,' Barry told his son, but Stuart blushed and said, 'They're in my room Dad – I borrowed them.'

His father glared at him and then hurried to Stuart's room and returned, uncapping the binoculars as Stuart was trying his best to write down the latest ominous message as the light winked on and off.

Barry lifted the binoculars and focused the thumbwheel. Not only could he clearly see that the light in the distance was the bulb of a flashlight, he could also see who was switching it on and off. It was a girl, perhaps in her early teens, or even younger, and she was dressed in a black jumper or a dark blouse of some sort, and her face was ghastly; a pale greyish face with black eye sockets and an open black oval where the mouth should be. She looked dead, inhuman. Barry almost swore, and then whispered, 'Jesus Christ, her face.'

'Dad, can I have a look?' Stuart asked, reaching for the binoculars in his father's hands.

'She's gone,' Barry muttered, 'she just vanished. The light went out.' Barry seemed unaware of his son's request to see the uncanny girl for himself.

'Dad, can I – '

'Wait! She's still there,' Barry almost grinned as he pressed squinting eyelids into the eyepieces of the binoculars. 'She's switched off the torch but she's still standing there in the dark, but I can see her face because its that pale. I think she knows we are watching her. Have a look!'

Stuart eagerly took the binoculars from his father and refocused them to his younger keener eyes. He could see the girl and her face was as frightening as his Dad had described. As Stuart looked on, the ashen face of the female vanished in an instant. 'She just vanished.' Stuart lowered the binoculars from his eyes, shocked at the girl's supernatural disappearance – and his father grabbed the binoculars and had a look at that window again to see that the girl had indeed disappeared into thin air.

Stuart began to decode the message, and it took him almost half an hour. The message – partly misspelt as usual - was very disturbing. It read: "DEATH DEATH DEATH TO FATHAR AND SON".

When Barry saw the message his son had decoded from the accursed Morse, he went cold. He made Stuart promise he would say nothing of this message to his mother. As you can imagine, Barry and Stuart had little sleep that night, and lived in fear of meeting an untimely end; after all, the two previous messages from that girl – whoever she was – had both come to pass. Barry slept with a crucifix under his pillow, whereas Stuart, who was not religious at all, lay in his bed that night in almost a foetal position, and every now and then when he dropped off he would kick out his leg with nerves and wake himself up again. By morning his nerves were shattered and he had to stay off school because he felt so ill and exhausted.

The days of mentally-grinding misery and nerve-jangling moods dragged by, and father and son thought each day would be their last, and wondered how they'd both meet their ends; would it be simultaneously or would one die before the other? Edna noticed her son and husband were hardly touching their food and asked what the matter was but they admitted to nothing as they knew she'd only be beside herself with worry, and so soon after losing her father.

It was Stuart who suggested that perhaps that girl – whoever and whatever she was – should perhaps be investigated. Barry reluctantly agreed to this and he had to make up a pretence to his wife about him and Stuart going to help a relative move into a house. Edna wanted to go with them but Barry said there was heavy furniture to be moved and told his wife that she'd only get in the way. Edna believed the story and at 8pm on a Sunday evening, father and son went to the house on Grant Avenue –and discovered that the front door was nailed shut, because that house had been uninhabited for almost three years. An elderly neighbour told them that the family had moved after a personal tragedy. Barry asked what sort of personal tragedy had occurred there, and the neighbour said the 13-year-old daughter of the family had hanged herself in her bedroom after her father had burnt all of her books on witchcraft. 'For the life of me I can't remember the girl's name now,' the old woman told Barry, 'was it Maggie? No, it was something like that. She had tried to commit suicide a few times because she wanted to know what it was like to die – that's what her auntie told me. The poor girl must have been deranged. She started messing around with upturned glasses and said the spirit of a murderer had contacted her. There was other stuff I can't go into in front of your son.'

Stuart's eyes widened and he looked at his father with a very concerned look.

'We've seen her at that window, flashing a torch,' Barry told the elderly neighbour, and the old woman erupted into a laryngitic cough and then she said, 'Seen who? The girl who died? Oh my God. A few have seen her I believe.'

'Yeah, we saw her at the window with a torch, and her face was very pale,' said Barry, and he looked up at the window of the derelict house – the very window he had seen the girl at through the binoculars.

'They had two priests out, the family did – and they were in there for ages. I don't know what went on, but there were unmerciful screams. Everyone round here heard them. I believe she – God, I wish I could remember her name – isn't old age terrible? I believe she started doing all horrible drawings on the wall in her blood – real horrible drawings of people being tortured and everything. I wish someone would move into that place. My bedroom is right next to the room that girl hung herself in.'

'Do you remember what priests were involved next door?' Barry asked the pensioner, and she nodded, and said she recalled one of them, and mentioned the local church he was from. On the following morning, Barry paid a visit to this church and managed to see the priest, a man in his late fifties. Barry told him about the ghost with the torch and the priest seemed very intrigued. He said the girl who had committed suicide had been a very bright student at her school, and when she had been confined to her room, she had used a torch to send signals to her best friend at night. Her friend, a girl named Amanda, had lived on Prince Alfred Road, and she in turn would use a flashlight to send messages back to her friend. Amanda was also into witchcraft and the occult, and after her friend took her own life, Amanda tried to kill herself by lying in a bath and cutting her wrists but her brother found her near to death and called an ambulance. Amanda died in the hospital for a few minutes but was successfully revived after receiving a massive blood transfusion. When she recovered from her suicide attempt at her home, Amanda was constantly watched by her mother, father and brother, who all took turns to make sure the girl never tried to kill herself again, and one night as the girl was being supervised by her father, she told him she could see her friend's ghost signalling to her, just the way she would before she hanged herself. Amanda's father saw the light winking on and off in the bedroom of the deceased girl, but he drew the curtains.

Barry was very unnerved by the priest's account, and he told him how he and his son now feared for their lives after receiving that chilling message from the ghost. The priest said Barry should have known better than to dabble in the Occult, and that he should have not heeded the light and that he should have dissuaded his son from heeding it too. 'No good can come from any communication with the dead,' the priest declared, and then he said he would dedicate the next Mass to Barry and his son to ward off any evil influence from the evil spirit of the suicide. Over the next two weeks, Barry and his son suffered from a mysterious illness which could not be treated by antibiotics or various other medicines. They suffered high temperatures, nausea, double vision, ringing in the ears, and palpitations that were so strong, they would rock the bed. At one point, Barry felt as if the forces of good and evil were battling over the very possession of his soul, and the priest later told Barry that he had said prayers three times a day to keep a terrible evil force from destroying his health and the health of his son. Then one Sunday morning as the bells of the local churches of Wavertree rang out, Barry and his son felt a strong sensation of peace descend upon them, and they left their sickbeds and asked Edna for breakfast.

The house on Grant Avenue is now occupied, but I have occasionally heard reports of a strange light that shines from the middle of Wavertree Park, always after dark, and this light is seen to go on and off at irregular intervals…

# CROSBY'S CRAWLING MEN

**Michael Perry-Lewis** remembers the spine-chilling incident of 1972 as if it happened only last night. It was a foggy evening, around half-past ten in November 1972, and Michael and his friend Ian – both aged 13 – were roaming the streets of Crosby, bored and prone to mischief in such moods. They considered knocking on the door of an old man on Hastings Road and running away, but decided not too, and as they reached Holden Road, a low mist rolled in from the Irish Sea and drifted towards them. The knee-length clouds of vapour looked just like the dry-ice fog they wafted on stage during *Top of the Pops* when

Pan's People danced about, Ian thought.

Then Michael saw two shapes coming down Holden Road towards them, going in the direction of Crosby beach. At first, Michael though the shapes were dogs, and he said to Ian, 'See them?' and pointed to the vague silhouettes, but Ian had much better eyesight and he could see something quite surreal and eerie – two people were approaching on all fours, and they were moving pretty quickly for someone moving along on their hands and knees. 'It's two fellahs,' said Ian, and stood rooted to the spot.

'What?' asked a bemused Michael, and now he could see it really was so – two men, possibly in their thirties, were crawling towards them out of the ground mist – but why. The boys got out of the way by crossing the road, anticipating that the two oddballs would be reaching them within the minute. Not another soul was about on this icy foggy night. A ship's horn groaned somewhere out at sea, and this heightened the unreality of the situation. Then the boys could hear he padding of the hands of the men on the tarmac, and as the figures moved out of the opaque mist, their forms became starkly clear.

Ian's mouth opened wide with shock.

The man in the front moving rapidly on his hands and knees had sustained some sort of horrific injuries, and his bottom jaw was dangling and swinging from the rest of the head, and blood was trailing steadily from the limp tongue. Not only that, but this unfortunate person's left foot had been twisted around so that the toes of his shoe pointed upwards. The hands of this man were also coated in glistening blood. The man behind him was also in a ghastly state, and

Michael Perry-Lewis felt faint and unsteady on his feet when he saw the condition of this second man. He was almost bald, having a much receded hairline, and the top right half of his head was simply missing, and a huge raw crimson section was showing instead, and parts of the jagged smashed skull were showing, and what looked like brains was also visible through this hole. The blood was pouring from this second man's face, and Ian noticed the right eyeball dangling from what was presumably the optic nerve or a shred of muscle. The legs of this man looked broken because of the way they were being dragged; they seemed limp and the feet were pointing away from each other. One foot had a brogue on and the other foot had a sock that partially covered it and it was soaked in blood. This second man was making a moaning, rhythmical sound as he went past, dragging himself with quite some force by his hands. Ian ran off at this point in utter terror, but Michael moved away slowly from Holden Street and watched the crawling men fade away into the fog as they reached Westward View. When Michael told his mother what he and Ian had seen, she believed her son had seen something but thought that perhaps a couple of students had been playing some prank, but other people saw the crawling figures that night, and one of them later wrote to me to tell me of her encounter. The witness was Jane Greer, a 21-year-old secretary who had just returned from a date with a man she would later marry. Jane had been crossing Holden Road on her way to her home on Warrenhouse Road when she had almost fallen over the second crawling man in the mist, and she had screamed in shock when she had seen his appalling injuries. Jane's brother John was a male nurse, and so when she ran home and told him what she had seen, John immediately hurried out of the house and went in search of what he imagined to be survivors of some gruesome traffic accident, but all John saw was a single trail of blood leading down towards the beach, and at the end of the trail he could see no one. Jane recalled seeing a young boy running up Holden Road that night, and this was probably Ian, fleeing from the creepy scene in shock.

I mentioned this case on a phone-in on Radio City one evening and six people in the Crosby area contacted me, and all of the six explanations given were in agreement. The crawling men were the ghosts of an horrific car crash that had taken place near Holden Road, possibly in the 1950s or early 1960s. The car the men had been travelling in had hit a truck, and driver of the truck suffered serious injuries to his spine but survived. The two men in the car were not so lucky. One had his jaw almost torn completely from his head, and the other had his head partly crushed in the impact. Both men crawled in panic from the wreckage and witnesses said the accident victims flitted from the wreckage covered in blood at quite some speed, shuffling along on all fours. Apparently, many accident victims who suffer traumatic or life-changing injuries try to run away from the scene of an accident, unable to accept that they are seriously injured or about to die. The lifeless body of the man with the dangling jaw was found on the beach in a kneeling position, his palms pressed together, as if he had been praying when he died, and the body of the man who had somehow crawled for half a mile with his brains leaking from his smashed skull, was found under a car in Leopold Road. He had placed his fingers into the hole in his skull, perhaps in a fruitless attempt to stop his brain matter and blood from oozing out.

Some of the people I spoke to say that on certain foggy nights, always in November, the crawling ghosts of the doomed men are seen coming down Holden Road.

# FLIGHT INTO HELL

**There are mysterious** openings in our world leading to God knows where, and they can be found on land, sea – and even in the skies of our planet. If you find the following story hard to believe, be mindful of the fact that eminent and highly-respected quantum physicists now know that there are mind-bending passages which would allow anyone travelling through them to visit any place or time in the universe within seconds. These passages are known by many names: wormholes, UFO window areas, Einstein-Rosen bridges (first hypothesized in 1935) and portals. From my research I have, over the years, compiled a rudimentary map of these portals for the British Isles and one of the most prominent ones, which I have provisionally designated Portal 3, opens and closes with some regularity over south Wirral, and sometimes extends itself as north as Bromborough and as westerly as Neston. One balmy afternoon in August 1919, a modified Avro 504 biplane took off from an airfield at Shotwick (later renamed RAF Sealand),

Flintshire. At the controls of the plane was Flying Officer H. L. Holland, and his mission was then cloaked in secrecy, but it is now known he was testing out a new radio transceiver, and this test involved flying over Lancashire, then turning west over Liverpool Bay, and returning to base via the airspace over Wirral. Radio contact was lost as Flying Officer Holland climbed over the Cheshire Plains, thousands of feet above Ellesmere Port. The August weather was fine and Holland was an experienced pilot who had flown from Shotwick to Baldonnel near Dublin and back, many times, so this outing should have been a piece of cake – but Holland and his plane seemed to have fallen off the map. Then two hours later, Holland's Avro 504 was sighted over Neston. He radioed the ground staff at the airfield in Shotwick and seemed to be very confused and excited, which was quite unlike a pilot of Holland's cool calibre. After a text-book landing Holland told Flying Officers C. R. Pithey that some 'terrible disaster' had befallen Liverpool. As he had flown over Speke, the skies had darkened, and he had entered billowing black clouds of smoke lit by an inferno that was engulfing Liverpool. It was like looking down into the pit of Hell, Holland remarked with a tremor in his voice. Every building in the town – even churches – seemed to be ablaze, and strange powerful beams of light shone up from various districts to rake the sky, almost blinding him. Holland's plane had even been shot at from someone on the ground. It was apocalyptic, like something out of an H. G. Wells novel – or the Bible's Book of Revelation. Holland asked Pithey and several other dumfounded officers present what had happened to Liverpool, and they all said they had heard of no such calamity. 'You must have! The devastation!' Holland exclaimed, and he swore a firestorm was raging in Liverpool. The other officers must have thought Holland was suffering from nervous exhaustion, but an engineer later pointed out something very strange: bulletholes and blackened dents in the fuselage of Holland's Avro 504. Had Flying Officer H. L. Holland somehow flown two decades into the future and witnessed a Liverpool being blitzed by Hitler's Luftwaffe? Six months after this incident, in February 1920, Holland and two other pilots vanished on a routine flight to Ireland. Their three planes were seen by fishermen crashing into the sea 85 miles south-west of the Scilly Isles – unaccountably 250 miles off course. The planes and the bodies of the three pilots were never recovered. How three experienced pilots became so disoriented on a routine flight across the Irish Sea and ended up in the North Atlantic is a real puzzler.

In March 1922, Flying Officer Brian Holding took off from Shotwick airfield, and he also vanished into the blue after all radio contact with the pilot was lost. Not a stick of any wreckage was ever found, and the fate of Flying Officer Holding remains unknown. The Air Ministry tried to suppress these disappearances at the time, but relatives of the missing men as well as families and friends of personnel working at Shotwick airbase naturally talked of the sinister vanishing acts and journalists also got wind of the disappearances and made their own inquiries. It is my belief that Portal 3, a vast invisible opening in the sky over south Wirral, is to blame for the disappearances and apparent timeslips of the type experienced by Flying Officer Holland in

1920. It's possible that the Portal also caused some sort of electromagnetic disturbance which might have affected the compasses of the planes and perhaps even caused some sort of cerebral disorientation.

# RODNEY STREET'S NOSY GHOST

**Not all ghosts** are seen or encountered during the hours of darkness; there are a surprising number of paranormal entities in our neck of the woods which are particularly active in the morning and afternoons. Take, for example, the eerie ghost that was seen almost every morning by a young mum named Amy. In the summer of 2011, Amy would get up most mornings around 5am to make a bottle for her baby, and the 22-eyar-old mum noticed a strange woman looking at her from the window of the house opposite one morning. It was just after 5am and the sun had not yet risen, but there was enough predawn light available to see the street outside – and the street in this case was Rodney Street, which, as regular readers of my books will know, has more than its fair share of ghosts. Amy had no interest in ghosts and had never read a *Haunted Liverpool* book, and as she made her baby girl's bottle, ghosts were the furthest thing from her mind, but glancing out the window, she saw a woman who looked as if she was in her thirties, gazing over at her from the window opposite. This nosy parker had her black hair scraped up into a bun, and she wore a strange high collared black top with long sleeves. Even from a distance of about fifty yards, Amy could see that this woman had a very pale face – almost white – and she also had dark rings about her eyes, and they were eyes that seemed to be protruding on stalks. Amy ignored the barefaced spectator at first, but on the following morning at the same time, again as Amy was making her child's bottle, she saw the same woman in black gawping over at her from the window opposite. Amy glared back at her, and then gave a sarcastic wave, and the woman returned the strangest, most unsettling smile Amy had ever seen. Her mouth looked like a black crescent, as if the woman had no teeth.

After the baby had been fed, Amy's partner Liam got up to go the toilet, and when he returned from the loo, Amy took him into the kitchen and told him to look across the road. Liam saw the nosy woman in black and asked who she was.

As Amy looked over at the woman she said: 'I don't know but have you seen the way she just stares right at us? She must have no life being up this early and snooping on people.'

'Amy, Are you sure she's not...' Liam suddenly trailed off without finishing the sentence, and then he turned to look at his partner with a worried expression.

'Sure she's not a what?' Amy wanted to know.

'She looks a bit weird to me,' Liam said, in a mumbling type of way and hardly moved his lips.

'I don't get what you mean,' Amy admitted.

'Are you sure she's not a ghost or something?' Liam asked earnestly.

'Do you like scaring the shit out of me or something?' Amy thinned her eyes and scowled at her partner, then turned and went into the bedroom as she heard her baby cry. 'She's not a ghost,' she said, as she went into the room.

The next morning, at a quarter to five, Amy was up

again and making a bottle for the baby, and on this occasion she was really tired as she had been watching a film on DVD until half-past three. She felt a bit nervous over seeing that watcher across the road, now that Liam had put it into her head that she might be a ghost, but thankfully, there was no sign of her at the window. For some company, Amy switched her iPhone to MP3 mode and listened to a few songs on the her earphones. She made the bottle, then glanced deliberately at the window opposite to see if the woman in black was there. She wasn't.

She was standing in the street below – on the pavement - gazing up at Amy's window.

Amy recoiled in shock. She took the earphones off and stared in horrified disbelief at the woman below, for she wore a long black dress that went down to the ground almost, and her attire was obviously Edwardian or Victorian. At these closer quarters, Amy could see that the eerie female had an unnaturally white face – as if he was dead – and her eyes were huge, bulging and encircled with dark borders.

'Liam!' Amy screamed and ran from the kitchen to the bedroom, where she startled her partner out of a deep sleep. He rose quickly into a sitting position as the baby bawled because of her mother's loud scream.

'What? What?' Liam asked twice, and Amy threw herself at him and hugged him as she shook violently. She could hardly get her words out because her throat had closed up with nerves: 'She's downstairs on the pavement! She was looking up at me!'

There then came the sound of someone rapping hard on the kitchen window, and the bangs on the panes sent Amy into a hysterical state. The kitchen window was over thirty feet up from the pavement, so how would anyone – besides a window cleaner on a ladder – manage to reach that window?

The couple were so afraid, they refused to go into the kitchen for almost thirty minutes, even though the rappings only lasted for about twenty seconds.

On the following morning, Amy made sure of two things; firstly that the roller-blind on the kitchen window was down, and secondly, that Liam was up with her as she made the bottle in the kitchen. The couple never got over the outdated observer and the tapping on the window, and four months after the incident, the couple moved out of their Rodney Street flat and rented a flat in Wavertree.

When I asked Amy to tell me the number of the house where the woman in black had been watching her so keenly, I looked up the address in my own files – which are very extensive for Rodney Street. On the second day of looking I found an eight-page note I had written up on an alleged ghost many years ago when I first began to systematically write or make typewritten records of hauntings. The note told me that in 1973, a 48-year-old widowed woman named Marcia and her 16-year-old son Gary had lived in the very flat which Amy would later occupy in 2011, and one September morning in 1973, Marcia had been up about half-past four, making a cup of tea for herself because she was unable to sleep, and whilst in the kitchen, she noticed a woman looking at her from the window of the house opposite. This woman seemed to be lifting her hand to her mouth from something she was holding. Her hand moved back and forth from what looked like a bowl to her mouth, as if she was eating something. Every morning this woman would be at the window whenever Marcia was in the kitchen. The latest Marcia saw her was about 5.45 am. One morning Marcia's son got up to get a cold drink from the fridge, and as he did, Marcia asked her son if he (having keener eyesight) could see what the woman in the window opposite was doing. Gary said the woman was eating something from a bowl. He went to fetch his astronomy telescope, and Marcia said, 'Hey, don't let her see you spying on her with that, she might think you're a Peeping Tom!'

But Gary had a look at the woman through the telescope, and he said she looked weird. She was eating what seemed to be cherries, and her eyeballs were huge with 'enormous black doll-like dots in the middle of them'. When the woman grinned, she had no teeth, according to Gary.

'Alright, that's enough,' Marcia told her son, 'get back to bed now, lad.'

All of a sudden, Gary's eyes widened as he looked over at the window across the street, and the lad said, 'Mam! Look at her!'

The woman in black was moving slowly up and down behind the window – as if she was floating about, and then she vanished.

Marcia was more fascinated than scared, but the way the woman had bobbed up and down and then disappeared really scared Gary. Thankfully, Marcia and her son never saw the woman in black after that morning, but they avoided going into the kitchen at that time in the morning after that incident, just in case they caught a glimpse of the ghost.

I have looked into the history of the house where

the ghostly woman in black was seen, and I have gone through the censuses and other records, and as of yet, I do not know the identity of Rodney Street's nosy ghost.

# DEATH OVERDUE

**Some occultists** - and the downright superstitious, believe that if someone cheats death, then death may wait for a while and try to catch its victim again, and this scenario has been used in supernatural literature over the years and has formed the basic plot of many horror films, such as the *Final Destination* series – but sometimes death – whether you imagine it as some dark cruel circumstance or as a chilling entity as personified by the Grim Greaper – really does seem to make further attempts at taking the life of someone who has escaped from its clutches. A case in point right off the top of my head is Helen Jones, a beautiful caring and selfless person who survived the Lockerbie bombing. This event took place on Wednesday 21 December, 1988, when a Boeing 747-121 named Clipper Maid of the Seas was destroyed by a terrorist's bomb of Libyan origin as it flew over Scotland at an altitude of 31,000 feet. The crew of sixteen and 243 passengers were killed in the incident, and eleven people on the ground also perished when large sections of the Boeing crashed down onto them at Lockerbie. One of the witnesses to the terrifying incident was an 11-year-old girl named Helen Jones. Young Helen saw flaming fragments of the passenger jet land on houses, killing families in an instant. The fuselage of the doomed plane which was attached to the wings contained over ninety-thousand kilograms of kerosene and the fireball incinerated a family upon impact to such an extent, no remains of them were ever found. One passenger was found near the site clutching grass in her hand, which means she must have somehow survived the fall of over 30,000 feet for a few minutes. Another passenger's body was found with the legs rammed into the torso from the impact. It was a truly horrific scene that night in the Scottish town of Lockerbie, and It was said for years that Helen Jones had cheated death because the debris had fallen all around her. Then, on the morning of Thursday 7 July 2005, there was a concerted series of bombings in central London, perpetrated by four Islamist "home-grown terrorists" (as the media labelled them) who detonated four bombs on the London underground, and on a double decker bus in Tavistock Square. All four bombers killed themselves in the explosions, which robbed the lives of 52 civilians – and one of them was a 28-year-old accountant named Helen Jones – the same Helen who had survived the Lockerbie terrorist bombing back in 1988.

In 1976, former Beatles roadie Mal Evans was shot dead by Los Angeles police officers who mistook Mal's air rifle for a real firearm during a domestic incident, and Lennon, upon hearing of Mal's death, stated: 'I'll be next, I just know it,' and talked about being stalked by the Angel of Death. Lennon was apparently convinced he would be shot, and just before he met his untimely end in December 1980, he was desperately looking for a place to move to, as he didn't feel safe in the Dakota apartments in New York. Lennon is said to have had recurring nightmares about being shot and "being brought to account" perhaps because of his irreverent remarks about the Beatles being bigger than Jesus and his atheistic "hymn" Imagine. In The Ballad of John and Yoko, the line: "The way things are going, they're gonna crucify me," really does ring true for Lennon's murder – shot four times in the back by Mark David Chapman outside the Dakotas, with Chapman allegedly saying a voice in his head had commanded him to pull the trigger, yelling: 'He's mine! Do it! Do it!'

On 14 October 2003, a 47-year-old woman named Linda Franklin had just finished shopping with her husband at a Home Depot store in Virginia. The time was almost 9.15pm. Just a few years before, Linda had been diagnosed with breast cancer and later underwent a double mastectomy, followed by a gruelling period of rehabilitation, but Linda had confronted her mortality head on and she was not a quitter. She survived the cancer and was getting on with her life – but at 9.15pm that October evening in 2003, a bullet struck her head and tore away the right side of her face, spattering her husband with her blood. Linda had been shot - dead - by John Allen Muhammad, the cowardly "Washington Sniper" who killed ten victims and critically injured three other people. The Sniper was eventually captured and executed by lethal injection (taking five minutes to die) on November 10 2009. Ironically, the young John Allen Muhammad had been traumatised at the age of five when his mother died from breast cancer – the same disease one of his later victims would survive, only to be murdered by one of his bullets – another ironic case of death returning to reclaim a person.

In March 1963, a Liverpool bricklayer named John Adams watched in horror as scaffolding around an office block in London collapsed. Two men fell to their deaths and Adams expected to be crushed by the scaffolding, but it fell around him, rather like that Buster Keaton stunt where the front of a house would fall onto the silent actor, but he would escape death because the open window fitted over him as it crashed down. The bodies of the two scaffolders landed with sickening thumps next to Adams, and one of them threw up bloody vomit all over the horrified bricklayer's feet after the fatal fall. From that moment, John Adams was convinced he had cheated death – but only for a fixed period; he was certain that death would call gain soon to settle the score. True enough, John Adams had six more close shaves with death. In April 1963 he was almost run down by a bus on Liverpool's Lime Street, and then in the following month he was thrown through a window in a gas explosion at his cousin's house in Manchester, but survived, despite serious lacerations to his face and neck from shards of glass. In June of that year, Adams went to the swimming baths in West Kirby and dived in, only to smack his forehead on the bottom of the pool. He was knocked out and lost consciousness, but was resuscitated by an elderly man who had been a lifeguard in his younger days. Adams told his wife and family he would be dead before the year was out, and talked of being followed by a strange shadowy being that he could only see out the corner of his eye. Finally in December 1963, John Adams was with his wife at a London hotel, when he suddenly told her 'This will be the day, I just know it.'

'The day for what?' his wife asked.

'The day I die,' Adams replied, sending a cold shiver down his wife's spine.

And true enough, that evening as Joan Adams lay in bed at the hotel, her husband entered the room at 9.40pm after enjoying a drink at the bar. As he came into the room he suddenly said, 'Goodbye my love,' and waved, and then collapsed. He hit the floor dead, with his eyes wide open. He had died from a burst blood vessel in the brain, and as Joan looked on in horror, she saw a sinister elongated shadow pass over the inert body of her husband and flit towards the window, where it vanished. Had death finally claimed John Adams?

# AIN'T NOBODY

**Some of the stories** I hear from readers defy all my attempts at supernatural classification; they may seem paranormal and yet not involve ghosts, but often in these indefinable accounts that come my way, the very nature of time and the linear past-to-future illusion we know as "our life" is shattered, and the following story is a perfect example of this. I don't know quite what to make of it, but perhaps the keener mind of some reader out there will be able to work out just what happened in this story. The woman who related the account to me is a very down to earth lady, and all who know her say she had never been interested in the supernatural, until one day in the 1980s...

At the age of 22, Leslie Kayle met Chris Forhilde, the man she would subsequently marry, in the early summer of 1983 at Liverpool's legendary Montrose Club on Whitefield Road, not far from the Cabbage

Hall area. At first he was a loving and considerate man but after dating Les for a few months he became very possessive with her, not allowing her to go out with her friends unless he was with her, and then he prohibited her from going out with any of her old friends or even family members, even when she told him he could go with her. Leslie's friends and family said that Chris was obviously a control freak and eventually they stopped asking Les to go out because of all the trouble it would cause between her and her boyfriend. Leslie said Chris wasn't being a control freak, he just liked being with her all the time and doted on her, and wanted her undivided affection and attention, but it seems Les was being blinded to the real nature of Chris's obsessive personality because she was looking at him through the tinted glasses of romance, and this was the first time she had truly been in love. They married within two months of their first meeting, and Leslie's mother thought the whole affair was just some flash in the pan, a whirlwind romance that would soon blow itself out.

After the marriage, Chris and Leslie soon fell into a fixed, rigid routine. Chris went to work (as a driving instructor) and Leslie had to stay at home because her husband preferred things that way. They ate at the same time each day, watched TV at the exact same time, and Chris even became mechanical in his lovemaking, which always commenced just after eleven each night. In the end, Leslie felt trapped in a clockwork existence, and many times she thought about deserting her husband. At the beginning of 1984, Chris came home early one day and let himself into the house in West Derby with his key, only to find

Leslie sitting in the lounge with a glass of gin and tonic as she listened to a cassette featuring an album by Rufus and Chaka Khan. The particular track that was playing on the album was *Ain't Nobody*, Les's favourite song of that year. Chris switched off the tape and asked his startled wife why she was drinking of a daytime and why wasn't she cleaning the kitchen, which, according to Chris, looked like "a midden". Leslie had had enough and she screamed at him and said he wanted to leave him. Chris eventually calmed his wife down and promised he'd change, that he'd be less strict, and he admitted he was still very much in love with Les. But he soon went back on his word and went back to his same old dictatorial self. Around this time, Les asked Chris why he never talked about any of his friends, and Chris said: 'That's simple – I don't have any.'

'Everyone has friends,' Les told him, but Chris smirked with a bitter look in his eyes and said he'd had a best mate once named Gordon, and he'd known him from infant school, but over the years, Gordon had become so boring in his ways; he'd abandoned all of his ambitions and become a drop-out. He had told Chris that one day he'd be a great songwriter, but by the age of 19 he had given up his dreams and had become a bus driver, and even then he'd stayed off work so much he'd been sacked. Chris had no time for no-hopers; the future belonged to the tryer, the go-getter.

Anyway, that night, just after eleven, Chris made love to Leslie, even though she was not in the mood, and she was glad when it was over.

'Are you sure you really love me?' Leslie asked Chris,

as he lay on his back, his head resting on his pillow with the back of his hand on his forehead.

He muttered something which sounded like, 'You know I do.'

She turned away from Chris, and looked at the crescent moon beyond the lace curtains of the window as her husband turned to face the wall opposite. He was soon snoring. Then something quite odd happened.

The snoring stopped. Chris turned to his wife in the bed and he said, 'Leslie, is that you?'

She thought he was dreaming at first, and she was going to reply: 'Who do you think it is?' but instead she said, 'Yeah. You okay?'

A very peculiar response was evoked by Les's words. 'You asked me if I love you, Les, and I should have said that I have never loved anyone the way I have loved you. You have no idea how much I missed you. Oh, I love you Les.' And Chris seized his wife by her shoulders and turned her to face him as if she was just a little doll. He kissed her gently, and held her so close she felt as if she'd be smothered.

'Chris, what's wrong? Are you okay?' Leslie's lips rubbed against his chest as she tried to push herself away from his strange bear hug embrace.

He asked: 'Have you ever heard of that old saying, "You don't know what you've got until it's gone?" Have you heard of that?'

'Yes,' Leslie replied, regaining her breath now that she had managed to pull away from his hold a few inches.

'It's so true, God it's true,' Chris said in a broken voice, and Les thought she heard him sniffle. She felt his eyes, and found them to be wet.

'Chris, what is going on?' Leslie asked, and now she felt a little scared, for he had never acted like this before and the thought of this strange behaviour heralding the onset of a nervous breakdown crossed her mind; he had been working a lot of late. She reached out and switched on the light.

His eyes were red.

'Chris, why are you being so emotional?'

'Leslie, if I told you, I don't think you'd believe me. It's so lovely to see your face again – '

Leslie got out of the bed naked and covered her breasts with her hands before going to grab her nightgown, which had been draped across the chair in front of the dresser. She put it on and looked at her husband. He was sitting up in their bed, and he had the most unearthly look in his eyes. Those eyes seemed much darker than usual, yet so full of longing for her. She had not seen this look in the eyes of Chris since that first week they met in the summer of 1984.

'Oh, you're lovelier than I remember,' Chris remarked, and wiped the tears from both eyes with his fingers.

'You're scaring me Chris,' Leslie admitted, 'why are you talking like this?'

Then came an enigmatic reply. 'I told you – you'd never believe me – and I couldn't blame you.'

'Try me, go on, just tell me.'

'Okay, okay. I'll be dead in twenty years. It's complicated this, but I am already dead in the future, and I was allowed to come back to just one day in my life by somebody – I'm not allowed to say who – and so here I am. I know I treated you like crap, Leslie, and

I remembered that night when you asked me if I really did love you, and I should have shown affection and I should have held you all night. I'm back here now for a while, but I'll have to go back to where I came from at daybreak.'

Well, you couldn't blame Leslie for being confused. She had not understood a word of the 'explantion' Chris had offered, and so she stood there gazing at him with her head angled in a quizzical manner and her hands resting on the back of the chair near the dresser. 'You have come back from twenty years in the future?' She asked, and at first she smiled, but she could see from the awfully serious look on Chris's face that he was not joking. He had to have had a breakdown; he didn't do drugs, Leslie knew that much, so she opted for the breakdown theory.

'I knew you wouldn't believe me – I should have said nothing. I could have just loved you anyway, but I just wanted you to know I was sorry.' Chris looked as if he was going to cry again.

'So if you're from the future, you'd look twenty years older,' Leslie reasoned, and then she scratched her messed-up head of hair and said, 'And what happened to the 1984 Chris? Where did *he* go?'

Chris shook his head, 'No, just my mind has come back, not my physical body – that's lying in a morgue. The mindline is the thing – it's hard to explain. Our minds have a thing called the mindline which connect our mind to every stage we lived through, from when we were babies right up to when we are old-age pensioners. This was probably a bad idea.'

'Let's go downstairs and have a cup of tea, and talk about all this, eh?' Leslie suggested, and approached the door sideways, keeping an eye on her 'unbalanced' husband.

Chris got out the bed, put on his Y-fronts, and then looked at himself in the dresser mirror for a moment with a slight grin on his face. 'I forgot I had a six-pack,' he remarked.

He went downstairs with his wife and into the kitchen, where he squinted at the flickering neon strip on the ceiling as it flickered to life. He grinned at the cooker and kept looking around at all the appliances in the kitchen as an increasingly concerned Leslie filled the kettle. Chris wandered into the lounge and said something about the television not being flat. The curtains were wide open and anyone passing the house at this late hour could possibly see Chris in his underpants, so Leslie led him into the kitchen and switched off the light in the lounge. He sat drinking a mug of strong tea, and Leslie sat facing him at the kitchen table, asking him how he felt now.

'You must think I'm having a breakdown or something,' Chris said with a chuckle. 'I couldn't even make this up, and you should know how unimaginative I am.'

'So, let's see then,' Leslie squinted one eye and gazed at the ceiling, 'if you're from twenty years in the future, you'd be from…'

'Two-thousand and four,' Chris quickly cut in, and he put the mug of tea down firmly on the Formica top of the table.

'We'll all be living on the moon by then won't we?' Leslie said in a tired and sarcastic voice. She was now wondering if this was all some joke, even though it would be entirely out of character for Chris to have such a prolonged sense of humour.

Chris had that tearful look in his eyes again, but they looked much less red now. 'I'm not allowed to say anything about the future, and I don't really care about the future; I'm more interested in the past.'

'Who let you come back, anyway?' Leslie wondered about this.

Chris shook his head. 'I am not allowed to say, but I am very grateful I was allowed to come back, if only just for a while.'

As the night went on, Leslie began to feel as if there was some eerie truth to the bizarre claims of her husband. He did seem much more mature than the Chris she knew, and if he was putting on an act it would take an awful lot of willpower and the skills of a method actor, and the Chris Leslie knew was a short-tempered and simple man. She didn't know what to believe. She thought perhaps she should just go with the flow, at least until morning, and if things with Chris were still the same, she could telephone her mother and ask her opinion, even if her mum suggested getting in touch with a doctor.

By three that morning, Chris had somehow managed to bring his wife into the lounge, where they drank a lot of gin, and Chris insisted playing the Rufus and Chaka Khan song *Ain't Nobody* – the song that he had caught his wife playing that afternoon when he came home early, and they had ended up having a unholy row. The cassette was played over and over as the couple kissed and embraced on the sofa. At one point, Chris asked his wife a favour: 'Please call my friend Gordon tomorrow, and tell him his songs were great, and tell him to try and get them recorded because he's very talented and he'll go far. Tell him I held him back because I couldn't write music. Here's his number - ' And Chris found a pen and wrote the number down along with Gordon's name in the margin of a newspaper on the coffee table. Leslie promised she'd call his old friend - the one he'd fallen out with all those years back.

Outside, the dawn was on its way, and already casting the pale milky light ahead of its arrival across the sky.

And now Leslie was tearful, for at last, she now believed Chris was telling the truth. She could not explain how it was so – how he had come back from beyond the veil of death to return to one day in his past, just to love her, but she believed him. That belief had grown in the euphoria of the third glass of gin and tonic, and then it was as if her eyes had been opened for the first time. 'Do you really have to go at dawn?' she asked Chris, and he was in tears too by now. He tried desperately to grin but it died on his lips and he closed his eyes as the tears trickled down his cheeks.

'Can't I come back with you? Please Chris,' Leslie pleaded.

'You can't, Les, you have to live your life and have so many things to do, but one day, I promise you this – ' Chris's throat closed up with the sheer sorrow building up in his heart. He inhaled and then finished the sentence: 'I promise you, one day, you'll be with me in a lovely sunny life after this, and we will never part.'

They hugged, and were both so upset they couldn't utter a word.

Then Leslie heard birdsong. Oh my God, Leslie

realised that the dawn had come. Pale blue-grey morning light was filtering through the curtains.

'I love you, Leslie, please forgive me, and please don't leave that younger Chris! He doesn't realise what he has. I love you, and will always love you...' Chris's voice faded. He slumped sideways onto the sofa and Leslie tried to wake him, but he was gone. He began to snore. She knew this was the Chris of today snoring, not the Chris of 2004 who had loved her so much he had returned to show her how much he had loved and cherished her now he had left this sacred sphere of life.

When Chris woke up on the sofa, he found he had a stiff neck, and he found Leslie in the kitchen, slumped at the table with her head rested on her folded arms. He asked her how he had come to be downstairs on the sofa and why he had the ghastly taste of gin in his mouth. 'You must have been sleepwalking, and sleep-drinking,' she said, without even looking up at her husband.

'Well I can't go to work like this, I could be breathalysed,' Chris grimaced and held his hand over his right eye, where a pain throbbed in his forehead. 'Are you not telling me something?' he asked his wife, 'I have never done anything like this before,' he groaned, and walked to the foot of the stairs.

'Go to bed and sleep it off, love,' Leslie advised, 'you'll be okay.'

And she said nothing about the 'visit' of the future Chris, and as the weeks went by, doubts began to plague her. Perhaps Chris had had some sort of mental disturbance. She telephoned a friend one day while Chris was at work and told her what had happened, and this friend said there were things called 'fugues' were people often acted very strangely and even wandered out of their homes in the dead of night, only to later have no recollections of what they had done.

But in 2004, Chris died on an operating table whilst having open-heart surgery. Only then, did Leslie think that something very strange had happened that night in the 1980s. She recalled the way Chris had remarked about the TV set not being flat, and of course, by 2004, many brand new TVs featured flat plasma screens, and where would someone as simple as Chris know about the concept of a "mindline"? To this day Leslie is not at all sure just what did happen that night, but the incident continues to haunt her, and she hopes that one day, she will be reunited with Chris, just as he promised that morning in 1984.

# BILOCATING BETTY

**A few years ago** a Dingle reader named John Tudor bumped into me outside a bookshop where I had just been signing copies of my work. We went to a café on Bold Street where he told me a strange but intriguing story about his younger days. In the 1970s, John was, by his own admission, something of a two-timing Lothario; a self-centred womanizer who didn't give two hoots about his despicable actions and the ensuing responsibilities. He was, in his late twenties, tall, quite handsome, always evenly tanned (because he had no qualms about stripping to the waist to bathe in the sun in the nearest park at the littlest glimmer of a solar ray) and with his shoulder-length black hair and strong masculine jaw, many remarked upon his close resemblance to Oliver Tobias - a heart-throb hunk of film and TV in that era. In his unending pursuit of the female, Tudor frequented various clubs of the Seventies; Pickwicks, the She Club, the Odd Spot, and even the more out-of-the-way venues such as the Master Mariners' Dining Club – housed within an ex-Royal Navy landing craft named *Landfall*, moored in the Collingwood Dock. And then he met and married a beautiful graceful and delicate 19-year-old Hoylake girl named Melody who loved John so much, she was blind to his deceptions and lies, but Melody's mother, Betty could see right through the philanderer. Although John knew Betty was onto him, he assumed there was nothing she could do about his unfaithfulness, but he was to be proved severely wrong in a very unearthly way. He told Melody he had to go and stay with his sick Aunt Jean one Saturday night, and Betty told her son-on-law he had on a nice aftershave as he was leaving the house. 'It's Old Spice,' he replied with a sneer, ' always reminds Auntie Jean of her late husband Ralph – he always wore it see.'

And that night at the back of the Back of the Moon club on Bold Street, John had his arms around a young lady, and was just about to kiss her, when a woman in the shadows with a familiar voice queried, 'How's your Auntie Jean, John?' It was Betty.

'What the frigging hell are you doing here? You been following me?' John looked absolutely stunned. 'Before you start getting the wrong end of the stick, this is my niece, Katrina,' John told his mother-in-law, and Betty smiled at her and said, 'Did you know your Uncle John's just been married? You have an Auntie Melody now – and she's round your age!'

'You're married? ' Katrina asked John, then gasped, 'You lying bastard!' and she slapped him hard and stormed off in tears. John threatened to have his mother-in-law sued for harassment but she suddenly wasn't anywhere to be seen. She'd been less than six feet away from him on Back Bold Street, and now that narrow alley-like passage was eerily quiet. When John got home to Melody, he found her and her mother sitting up, drinking tea, but it transpired that Betty had not told her daughter about Katrina.

A week later, John told Melody he was going for a job interview at C&A on Church Street, but that afternoon as he whispered sweet-nothings to a very naïve young secretary named Sally in the Carnarvon Castle pub on Tarleton Street, he glanced in the mirror behind the bar to admire himself in action – when he saw Betty in the reflection with her arms folded, and a look of seething indignation on her face. John swung his head round, expecting his mother-in-law to be standing behind him, but saw no one. He was so spooked by the creepy incident he left the pub – and Sally too. At every clandestine rendezvous – including one in Chester - Betty would somehow spookily turn up, and so John eventually gave up his cheating routines. He went into a relapse at one point but when Melody became pregnant he remained faithful to her for life. John often asked Betty how she did her omnipresence "trick" but she never did tell, and she took her secret to the grave when she passed away in 2009. I made inquiries about Betty on a radio station and also on my website, and a woman named Mary Jones who had worked with her at Littlewoods in the early 1970s told me she was well aware of Betty's uncanny ability of being able to be in two places at once. Mary said that Betty had on one occasion been seen in Birkenhead Park by one of her supervisors at Littlewoods around noon, and he had wondered why she was not in work. However, when he made inquiries, he discovered that Betty had been in work at that time, so he assumed the woman he had seen in

Birkenhead Park had just been someone who looked like Betty or even a relative. However, on a further occasion, the same supervisor saw and spoke to Betty one afternoon at Littlewoods, and later discovered that she was, at the time, in bed, suffering from a bad bout of the flu. When Betty moved to Hoylake, she was seen by many of her former neighbours in the streets around her old neighbourhood off Edge Lane, and on some occasions she was seen to disappear into thin air when approached. Mary believed Betty's supernatural 'talent' was down to witchcraft, because on several occasions Betty had said he had learned to read tealeaves and cards from her mother, who was said to have had the gift of second sight. Betty had also resorted to divination to tell some of her closest friends how their relationships would go. 'She would prick a lit candle wick with a needle and recite some strange rhymes,' another of Betty's friends recalled, 'And things she predicted would always come true.'

The art of projecting the image of oneself to another place is known in the world of the Occult as bilocation, and even the Church accepts the validity of this phenomenon – in fact, several saints have bilocated throughout history, and bilocating Betty is just a secular example of a phenomenon that is well documented in the history of Christianity. When St Anthony of Padua was preaching in the Church of St. Pierre du Queyroix at Limoges on Holy Thursday, in the year 1226, he suddenly recalled that he was supposed to be at a service at a monastery in the other side of town, and so it is recorded by many witnesses how St Anthony drew his hood over his head, then knelt down in silence for a few minutes, seemingly deep in prayer, while the congregation watched him with some impatience. Meanwhile, over at the monastery, St Anthony appeared – still hooded – and read a passage from the Bible. He then vanished into thin air before the monks. Another Holy personage used his talent of bilocation was St. Alphonsus Liguori, an Italian Catholic Bishop and mystic. On 17 September, 1774 he went into a strange trance and threw himself into his armchair, and he would not move from that chair for almost 24 hours. Those around Liguori thought he was ill, that he'd had a funny turn, but when he came out of the trance he said that he had just paid a bedside visit to Pope Clement XIV at Rome - and the 68-year-old Pope had been dying. Rome was four days of travel away, but sure enough, the news of the Pope's death was soon confirmed, and those who had attended Pope Clement XIV's death recalled seeing Liguori at his bedside. In more modern times, in the 1950s, there was a certain priest in St Anne's Church, Edge Hill, who is said to have bilocated to a church in Ireland during a Mass. He was seen to become partially transparent in the pulpit for about a minute, and during that time he was seen at a church in Dublin by an old woman who had come to pray for strength from God because her husband had just been killed in a car accident. The priest was seen to comfort this woman and then vanish.

How does one bilocate? The writer and mystic Aldous Huxley was able to bilocate, and used pure willpower. He would stare intently at a person who was sleeping and will himself into their dreams, and sometimes the waking saw him too. The author John

Cowper Powys could also voluntarily bilocate, and even told fellow writer Theodore Dreiser he'd appear to him later in the evening. True to his word, Cowper Powys appeared to Dreiser as the latter sat reading a book in his home in New York that evening. Dreiser slowly got up and tried to approach the apparition but it vanished. He then telephoned Cowper Powys at his home in the Hudson valley, thirty miles away, and Cowper Powys answered and confirmed that he had just projected himself. There is no doubt that some form of hypnotic trance and concentrated willpower is the secret, coupled with good visualisation techniques. I mentioned the discipline needed for bilocation at a talk many years ago, and one of those present was later imprisoned in Walton Jail (for armed robbery), and finding he had a lot of time on his hands, he began to make daily attempts at bilocation, and after about a week of trying, he allegedly appeared in his home where his girlfriend and two of her friends saw him appear. One of the girls suffered an asthma attack because she mistook the bilocating prisoner for a ghost. I interviewed the girls and they confirmed the story. Several friends of the prisoner also saw him at various places around Liverpool, so perhaps anyone – given sufficient training – *can* be in two places at once.

# WRITTEN IN THE STARS

**Are you one** of the millions of people who regularly turn to the horoscope column of a magazine or daily newspaper to see what the stars have in store for you? Perhaps you read your internet horoscope each day on your laptop or mobile. Recent research has established that 60 per cent of people who read horoscopes actually believe in them, but surely there is no scientific evidence that astrology works? The following may surprise the sceptics amongst you.

In 1950, a young French statistician, Michel Gauquelin, set out to disprove that there was any connection between planetary positions at a person's birth and that individual's future development. It is a legal requirement in France to register the time of a child's birth, and this useful data enabled the sceptical statistician to calculate the horoscopes of his randomly-chosen 25,000 subjects. However, instead of disproving astrology, Gauquelin's findings apparently supported it! The birth data of 508 doctors in the study showed that they had been born with Saturn at or near mid-heaven. Saturn has long been held to be the ruling planet of scientists and those in the medical profession. Similarly, 134 soldiers were born with Mars high in the ecliptic, and the red planet Mars, of course, was regarded as the god of war for centuries. The study also produced other intriguing results. A group of 190 artists, actors and writers were born when the planet Venus was looming in the western sky.

There were many other unexpected and significant correlations produced by Gauquelin's study but, unfortunately, the Frenchman was quickly ridiculed by the scientific establishment. All the same, Gauquelin continued his research with an open mind. From all over France he collected more birth data for groups of prominent military men, politicians, writers, actors and sports people. Once again, the results of the astrological study were disquieting: 3,141 politicians and almost all of the military men and sports people in the study had Mars past the ascendant or mid-heaven in their horoscopes; 3,305 scientists from the sample were born when Saturn was rising or at mid-heaven, while once again Venus dominated the horoscopes of the artists, actors and writers.

Further studies into the validity of astrology have uncovered many incidences of "astrological twins". Here are just a few. The eminent German physicist Albert Einstein, and fellow Nobel Prize-winning scientist Otto Hahn, were both born on 14 March 1879, which makes them Pisceans. A set of notable

Gemini astro twins were Vincent Price and fellow horror-film actor Peter Gushing, who were born on 27 May. Nazis Herman Goring and Alfred Rosenberg were not only born on the same day in the same year, they also died on the same day in the same year - 15 October 1946 at Nuremberg. Rosenberg was hanged as a war criminal, while Goring took poison in his cell to cheat the hangman's noose.

So, does astrology really work? Can horoscopes in the newspaper accurately predict what the future has in store for someone on a personal level? This certainly seemed to be the case in the following chilling incident which was reported in a French newspaper in the early 1970s.

In 1971, a French bus driver, Alain Bosier, told his girlfriend that the horoscopes she consulted everyday were nonsense. She said he was wrong and that, nine times out of ten, her horoscope had been fairly accurate - especially the horoscopes written by the French astrologer Madame Du Berzil.

Alain told his girlfriend to read out his horoscope, which was Gemini. His girlfriend said, "Okay, here's your horoscope: 'Take extra care on the road as the moon is waning and your planet - the fleet-footed Mercury, is in conflict with the balance of the ecliptic. A relative or close friend will lose his head in an unsavoury situation, and this could end or damage your career or vocation.' "

"Complete rubbish!" Alain laughed and shook his head. "Mercury and the moon, and all the stars in the sky have no influence on me whatsoever." And he kissed his girlfriend, but she elbowed him in the ribs because of his mocking tone. She really believed in astrology and non-believers irritated her.

"Go to work!" Alain's girlfriend shouted out, and as he got to the door, she added, "You'll see. It'll all come true - so take care on the road. I still love you even though you're a sceptic."

It seemed like another uneventful day. Alain drove the bus from the station and took it on his usual route around the outskirts of Rouen. At around 6 p.m. the roads started to get busy, and Alain saw a wagon speeding up to him from behind. It must have been doing around 60 mph (96 kph) and was closing fast - and there was a sharp bend on the road ahead. Alain stuck his head out of the side window and waved at the driver of the wagon then gestured for him to keep his distance. The wagon driver put two fingers up at Alain, then gradually slowed down. "The same to you!" Alain shouted, and he said to the passengers, "That idiot was trying to overtake on the bend." One of the passengers, a young man, commented, "He's crazy. He has sheets of corrugated iron on the back of the wagon and they look like they're going to come off. He hasn't tied them down properly."

The wagon driver followed the bus round the sharp bend in the road without keeping the correct separation distance. He even beeped his horn at Alain. "I'll report that madman to the police!" said the bus driver. He asked the passengers to get the wagon's registration, but a young woman said, "Oh just forget him and drive on will you? I'm already late."

Alain calmed down, took a deep breath, then glanced in his wing mirror. He saw a speck coming up the road from behind the wagon. As the speck drew nearer, Alain could see it was his old friend Pierre, who used to work as a busman a few years back. The two men were very good friends and often played chess together. Pierre was now a motorcycle fanatic, and was driving a Harley-Davidson Soft-tail Classic.

Pierre flashed his headlight at main beam for a second to acknowledge Alain, and then the bike revved and came tearing up the road towards the bus. As it was passing the wagon, something horrific happened. A sudden cross-wind roared out of a gap in a hedge and lifted one of the sheets of corrugated iron off the wagon. The thin cables holding it came undone and the sheet flew off the top of the stack and glided down at an angle towards the motorcyclist. In one swift movement the sheet of iron took off Pierre's head with a clean cut. The body of the headless motorcyclist went into various spasms and nervous twitches, and the bike continued to roar up the road as the headless corpse gripped and twisted the throttle. It passed the busload of horrified and traumatized passengers with blood spraying out from the stump of Pierre's neck. Jets of arterial blood spurted across the windows of the bus as the passengers screamed or turned away in terror. Meanwhile, Pierre's helmeted head bounced along the road like a football, and actually rolled into a field where three schoolgirls were picnicking. The bemused girls first thought that the object was a football; then they all saw the blood, and the limp tongue hanging out of the severed head, and they ran off screaming.

When Alain saw the headless motorcyclist pass him, he went into shock and swerved to keep away from the gruesome spectacle - and the bus skidded out of control and mowed down an old man who had been walking down the side of the road with his dog. The man and his dog died instantly.

Alain left his job and was under psychiatric observation for months. Only the love of his girlfriend pulled him through the trauma. As a macabre keepsake, he cut out the horoscope of that fateful day; the horoscope that had told him to be careful on the road; the horoscope which had uncannily said that a close friend would lose his head and that Alain's career would be subsequently ended as a result. He agreed that there was more to astrology than he had ever suspected.

In our neck of the woods, here in the North West of England, there is another intriguing account of astrology being used – to solve several crimes. Our story takes place in the late Victorian period, in 1887, the year before the infamous Jack the Ripper murders. In December of that year, upon Christmas Eve, the spirit of altruism had well and truly descended, along with the snow, upon Liverpool, and in many a home the Yule log cheerily blazed, with holly on the mantelpiece and evergreen entwined in the gasalier. A frost had hardened the mantle of snow upon the great thoroughfare of Bold Street, and flickering yellow flames of gas in the lanterns of the lamp posts lent an amber haze to the foggy arcades. It was only two in the afternoon but many engaged in the last minute rush for Christmas gifts that Saturday believed it was much later because the fog had cast a Cimmerian gloom over the second city of the Empire. The window-dressers of Bold Street had done their shops proud with green seasonal wreaths gemmed with scarlet berries and rainbows of ribbons and intricate multicoloured paper decorations festooning the arrangements of gifs and wares. A Salvation Army brass band was playing *God Rest Ye Merry Gentlemen* on Waterloo Place, next to the Lyceum, and at the other end of Bold Street, a ghostly ethereal sound could just be heard, and this was the strains of the choirboys of St Luke's offering up a carol to the twilit heavens. Over at the Royal Alexandra Theatre on Lime Street, there were snaking queues of red-nosed adults and gleeful children, waiting patiently in a line stretching to the North Western Hotel for tickets to the 7pm show of Mrs Saker's celebrated pantomime "Forty Thieves".

Standing before the impressive window of William Creamer & Co (Furriers in ordinary to Her Majesty the Queen and Her Royal Highness Princess Beatrice), at 56 Bold Street, was a 24-year-old bachelor named Edward Sinclair, a self-styled private inquiry agent who had a tiny cramped office (which also served as his living quarters) further up the street over a chandlers shop. He was gazing into Creamer's window display at a nine-guinea sealskin coat, but he couldn't decide whether he wanted this coat for his grandmother or the squirrel tail and bear boa and leather gloves for ten guineas, as "Nanna" loved to wear a boa. He had little money to spend this Christmas because of the extortionate rent increase of his office by the Draconian landlord Mr Chesney. He wondered if he should give up his career as a desperate detective and find a more mundane occupation, and with those depressing thoughts he turned away from the window, intending to try the cheaper stores such as Owen Owen and the Bon Marche, when a familiar silky voice called his name.

'Eddy!'

He turned to see the beautiful 19-year-old Charlotte McLennan, such a welcoming sight to a lonely young man in the foggy gaslit gloom of Bold Street. She was wearing a pink bonnet adorned with velvet flowers, and a smart long coat featuring her family tartan. Lottie (as Edward knew her) had been born in Edinburgh but raised in Liverpool, but there was something distinctly pure and Celtic about her flawless complexion, and to Edward her eyes always seemed full of mystery and magic. Lottie was a friend of his cousin Amelia, and she had known him since he was a child. He had fallen in and out of love with her so many times, and he knew she'd haunt his thoughts tonight when he'd be wallowing in self-pity in his little lodgings before that inadequate fireplace. However, when she heard that he would not be spending Christmas with his family, Lottie insisted on him having dinner with her family. Edward felt so low of late, so inferior, a washout who had let his father down by not following him into the sphere of civil engineering. 'Eddy, you must have dinner with us,' Lottie pressed her gloved hands together in a begging gesture until her old friend relented.

Later that evening, after Edward had purchased the few little gifts he could afford for his grandmother, father and mother, he returned to his lodgings and used the bellows to kindle a flickering flame in the grate. At half-past six that Christmas Eve, Lottie called, bringing a little straw basket crammed with her mother's home-made plum pudding, biscuits, a wedge of iced Christmas cake, a few tangerines and a small box of expensive French chocolates. She had told her parents she was taking a gift to her friend Rose on Huskisson Street, she informed Edward, and he smiled and fidgeted with a tangerine as they both stood before the orange glow of that tiny fire. There was an awkward pause, and Edward cleared his magazines and newspapers from a seat and asked Lottie to sit down. He explained how business was very slow at the moment, but how he expected it to pick up in the New Year. He then chatted with Lottie, and asked her what she'd been doing since he had last seen her almost two years ago. She wanted to make pottery, to paint, to make greeting cards and to create things. But she had also been absorbed by another interest over the past year or so, and this was astrology. At first Edward thought Lottie was talking about astronomy, and said he had a small brass telescope somewhere she could have, but Lottie smiled, and she took off her bonnet, shook her dark hair loose, and leaned forward to gaze into the flames of the grate. 'No, not astronomy – that's a singularly dull branch of physics, studying the moon and meteorites and all that. No, my interest lies in astrology – the signs of the Zodiac.'

Edward found a little bundle of stickwood, and he fed the flames, then made some cocoa in a rather self-conscious manner by pouring milk into a kettle suspended by a chain over the fire.

'I should have thought that astrology was of little practical use in today's scientific world,' he reasoned with a blush.

'On the contrary,' Lottie replied, 'I find it very useful indeed.'

'How so?'

'I sincerely believe that planetary combinations and the positions of the stars wield an influence over our lives,' Lottie told him, 'and I know that the human race are divided into personalities of twelve distinctive types, ranging from the duplicitous two-faced but creative Gemini to the quarrelsome but loyal Capricorn. From the moment we are born, we travel along a particular orbit through this life, and just as astronomers can scientifically predict eclipses of the sun and moon, as well as meteor showers, the astrologer can predict incidents and predicaments that are in store for anybody.'

'Which seems little more than fortune-telling, Lottie,' Edward smirked, listening to the milk simmer in the kettle.

Lottie went to the window, parted the curtain and looked out into the night sky with her hand cupped around an eye to shield from the light from the gas mantle. 'Ah, there's Saturn,' she said with a slight grin, and beckoned Edward to come over to the window. She pointed at the tiny pinpoint of emerald green light just above a chimney stack. 'Saturn, and its in the constellation of Cancer; now that means...'

And Lottie rambled on about the houses of the Zodiac and what the positions of the planets and stars meant for the world at large, and Edward hardly heard a word she was saying because he was so beguiled by her beauty; the way her lips moved and the way her nose screwed up when she spoke and the funny cute way she unconsciously pulled faces. When Lottie realised he'd not been paying attention she accused him of being "a typical inattentive butterfly-minded Cancerian".

'Steady on, Lottie,' Edward recoiled with a smirk on his face, and when he handed her a mug of hot cocoa she waved it away saying, 'I don't want it, it smells awful.'

'Look, Lottie, I'm sorry I'm not interested in this mumbo jumbo, but it really is for the birds!' Edward glared at her and clunked down the mug on a tiny rickety table.

Lottie seemed lost for words at the vicious scepticism.

Edward continued his attack. 'I mean, let us look at the scientific facts and statistics shall we? There are eighty babies born every minute in this world, so that means each of these eighty babies will share the same course through life as governed by where the stars and planets are! That's preposterous.'

'Ah, well that's where you are wrong Mr Know-it-All,' Lottie retaliated and her beautiful dark eyes seemed to glint with the reflected light of the fire. Edward found the effect so mesmerising.

'How am I wrong Lottie?'

'Well, for a start,' Lottie said in a firm but condescending voice, 'each of these eighty babies being born at the same time will not be in the same place will they? They will be born at various latitudes and longitudes, from places as diverse as Calcutta to Liverpool, and that makes all of the difference, because longitude and latitude dictate a great part of the horoscope, but you obviously didn't know that!'

Edward sipped the cocoa and then his eyes looked to the ceiling as his eyebrows arched high – and this mannerism, which had long been noted by Lottie, always meant he'd had an idea. 'You and I were born within a day of one another, and yet you called me a typical butterfly-minded Cancerian! Now, you might have been born in Edinburgh and I was born in Liverpool, but on the scale of this world that's but a tiny distance apart! So can you explain why we are so different?'

'People who are born close to one another are often close in life,' Lottie said, all matter-of-fact. 'That's why twins are so close – they have almost identical horoscopes and are born under the same sign.'

'Yes, but I'm a Cancerian and you're a Leo – ' Edward was trying to argue his point but Lottie cut through his words.

'Edward, you were born on 20th day of July, and I was born on the 21st day of that same month, but that makes me a Leo, and that's an entirely different sign, although I agree I may share some of the traits of the Crab, but certainly not the butterfly-mindedness you exhibit!'

Edward shook his head and smiled. 'I believe in logic and science and reason. In my everyday life and in my work as a private inquiry agent – '

'Then perhaps it's time for you to give astrology a chance – for it may help you in your work,' Lottie suggested, but her voice was now almost a whisper, and she looked quite hurt by the criticisms hurled at her by someone she obviously had feelings for. 'I use astrology, and, dare I even mention this, but I also dabble in tasseomancy – the reading of tealeaves – as method of divination.'

'Ha! All this jiggery pokery is, as I have said, all for the birds – ' Edward was about to launch into another scathing disparagement of poor Lottie but seeing how hurt she was, and feeling decidedly ungallant, he backtracked somewhat. 'Although, I mean, er, by all means, I'd be willing to give all this a chance, a trial period, I can see no harm in that.'

And by a strange coincidence, on the following day, the perfect situation arose for Edward to test this suggestion to Lottie. He had enjoyed Christmas dinner at her home in Aigburth – a large sprawling four-storey house – when the butler, Mr Jones came to the dinner table and whispered something in the ear of Lottie's father, George McLennan. 'What? Are you sure man?' George said in his rough, Scottish way of speaking. He told his wife and then he told everyone present that there had been a break-in at the house. It transpired that the butler Mr Jones had heard a racket upstairs in the upper rooms and he had gone up with a parlourmaid to see what the trouble was. At first the butler thought the strong winds outside had blown open the attic window, but the cause of the cacophony had been something much more sinister. The parlourmaid saw nothing but the butler caught a fleeting glimpse of a very strange man, dressed in black, with a long black cape, running up the stairs to the attic. Jones the butler bravely gave chase and witnessed a very sinister-looking man in black in a long black cloak open the skylight window and run along the rooftop – which was covered in snow. The man then jumped from the roof and sailed upwards into the night. The butler called to three servants (all of them Irish) and pointed out of the open window of his own quarters, and all of them saw a strange black shape flit back and forth across the waxing gibbous moon high up in the sky. Jones said the thing was either Spring-

Heeled Jack or the Devil himself. The door to the master bedroom of the McLennans was found ajar, and the jewellery box belonging to Christina McLennan – Lottie's mother – was found empty on the bed. It was estimated that some two thousand pounds' worth of jewellery had been stolen. The incident had happened around 8pm as the Christmas dinner was in progress.

Edward Sinclair examined the roof just before the police arrived, and he saw U-shaped markings imprinted in the hard snow covering the slates of the roof. There was also a curious long track, about five inches in length in the snow at the top of a chimney stack. But Edward could not work out what had made such a mark. The superstitious trio of Irish servants knew of only one individual who could leave U-shaped marks and fly up from a roof – and that had to be Old Nick himself, with his hoofed feet and bat-like wings. His pointed tail had no doubt left that mystifying groove in the snow on top of that chimney!

Edward, being a very rational man, simply couldn't accept all this nonsense about the Devil robbing jewellery. Even if he existed, why would he waste his time carrying out such a petty crime when he could steal the Crown Jewels – or even the Tower of London itself along with all the ravens if he wished? And according to folklore, the Devil was not a thief, but a supreme tempter and a collector of souls. Edward climbed back into the attic from the snowy, slippery roof as a worried Lottie looked on, and he told her the jewellery had been spirited away, but not by some supernatural being. 'I think those so-called hoof marks were put there by someone in this house, and my money's on Jones the butler,' said Edward as he kicked the snow from the toes of his boots.

'Jones has been our butler for yonks,' Lottie said with a disdainful look, 'don't let father hear of your suspicions. He'd trust Jones with his life.'

'Yesterday you urged me to open my mind to new possibilities,' Edward reminded Lottie as he looked out the attic window at the iced rooftops glistening in the moonlight, 'so perhaps you should practice what you preach.' Edward looked around the attic, and here and there on the bare wooden boards of the floor he noticed small traces of sawdust. Lottie also picked up a few tacks made of a dark blue metal. Were these clues in the jewellery theft or merely incidental finds unconnected to the crime? Eddy couldn't quite make up his mind on this matter.

An Inspector Chandler from Lark Lane Police Station arrived at the house and interviewed everybody. No guest was allowed to leave the house, and Chandler and a policeman climbed out onto the roof to view the strange hoof prints by the feeble light of a bull's eye lantern. When the inspector heard about the way the jewel thief had flown off into the night he first returned a puzzled look, and then a grin almost materialised across his craggy face. 'He probably had an accomplice, and threw the loot down to him,' Chandler reasoned, 'because it is not humanly possible for anyone to escape over the rooftops outside – they're treacherous.'

'So where on earth did he go, inspector?' asked George McLennan. He held his wife, a little woman, in his arms with her face to his breast, and she looked as if she was about to cry.

'I think he probably went back into the house from the attic window and probably left via the tradesman's exit, while you were all at the dinner table,' Chandler replied, taking off his tight black leather gloves. He produced a small pencil and scribbled a few lines in a notebook.

'But what about those marks that look like hoof prints, inspector?' Lottie inquired.

'They could be nothing more than the impressions of bird's feet that have partly thawed,' Chandler said in a rather smug manner, 'I've seen similar marks left by badgers and foxes when a thaw begins to set in.'

Edward cast a sly glance at Lottie's eyes and that silent look was saying, 'Can you believe this nonsense?'

Lottie pointed out the sawdust on the floor of the attic to Chandler, and showed the inspector the tacks she had found, but he shook his head and said: 'Nah, they're nothing to do with this; no bearing on this case at all.'

The servants were interviewed one by one in the drawing room, as were the guests and of course, that included Edward, and when the latter stated he was a private inquiry agent by trade, Chandler sniggered and said, 'And have you had any successes so far?'

Edward didn't answer, because he'd only been involved in cases concerning missing dogs and one investigation where someone was sneakily painting a woman's front door white – and the culprit turned out to be a 12-year-old child.

The investigation came to nothing, and Chandler advised Mrs McLennan to invest in a good safe in which to keep her valuables from now on, and then he left.

Around midnight, most of the servants had retired, and Mr and Mrs McLennan had gone to bed after the most traumatic Christmas they'd ever experienced. In the parlour, before a mellow fire, Edward and Lottie sat at a table, and spread out upon that table were strange diagrams – horoscopes – almanacs, a crystal ball, a pot of tea, and a single china cup – the interior of which Lottie had been studying for a good quarter of an hour. Edward watched the girl at work; she was like some 19th century witch. She had asked the servants and the Butler to give their birthdates for a novel game she wanted to play, and now she had the data and had determined that the finger of suspicion pointed to the Butler – a Scorpio, and from his date of birth, Lottie had worked out that he was unusually prone to greed and selfishness, but tempered with a quick-witted mind, especially with being a water sign. All this was double Dutch to Edward, and he was trying to work out what that impression in the snow atop of the chimney stack was. It was as if some rod had been lain down in the snow there.

'This is the cup Mr Jones supped his tea from – ' Lottie muttered as she turned the china cup and scrutinised the patterns of the leaves within it.

'Yes, you told me that before,' Edward replied, and he turned to look into the flames of the fire as he rested his jaw on his clenched fist. Come on, how did he get those jewels's away? He thought, grinding his teeth now.

'Edward, look at this!' Lottie pointed her little finger at a clump of tea leaves which had collected into a geometric figure – almost a diamond in shape. Edward could see it.

'Look's like a diamond,' he thought, and then those eyebrows lifted and he looked at Lottie. 'And, a diamond is a…jewel.'

'No, not a jewel,' Lottie said calmly, squinting at the shape in the cup, 'it has a wavy lines coming from one corner – like a piece of string. See?'

'A kite!' Edward exclaimed. 'Wait; yes, a kite. And the servants saw something black fly past the face of the moon, and they thought it was our demonic burglar because Jones put that in their minds, saying he'd seen the man flap his cloak and step off the roof and fly into space. By Jove Lottie, we're onto something!'

Lottie's eyes sparkled with another realization. 'The butler could have imprinted those U-shaped marks on the roof with a horseshoe – knowing how superstitious the Irish servants are!'

'And that mark – that line in the snow on the top of the chimney stack – that was probably made by the string or twine of the kite, but wait a minute, what are we saying Lottie? That Jones attached the jewels to a kite and guided it across the skies without being seen?'

'Perhaps it was a dark-coloured kite, a black one even, made from black silk,' Lottie imagined such a black diamond kite soaring up from the roof of her home. The winds were blowing like mad last night – but where did that kite go? She raised this important question and Edward said there was probably an accomplice somewhere downwind of the house near Jericho farm – to the south.

'If our theory holds some truth, Lottie, why, it would certainly explain the sawdust and the tacks in the attic; the frame of the kite could have been cut and the fabric tacked onto the frame up there. Yes, it's making sense,' Edward voiced his train of thoughts out loud and then smiled.

'We've got to go and look!' Lottie suggested, and she got up from the table and walked to the door, but Edward said he could not allow her to put her life a risk, for there might be violent criminals out there, and if they knew someone was onto them, they'd resort even to murder to prevent the truth being discovered. 'Ha! Then I shall go armed!' Lottie announced, and she left the parlour and ran upstairs. She returned a few minutes later with a loaded revolver.

'Lottie! Where the deuces did you get *that*?' a horrified Edward asked.

'Never you mind, Eddy, but I'll let them have it if they try and harm a hair on your head!'

And they went out into the snow-covered lane, through Fulwood Park, until they came upon a curious but eerie sight in a field adjoining the Otterspool Road which was covered with a crust of frosted snow four or five inches in depth. There in the middle of the field lay an enormous black kite, almost seven feet long and four feet in breadth and a length of twine lay coiled by it. A little black velvet bag hung from the tail of the kite frame, but it was found to be empty, and two trails of footprints led to and from the giant black diamond. Eddy and Lottie followed the trail of footprints from the field, hoping they would lead to the house of the thieves, but unfortunately the trail vanished into the grass that lay untouched by snow because it had been sheltered by a clump of trees near Otterspool Farm. On the other side of the wooded area, the impressions of hansom cab wheels were clearly evident. The trail had ended, the thieves had got away Scot free, and although nothing could be proved, Jones the butler suddenly decided to seek employment elsewhere when Lottie mentioned the discovery of the black kite to her father. It was a disastrous first case, but at least Edward had found his mind opened to the intriguing powers of Lottie McLennan, a veritable astrological detective, and they teamed up and went on to tackle many more cases in a unique partnership of science and the arcane, and it seems that love and marriage was written in *their* stars too, for they later wed.

# EYES IN THE SKY

**I get some** very strange reports from readers...

Sunday 9th June, 2013 was an untypical beautiful sunny day across Liverpool. It really looked as if the summer we hope to see each year had finally arrived, despite the imprecise ramblings of the weather people on the TV and radio who seem to always say "rain's on the way so enjoy the sunshine while you can".

Well, one person who was enjoying the sunshine and the clear blue sky that Sunday was a 21-year-old university student named Heather. She and Brendan, her boyfriend of two years found a fairly secluded spot in Calderstones Park and lay on a huge Little Mermaid bath towel that Heather had bought in Disneyland, Florida a few years back. The couple lay on their backs, Heather in a white Power Puff Girls tee shirt and pink shorts, and Brendan stripped to the waist in his knee-length black shorts. He was about to put on the earphones connected to his mobile so he could listen to his collection of MP3s when he saw something very strange indeed. Heather's body lifted up into the air about five inches, then fell back onto the grass. 'Whoa!' she yelled, and she turned to Brendan, who was gawping at her open-mouthed. 'Did you see that?' she asked in a high-pitched voice.

'Yeah; what happened?' Brendan seemed to be in shock.

'Oh my God, I felt something lifting me up for a

moment, by my navel area, and then it let go,' Heather struggled to find words to describe the weird and unsettling sensation. She and Brendan went on about the incident for about fifteen minutes, then saw the funny side of it and settled back down. As they lay there, Heather couldn't put the weird incident out of her mind, but Brendan was dozing off in his sunglasses as he listened to retro music such as Radiohead and Pink Floyd.

Then, all of a sudden, the sensation returned, but ever so slowly. It began with the feeling of butterflies in the stomach, of a strange tugging sensation from above, as if Heather was a paperclip and a huge magnet was hanging over her. She felt herself rise up, but this time, as she went to speak, to alert Brendan, she found that she was unable to move. She couldn't move her mouth, and even moving her eyes seemed difficult, and this made her panic.

Heather began to rise up from the grass, only she knew it wasn't her body that was going up through the air, but her consciousness, her soul perhaps, and she could see this odd-looking, almost triangular fluffy cloud miles up in the blue, and she somehow knew the thing pulling her up into the sky was in that cloud. He stomach fell away. Heather immediately recalled the sensation she had felt when she was a little girl, careering down the helter skelter at the fair, and that turn in the stomach she'd get on a roller coaster. This felt like this, and the only way Heather can describe the sensation is if you imagine lying on your back in a park, gazing at the sky, when gravity is switched off, and you "fall" into the immense depths of the upper atmosphere. As she went up, she could feel

Calderstones Park falling away, and somehow she managed to look around. She saw the patchwork quilt of green and grey fields and streets far below. Then she could see the Wirral peninsula and the unsettling sight of the thin black line of Blackpool Tower in the hazy distance. The Isle of Man stood out in the grey Irish Sea, and the white flecks moving by far below were seagulls. Heather tried to scream for Brendan, but she couldn't utter a word. She looked up and saw that massive long triangular cloud, and she estimated that it was quite a few miles in length, and its enormity filled her with horror. Should it suddenly stop attracting her now and let her fall, she'd be ketchup with clothes on top when she reached the ground. Heather was by no means a religious person, but she begged God to stop this evil thing in that cloud from taking her. As she looked up into the rolling mists of the cloud, she thought she saw something dark and circular, and as she got nearer and nearer, she realised the dark disk-like thing was some sort of eye. By now Heather looked to her left and saw the Isle of Anglesey off the Welsh coast, and cloud-kissing Snowdon close by on this scale. In her mind she screamed for God to save her, but she seemed to be accelerating now. Then a weird, low groaning monotone voice boomed in her mind, and it said to Heather: 'I'm keeping you.'

Heather wanted to cry but couldn't even show such a basic emotion.

Then she noticed another cloud sailing into view, just to the right of the one she was being drawn to at a phenomenal velocity. This cloud seemed a bit smaller but it had the similar triangular shape to it as the other one. Now a voice of a different cadence echoed in

Heather's racing mind. It said: 'Put it back! Put it back!'

'No!' roared the deeper voice, but Heather felt the rate of ascent slow down.

'Put it back! You will put it back!' the second voice shrieked.

Heather stopped in mid-air, and she was at such a high altitude she could see the sky darkening above the two quarrelling clouds – as if she was on the edge of space.

A blinding bolt of lightning flashed from the smaller cloud and struck the bigger one, and a deafening voice cried out as if it was in pain.

Heather fell like a stone and as she did she heard deep gruff laughter fading away. The only two clouds in the otherwise perfect blue sky were getting just a little bit smaller. The ground was coming up fast. Coloured ants moving along the roads below began to speed up as Heather recognised them as cars, and the green patch that was Calderstones Park was getting bigger and bigger. The white flecks were easily recognisable as seagulls gliding about at the bottom of the atmosphere. Heather really believed she would create an impact crater pretty soon, and made up prayers as she fell faster and faster – nine metres per second per second...

She briefly saw the ant-sized couple below – one in the white tee shirt with some pink about her and the other one – Brendan, looked like a weird flesh-coloured insect. Heather chose to look upwards in the seconds before she died. She was puzzled, and to say she was upset would be a silly understatement, for the girl was preparing to meet her death.

She heard a bang in her head, a sound like a shotgun, and she opened her eyes and screamed a profanity. And then she saw the blue sky above and those two clouds sliding sideways ever so slowly overhead. Heather rolled towards Brendan, and grabbed him as she let out a scream. He yelped because he had been startled out of his sleep, and he asked Heather what the matter was. She couldn't find the words to describe her surreal ordeal at first, and instead she dragged Brendan along as she got to her feet, leaving the towel on the grass. Her legs felt like jelly for about a minute. 'Let's get out of here! Come on!' she cried, and looked heavenwards at the two clouds with an expression of pure terror on her sun-reddened face.

'You've had a nightmare!' Brendan growled, 'Calm down Heather!' he found himself actually scared of the strength this slim girl possessed, and she continued to drag him along towards the cover of some trees.

When they got back to their flat, Heather told Brendan what had happened, and at first he wondered if someone had spiked the Coke his girlfriend at drunk before they went to the park, but this was highly unlikely as no one had been near them as they both drank soft drinks purchased from a corner shop near Rose Lane. And then, Brendan recalled that strange incident when the couple had been about to soak up the sun – when Heather had seemingly been physically lifted up by something. The couple still refuse to go anywhere near Calderstones Park, just in case the thing up there – whatever it is - is still active, and Heather now has a phobia of sunbathing in wide-open spaces.

# THE BLACKLERS GHOST

**Sheila Cranham awoke** from a nightmare that cold morning of 31 October 1971 – Halloween. She'd dreamt her violent husband – from whom she was separated – was strangling her, and the bad dream had been so realistic she had felt his hands closing hard around her throat, crushing her windpipe. As she rejoined waking reality she was relieved to recall that she was in the spare room of her mum's home on West Derby Road. She's been staying with her mother now for almost a fortnight, and had no plans to ever go back to a wife-beater. Şheila reached for the clock on the bedside cabinet and was shocked to see that it was almost ten-past six; she was supposed to be in work at half-past six this morning. She sprung out the bed, got washed, teased her good head of hair into shape, and grabbed her pale blue overalls, navy skirt, and managed to locate a pair of tights in the chest of drawers. She put on her foundation in record time and as she hurried about, looking for her shoes, she thought of the dream of her estranged husband throttling her. By 6.20 am she was rushing along the dark and windy October Street to the bus stop – and she saw how quiet the roads were. One single vehicle was cruising past – a milk float. She waited and waited, and no buses came, and as the wind made a mess of her hair, she swore under her breath. She'd only just started as a cleaner at a store on Ranelagh Street and didn't want to blow it by being late. The money wasn't great but every penny of it was accounted for, and soon she would have to find a place of her own and have to pay rent on it. Her head was "chocker" as her late Nan would say. A white mini passed – then reversed – it was Sid, the dopey soft-spoken boyfriend of Sheila's younger sister April, going home from his night-watchman job at a factory. 'You're not waiting for a bus are you? It's – ' he was saying in his usual low whispery voice when Sheila rudely interrupted him and virtually demanded a lift. All the way to Ranelagh Street, Sheila talked about her brute of a husband, and how he was like a Jekyll and Hyde character in drink, and Sid couldn't get a word in edgeways. He dropped her off at Lewis's corner and seemed glad to see the back of Sheila as he drove homewards. Then, as Sheila saw her workplace was closed, she realised it was Sunday, and she also recalled that the clocks had gone back an hour that morning; so it was 5.40am. That's why Liverpool was like a ghost town. She turned to glance at Renshaw Street, hoping Sid might be stuck at the traffic lights in his mini, but he was nowhere to be seen.

'Oh I'm getting worse,' Sheila groaned to herself, 'I don't bleeding believe this!'

'Excuse me,' said a very effeminate voice, and Sheila turned to see a man – well over six feet in height – in a black trilby-like hat of some sort, and a long black knee-length coat. He had huge hands clad in brown leather gloves. He had peculiar swept-back eyebrows and the eyes beneath them looked menacing and positively sinister. He had a pencil-thin moustache and below this he wore a false lopsided grin. He walked rapidly with a strange gait from the direction of a doorway of Blacklers, and Sheila instinctively ran from him. She screamed for help as she bolted towards Renshaw Street in the middle of the road, but the eerie tall man screeched with laughter and shouted something Sheila couldn't make out, but it could have been "You have a pretty neck". She got as far as the YMCA on Mount Pleasant and thought she had lost the lanky maniac, but he seemed to reappear out of nowhere and he ran after her with his gloved hands reaching towards her. Not another soul seemed to be about that Sunday morning, and Sheila was in tears by the time she reached Hope Street, out of breath, with a stitch in her side. Then, all of a sudden, as the gangly weirdo closed in on her with his long outstretched arms and big gloved hands, a hackney cab came round the corner from Oxford Street and screeched to a halt, and the tall man in black walked calmly away into the shadows. Sheila ran to the cab and the little bald corpulent driver helped her into the vehicle. He slammed the door, jumped back into the hackney, and swerved it into a u-turn. 'West Derby Road, please, driver,' Sheila said, and wiped the tears from her eyes with a crumpled tissue handkerchief she found in her coat pocket.

'That fellah, love,' the cabby said to Sheila as he scanned the rear-view mirror, 'is, well, you won't believe this love; he's a ghost. Yeah.' He nodded at Sheila's face reflected in his rear-view mirror. 'That's true as Gospel girl, on my kids' life.'

'I believe you, he – ' Sheila started to reply.

The cabby talked over Sheila, telling her that the stalker was a ghost he had seen many times over the years. It was known as the Blacklers ghost because it always seemed to come from the Blacklers store on Great Charlotte Street. Sheila was dumbfounded, and she noticed how nervous the cabby was telling her about the creepy entity.

When she reached her mother's home on West Derby Road, the cabby refused to take any money from his fare, and Sheila thought this was very gallant, and she invited the cabby in for a cuppa. 'Nah, I've got to get home,' he said, 'been on the job since 7pm Saturday night,' he told her with a weary grin.

Sheila insisted upon him coming in, and realised she fancied him. 'Oh come in and have a cuppa and I'll make you some breakfast if you like, and you can tell me more about that ghost.'

'Well I can't refuse an offer like that,' the cabby replied, and then he ruefully added, 'Beats going home to an empty house.' He later explained how he had been divorced for five years and never seemed to have the time to go and 'court'. Sheila later divorced her husband and married the cabby.

But what of the Blackler's ghost? Whose shade is he? I once mentioned this ghost on a local radio programme and received quite a few calls and emails about the apparition. The earliest account of the Blacklers ghost dated from 1959, when it was seen by two policemen as they went along Lime Street in a patrol car. They saw the figure cross from the direction of the Adelphi Hotel, and followed it as far as Great Charlotte Street, where it went into a doorway. When one of the policemen rushed to the doorway to confront the suspicious figure, he was surprised to see it wasn't there. Thinking that perhaps the unknown man had somehow got into the store with a key, the policeman informed his colleague in the patrol car and they both shone their torches into the building. A passer-by asked the police if they had seen the ghost too. One of the policemen asked the passer-by what he meant, and in reply the man gave an exact description of the ghost's attire and unusual; tallness. Later that night, the same policemen once again saw the tall figure in black with a strange-looking hat walk to the same doorway from the direction of Elliot Street, and once again the figure vanished in the same doorway, or possibly simply passed through the locked door.

They say this unidentified ghost now haunts the pub named after one of Blacklers founders – the Richard John Blackler – and this drinking establishment stands in the very building that once housed the Blacklers department store. That pub, incidentally, is also haunted by two other supernatural presences, and it has also been the scene of some intriguing timeslips.

# THE BARBER'S HAUNTED LOOKING-GLASS

**Way back in** the late 1950s there was a certain barber's shop off Scotland Road where a strange series of inexplicable and frightening incidents took place. The first of these incidents occurred one rainy but warm Saturday afternoon in August 1959 when a local 37-year-old furniture salesman named John Campbell went to have his monthly trim. The barber, a man named Bob, informed John that he had just had a new eighteen foot by five foot mirror mounted on his wall. The previous mirror had been shattered by a ball-bearing fired from a high-powered device resembling a cross-bow in its construction, with a specially-cut strip of bicycle inner-tube tyre to propel the steel ball. The ball had narrowly missed a customer's head and the culprit, though never caught nor identified, had dropped the home-made weapon fifty yards from the shop after the senseless 'shot'. John Campbell could see that the new mirror was a lot longer and taller than the former one, and he sat in the barber's chair and virtually said nothing as Bob wet and straightened his hair with a steel comb and a water spray. The sumptuous padded reclining chair always made John feel a bit too relaxed, and he often assured Bob he'd pay him good money for that chair if he ever wanted to replace it with a new one. John was an insomniac but that barber's chair always made him feel sleepy and already he was feeling a little lethargic, but something was glimpsed in that new barber's mirror which would startle him out of his dreamy state. As Bob snipped away, John saw what he could only describe as faint movement in the mirror, just to the left of his reflection. Then the movement became a partially transparent figure of a woman who looked as if she was dressed as the women were fifty years or more before. Her hair was combed back and arranged in a bun at the crown of her head, and she seemed to be only around five feet in height. Her clothes were dark brown or black, and her blouse or jacket had a high collar on. Her face looked foreign and her eyes were very dark and large. She seemed to be aged about sixty. Then the second figure appeared, and he was a man, possibly as old as the woman, and he was a lot taller but had a fair bit of grey in his hair, which was neatly centre-parted. The outdated couple appeared to be fighting, and the woman was slapping the man across the face and hitting him on the chest, and he was trying to box her blows and parry her hands. 'What the hell!' the barber exclaimed, and almost snipped at the top of John Campbell's ear when he saw the animated images in the mirror.

And then they were gone, as mysteriously as they had appeared. An elderly man named Mr Jenkins walked into the barber shop and said "Good afternoon" or words to that effect, but both the barber and John Campbell said nothing in reply to the venerable old customer because they were still staring into the mirror, wondering if they'd see the ghostly couple reappear, but there were no further ghostly goings-on in the mirror that day, and the barber accompanied John outside after he finally managed to trim his air and said, 'Look, John, I would really appreciate it if you said nothing about those things we saw in the mirror; it might be detrimental to my business, you know, a lot of people being superstitious and that.'

John Campbell nodded and assured Bob he'd not breathe a word to anyone, even his wife, but as soon as the furniture salesman got to his home on Kirkdale Road, he found he couldn't help himself, and he told his wife, sister and brother-in-law about the haunted barber's mirror, and the eerie rumour spread across the neighbourhood and beyond, well within a day or two. When John happened to pass Bob the barber on Great Homer Street three days later, the hairdresser ignored him and walked on with a very sour expression, because he knew John had obviously told people about the ghosts.

About a month later, a seven-year-old boy named Paddy from Heyworth Street was brought to the barber's shop near Scotland Road by his grandfather, a regular client of Bob's, and Paddy was that small, Bob had to put a special plank of wood across the arms of the chair that the lad could sit on. 'Give him a short back and sides Bob,' Paddy's grandfather told the barber, and then the old man sat down and read a newspaper. Paddy's hair was thick and tatty, and Bob tried his best to straighten the entangled mass, but the boy kept saying, 'Ow!'

Bob finally managed to straighten the busby, and he

began to sing along with a song on the radio as he snipped away. Hey, what's that?' Paddy asked the barber, who stopped singng.

'What's what?' Bob asked the boy.

'I just seen some fellah in the mirror,' said Paddy, with a very serious look upon his cherubic face as he gazed at his reflection.

'That's your grand-dad!' Bob joked, but he was already feeling rather nervous, and sensed he was about to see those ghosts appear again.

'No, it wasn't him, this was a funny-looking fellah, and – and he had like a big razor!' Paddy told Bob, and began to fidget as he sat on the plank.

'Keep your head still!' Bob told the lad, and he tried to distract him from gazing in the mirror by asking him what he wanted to be when he grew up, but Paddy's eyes suddenly widened and the boy let out an ear-piercing scream which made the barber jump. The child's grandfather dropped the newspaper in shock and looked up at his grandson.

All three saw a ghastly, nightmarish sight which would haunt them till their dying days. In the mirror, a man was standing behind an old-fashioned barber's chair on which a boy of around Paddy's age was seated. The child had a white linen cover tied around his neck, and that linen was draped over the boy as far as his shorts. The barber in the mirror held the boy's detached head in one hand, with the fingers of this hand around the child's tuft of hair, and in the other hand the barber held a long razor that had beads and smears of vivid blood upon it. The eyes of the severed head were open wide in shock, and the little mouth was opening and closing like the mouth of s goldfish, and blood was trickling from this mouth onto the blade of the barber's steel razor. Blood was simultaneously blossoming in widening crimson stains upon the linen covering the boy's torso.

As the image of this stomach-turning child murder vanished in a heartbeat, little Paddy fainted, and he fell forwards and knocked his head on a porcelain sink. Bob lunged forward and hauled him up and walked him over to his grandfather — and saw that the old man was in a strange position; he was crouching on one bended knee with his hands on his chest. He'd suffered a "funny turn" upon seeing the horrific decapitated child. The barber pulled open his door with its jangling bell with one hand, and rushed out into the street carrying the unconscious Paddy. The barber wasn't very coherent as he ran into a cake shop and rambled on about a barber cutting a child's head clean off with a razor. As chance would have it, a doctor was present at the confectioner's, and he accompanied Bob back to his barber shop and treated Paddy and his grandfather. An ambulance soon arrived and whisked the old man off to hospital, where he was treated for low blood pressure and shock. A detective visited Bob and asked him what all this talk about a child having its head cut off was about, and in a long roundabout way, the barber eventually told the detective about the ghostly visions people had been seeing in his mirror. As you can imagine, the detective did not take the barber's account seriously.

There were more strange visions seen in the poor barber's mirror, and finally, in the following year, in March, before three customers, a very alarming and frightening sight was seen in the mirror. As Bob was shaving an Italian client one afternoon, the ghosts of the man and woman Bob had seen in the previous August appeared once more, but on this occasion, muffled sounds were also heard in conjunction with the apparitions. It sounded as if someone was shouting through a wall next door. The paranormal scene this time within the mirror was a gaslit one, as if events taking place were happening in the evening. The Italian and two customers waiting to be seen by Bob saw the ghosts, and this time, the woman in the mirror was brandishing a pistol. She pointed it at the man and shot him, and as she did, a dull bang could be heard. The man seemed to have been hit by the bullet, and he slumped down to his knees. As he went down, the woman fired again – and then the ghosts vanished, leaving nothing but the reflections of four astonished faces in the looking glass. The Italian subsequently left the chair with parts of his face still lathered, and the two customers who had been waiting for their turn in the chair promptly left. The barber became so enraged by the way the ghosts were killing his business, he picked up one of the chairs customers waited in, and he hurled it at the mirror. The first attempt was unsuccessful, but when the chair was thrown again, the mirror cracked from one end to the other. The barber slumped down onto the chair that was still warm from the Italian who had just vacated it, and his tearful eyes surveyed the damage. A week later, another mirror was installed, and although it was a lot smaller than the previous one, it was not haunted, and no more ghosts were seen in it. James, the son of the barber told me this intriguing story at a talk I gave on ghosts in the Great Hall of St George's Hall. The talk was well-attended with over 3,000 people turning up, and so I was pushed for time when people came forward in the interval to tell me of their own experiences. I did, however, mention the story that James, the son of the barber had told me on the radio, and a fairly well-known local historian immediately telephoned the radio station to say that the tale was nonsense, because he had not heard of any murder in a barber shop near Scotland Road. I told him I would look through the newspaper archives myself to check, and he did the same and drew a blank, but I delved deeper and struck gold. Firstly, I re-interviewed the son of the barber and discovered that the haunted mirror had once been mounted on the wall of a barber shop on Great Nelson Street, near Scotland Road, and that titbit of information provided the key to the mystery. I discovered that around 9pm on Thursday 17 March, 1881, at a barber shop on Great Nelson Street, Louisa Fredericka Rosina Wasmuss, the Hanover-born wife of German barber Heinrich Franz Wasmuss, attempted to murder her husband. She fired a revolver at him and the bullet entered his chest and penetrated his left lung. Heinrich fell after he was hit, and he was lucky he fell when he did because the next bullet from his wife's gun was aimed at his head, and missed him as he collapsed. Someone subsequently charged at the woman and seized the gun from her. Louisa had tried to kill her husband because he was a womaniser who had been making secret preparations to marry a young Shropshire lady named Martha Rowe – and thus, commit bigamy. He'd even removed furniture from their home and was about to start anew with young Martha. Heinrich had also been blackening the reputation of his wife by telling everyone he never slept under the same roof as her because she was a bad woman, and when the rumours of her being some loose woman reached the ears of Louisa, she resolved to kill her husband in an act of revenge. Heinrich Wasmuss was taken to the Northern Hospital and saved by a Dr Batty, the house surgeon who operated on him immediately. Louisa was arrested and eventually committed to the Liverpool Assiszes for trial, but was subsequently released due to the mitigating circumstances of her husband's infidelity and the way he had deliberately attempted to slander her good name.

This find seems to throw some light on the ghosts of the barber's mirror, but what of the child who was seen to have its head cut off in the barber's chair? The hairdresser Bob swore the murderer was the same man he had seen in the mirror before – Heinrich Wasmuss – so, if Bob is not mistaken, is it possible that Wasmuss had an even darker side – that of a child killer?

# TIMEWARP BOUTIQUE

**Some people have** a talent for psychometry but don't always fully realise they have the gift for reading objects. In 1842, an American scientist named Joseph Rhodes Buchanan (1814-1899) of Covington, Kentucky, discovered that around eighty per cent of his students could somehow 'sense' the effects of drugs Buchanan handed to them during his classes. Most students who were handed an unlabelled bottle containing an emetic and asked how they felt would tell Buchanan that they felt their mouths watering; that a salty taste was detectable at the back of their tongue and that they felt as if they were going to vomit. If an opiate was handed to students in a bottle wrapped in brown paper (to prevent the student from seeing what the medicine was) a majority of the pupils would say that they felt sleepy. Buchanan, being a respected Professor of Medicine, could not explain how the students were 'tuning in' to the drugs in the bottles, and he knew of nothing in the field of science which could explain the strange talent. He coined the word "psychometry" to describe the ability of a person to gain information about an object's properties or history just by holding it. Buchanan's discovery was investigated by a Boston Professor of Geology named

William Denton, and he was an open-minded man like Buchanan. Denton wondered if people could somehow read the fossils and meteorites he collected and if they could perhaps provide him with some history of the objects. Psychometry test began, and Denton made a peculiar discovery: women were better at reading objects than men. One in ten men managed to extract information and historical data about the items they handled, whereas four in ten women gave vivid and highly accurate information about the items handled and also went into detail about the environment to which the item had belonged. Denton was impressed by this testable ability of everyday people and mused on the concept of psychic Archaeology – but of course, the sceptical scientists had a field day with the whole notion of people obtaining information from an object just by holding it. All the great concepts in the history of human progress were laughed at in their day and many potential developments which would have advanced human knowledge were put back decades by the pressure of scientists who thought they knew better. Radio was suggested much earlier than the Marconi era, and antibiotics were known in their crude form to the Egyptians (who had long recognised the medicinal value of fungus on cheeses). We could fill this book and many others with the endless examples of scientific world-changing ideas that were originally rejected by scientists of the day, and psychometry is an idea whose time has come. If we could enhance the powers of a person blessed with psychometry, we'd make enormous strides in the field of archaeology and criminology; by merely handling a murder weapon we would feel the identity of the murderer coming through and the motives behind the crime.

Are *you* a psychometrist? Find an old object; a key, an antique coin, anything which is old – it doesn't have to date back a hundred years, but it would help if it was at least over five years old. Perhaps you could ask a friend or family member to hand you an item, but they can either put it in an envelope or a box so that you can't see what it is. See if you can tune in to the object and perhaps sense who the previous owner was. I recall a case many years ago where a woman named Kim kept having the same heart-breaking dream each night; she would walk into a church with a man on her arm who seemed to be her father (for that's what she felt, anyway) and he would take her down the aisle, where crowds of people crushed into the pews were waiting for her to arrive. Upon reaching the gate leading to the altar the priest would smile and wait for the groom to arrive, and time would drag by until it was obvious that the groom was not going to arrive. Kim would then begin to cry, and she would turn and run past all of the faces of those attending the disastrous wedding ceremony. Kim would awake in tears. Now, Kim was happily married and she could not explain this dream. She wrote to me and I interviewed her, and I wondered about the dream from the psychometry viewpoint. I asked Kim if he had recently come into possession of a ring, and she must have thought I was psychic. She said she had and she showed me the old ring she had found in the garden of her home, just after she and her husband had bought the house. It was a silver ring with an assay mark stamped inside it which, I discovered, showed what looked like a girl's face in profile next to the letter F. This hallmark meant that the ring was made in Exeter in 1882. I mentioned the ring on the radio and also trawled through many censuses, electoral registers and street directories to find out who had lived at Kim's house in the past. I traced an elderly relative of a woman who had died at the house in the 1970s and this relative told me a story that sounded very familiar. Her aunt, Lydia had died a spinster after being stood up at the altar in the 1950s. She never bothered to date after her fiancée deserted her for another woman, and died broken-hearted. I asked her if Lydia had ever worn any rings, but the relative couldn't recall any – however, there was a connection to Exeter, the place the silver ring had originated from: Lydia's grandmother was from Topsham – a suburb of Exeter. I imagine the silver ring Kim found must have belonged to poor old Lydia, and somehow, all of the emotional negative energy from the spinster must have 'charged' that ring before it was lost. Kim only had the recurring dream about being jilted whenever she wore the ring, but her husband, a veritable Doubting Thomas, said it was all a case of suggestion, and he couldn't accept the idea of his wife being a 'sensitive'. Kim, however, told me that she had, more times than she could remember, somehow sense what was in envelopes when she heard the postman pushing them through her letterbox of a morning, even though she was upstairs in bed at the time.

Well, this story is about the talent of psychometry, and was reported to me a few years back.

In 2009 a 15-year-old girl named Taylor felt she needed a Saturday job, not just for the money, but because she was bored with the same company she kept each weekend. Her school friend Alyssa would usually visit her on Saturday mornings and talk about nothing but her hair and clothes, and Taylor had had enough. Through a cousin she heard about a certain shop in Liverpool city centre that sold vintage clothes, and after visiting this period-clothes shop one morning with her cousin, she met the proprietor, a girl in her twenties named Kate, and after buying a pair of genuine 1970s platforms, she cheekily asked Kate if she could help out at the shop at weekends. To Taylor's surprise, Kate said she could, but said that with the recession and that she could only pay Taylor twenty quid, and that was for two days: 9am till 5pm on Saturday and 10am till 4pm on Sundays. There were the usual breaks for lunch of course. Taylor grabbed the opportunity with both hands and began her new job on the following Saturday. In the school summer holidays of that year, Taylor was at the shop every day, and loved the atmosphere of the place. She told me that she could often 'feel the past coming through' in that shop because of all the vintage clothing items being in one place. All of the different eras seemed to intrude upon the 21st century in that 'boutique' as Kate liked to call her shop. One Saturday morning when Kate went to Subway to get her and Taylor a sandwich, a girl in a straw boater with a yellow ribbon tied around it came into the shop. She wore a long black coat with dull metal buttons, black stockings and flat buckled shoes. She had rosy cheeks, huge blue eyes and mousy blonde pigtails dangling from under her boater. She wandered around the shop, eyeing the goods and whispering or possibly singing to herself. Taylor thought she was a girl from some upmarket college at first, but then she realised the school holidays were on. Out of curiosity she followed the girl in the hat around a corner and through an archway into another part of the shop – only to find that the girl had vanished. This naturally gave Taylor a start, but things got even creepier because the teenager began to feel as if someone was watching her. Kate returned with a sandwich, but then she received a call on her mobile from a friend who told her that she had just been given the entire wardrobe of an old woman who had just gone into a care home. The clothes dated back to the woman's grandmother in Edwardian times, so Kate told Taylor she was going to get these antiquated clothes and said she'd definitely be back no later than one o'clock. She then told Taylor not to leave the till unattended on any occasion, and if any scally should come into the shop, she should immediately alert Mr Marks, a stocky man who had a shop opposite the boutique. Kate then left. Taylor's friend, Alyssa paid a visit to the shop about ten minutes later, and as she walked in, Taylor said, 'God, am I glad to see you,' but before she could tell Alyssa about the ghostly girl in the straw hat, Alyssa looked towards the back of the shop and said: 'Who's she looking at?'

'What?' Taylor turned to look and saw no one. All she saw was a pillar in the middle of the floor and several long clothes rails overloaded with vintage garments.

Alyssa turned to Taylor and her mouth hardly moved, as if she was a ventriloquist operating a dummy. In a low voice she said, 'Is she mental?'

'Who, Ally? Who are you talking about?' Taylor asked, quite puzzled.

'The girl with the hat on, there, by the pillar,' Alyssa said out the corner of her mouth.

Taylor could see no one, and as she went to ask her friend where about this girl with the hat on was, a young man of about sixteen walked into the shop and looked at Alyssa.

'Oh hiya,' Alyssa said, and the boy said something unintelligible to her, to which Alyssa said, 'What?'

'I said "I thought it was you coming in here then".' He mumbled, and blushed.

Taylor paid hardly any notice to the teenaged boy; she was becoming too increasingly unnerved by Alyssa's mention of the hat which the unseen girl was wearing.

'This is Dan,' Alyssa told Taylor, and then took her phone from her trouser pocket and started messing with a menu on it in a rather self-conscious manner.

'Ally, I can't see any girl down there,' Taylor declared, and squinted as she scanned that darker end of the shop floor.

'Do you reckon my hair's grown since I saw you last Thursday?' Alyssa asked Dan, with a curl at the side of her head between her finger and thumb.

Dan shrugged.

'I reckon it has, like,' Alyssa said, craning her head back to look up at tall Dan.

'I don't think it grows that fast, unless like you shave your head, cos I've done that, and it's definitely grown faster after you do that.'

This inane conversation continued between Dan and Alyssa for about a minute, during which Taylor bravely went to the other end of the shop. She turned around upon reaching the pillar and said to Alyssa, 'Has she gone now? Hey? Ally?'

Alyssa tore her gaze away from Dan, who was now showing her a picture of a huge burger he'd eaten earlier on his mobile. 'Yeah, she's gone.' Alyssa then turned back to Dan and asked him something.

'How could she have gone, Ally? Taylor asked her dizzy friend, 'She'd have had to pass us to get out, there's only one way out.'

'We're getting off now,' Alyssa suddenly announced as Dan turned and went towards the doorway of the boutique.

'Oh, have you got to?'

'Dan's going to get a tattoo,' Alyssa said as she turned to leave, 'and I want to have a look at some tattoo designs too.'

'Ally can't you just stay for a bit? I think this shop is haunted.' Taylor hurried back towards the counter.

Alyssa seemed to think Taylor was just joking about the place being haunted, and as she said, 'See you later,' two girls, aged around twenty, came into the shop. Taylor now felt a bit safer, and she wondered if Alyssa had been pulling her leg about the girl in the hat, but then she immediately recalled the girl in the straw boater who had vanished around that corner.

'Looking for anything in particular?' Taylor asked the couple of potential customers as they passed the counter.

'Just browsing,' one of the girls said and smiled as she headed for the far end of the shop.

Taylor searched for the DAB radio behind the counter, and located it behind a pile of shoeboxes. She put on the Kerrang! station and found that the music – as sell as the temporary company – dispelled the spooky atmosphere and icy isolation of the shop. One of the girls returned to the counter with a long flowery ankle-length skirt and asked if she could try it on.

'Yeah, there's a little cubicle thingy round the corner there, just through the archway,' Taylor told the customer. As the girl went to try on the dress, her friend asked her how business was.

'It's okay, yeah,' Taylor told her.

'I wanted that gypsy skirt, but that bitch saw it first,' the girl joked, referring to the floral skirt her friend was trying on.

'I had my eyes on that one as well,' Taylor replied. 'She pointed to a corner of the shop. 'I think there's more of them over there.'

'I love them,' the girl remarked, 'they're like the ones Stevie Nicks wears – '

A scream ripped the air, making Taylor and the girl jump.

The girl who had gone to try on the gypsy skirt came hurrying from the archway, and her eyes were bulging with fear. 'Just saw feet and there was no one there!' she told her friend and Taylor with a trembling voice. She threw the skirt onto the counter and headed for the door of the shop.

'What are you talking about?' Taylor asked.

'I saw someone's shoes walking under the gap in the curtain in the cubicle, and then the curtain went back on its own and there was no one there!' the girl replied, then hurried out of the shop. Her friend shot a quizzical look at her then turned to Taylor and raised her eyebrows. 'A ghost!' she said, and gave a blatant false laugh – before hurrying out the shop after her spooked friend.

Taylor was now so afraid, she did a very stupid thing. She walked out of the shop, crossed the street, and went to see Mr Marks, a tall stocky shaven-headed man with a sand-blasted face who knew Kate quite well. He was serving in his shop when Taylor approached him. When she told him Kate's shop was haunted, Marks smirked, then he saw the fear in the teenager's eyes and realised she was not joking. He got his nephew Shaun to look after the shop while he accompanied Taylor back to the boutique across the road.

'Have you left the till unattended?' Mr Marks asked the teenager as he eyed the open door of the vintage clothing shop with an ominous foreboding.

'Yeah,' Taylor told him, then as he closed his eyes and slowly shook his head she added, 'I know. I was scared.'

They went into the shop and luckily, nothing was missing from the till and no items appeared to have been lifted from the place.

As he looked around the shop, Marks advised: 'Look kid, next time you get scared or for whatever reason, use your mobile and give me a bell; don't go leaving the shop unattended.'

Taylor merely nodded, and it was obvious she was still scared, so Marks opened the mini fridge in a tiny stockroom and gave the teenager a can of Pepsi Max. He opened a carton of milk, took a sip from it, and he kindly stayed there for about fifteen minutes. He talked about the way some old shops had spooky atmospheres just because the lighting was abysmal,

'And boy is this place dreary,' said Marks, looking around the boutique. He cheered up Taylor a little and seemed to dispel the faint menace that had tinged the very air. Three female customers came into the shop just after Marks had left, and then Kate and her friend returned to the premises much earlier than expected with boxes of clothes.

Taylor gradually got used to the uncanny vibes of the shop, and one afternoon when Kate was out collecting more stock, she noticed something decidedly eerie yet intriguing. On a high shelf in the shop, there was a polystyrene mannequin head with a straw boater perched on it, and this hat had the exact same type of yellow ribbon that Taylor had seen on the boater worn by the vanishing school girl. Taylor went cold when she saw the hat, and she later learned from Kate that the boater had been found with several more in the loft of an old school in West Derby. The hats were believed to date back to the 1920s, perhaps earlier.

One afternoon a tall elderly lady in black breezed into the boutique and browsed through some psychedelic and Indian kerchiefs. She then turned and looked at Taylor and thinned her dark eyes. She went over to the teenager and told her she had quite an aura.

'Oh, really?' Taylor asked, in no doubt that the customer could probably see something. She was becoming very open-minded to many of the psychic types that had been visiting the shop in recent weeks. The woman introduced herself as Magda, and said she was a white witch, and this admission greatly intrigued Taylor. After reading Taylor's palm – and saying nothing about what she had seen in the lines and mounts (which worried Taylor) – she told the girl she had the talent of psychometry and that she had inherited it from a female ancestor who had lived at the time of the Wars of the Roses.

'I've heard of psychometry; what is it?' Taylor asked, neglecting a customer who was waiting to be served for a while until the lady coughed.

As soon as the customer had been served and had left the premises, Magda said to Taylor: 'You can read objects, just by holding them in your hands. Many items in a person's life – especially ones of sentimental value – often store memories and emotions of their owners, and people like you can read them. I'll show you how. We're certainly in the right place to do this.'

'Yes, we are,' Taylor nodded, knowingly, and her eyes and Magda's eyes flitted about, looking for an object to read. Magda found an ornate bangle in a wicker bowl. She picked it up first, and seemed to gaze up into space as she held it in her right closed hand. Taylor watched, spellbound. Magda then handed the bangle to the girl and said, 'Just clear your mind first, and relax a little, then gently focus on the bangle and tell me what you see.'

Taylor held the bangle in her right fist, and at first she said she could see nothing. Magda asked her what hand she wrote with. 'Left,' Taylor replied, so Magda told her to put the bangle in her dominant hand, and this time, Taylor saw a piano keyboard for a few moments in her mind's eye, and she could see female hands with red nail polish on playing chords and picking out a melody, but she couldn't hear the music. The wallpaper above the upright piano looked decidedly of the type she'd associate with the 1960s.

Taylor opened her eyes.

'Did you see her?' Magda asked, smiling.

'Yeah, she was –' Taylor started.

'Playing a piano,' Magda interrupted in an enthusiastic voice.

'Oh my God, how did you know that was what I saw?'

'Did you get the name of the piano?' Magda asked.

'No, but I saw the wallpaper, and it had a 1960s design,' Taylor recalled the orange brown and black abstract geometrical patterns of the paper.

'It was a Bentley,' Magda closed her eyes. 'And I think she had a metronome on top of the piano.'

'Are you on Facebook?' Taylor asked the fascinating woman, and Magda grinned and shook her head. 'Don't even have an email address thingy,' she added. She told Taylor how to practice her gift, and then left the shop, saying she'd pop in again some time, but Taylor never saw Magda after that. She mentioned the bangle to Kate and asked her if it had belonged to someone who had played the piano, but Kate said she couldn't remember where she'd got that bangle from.

Taylor practiced her psychometry but it proved to be a big mistake. One day she was introduced to her mother's new partner – a man named Mike. Taylor's mum Louise had just been divorced and right away she had started seeing a man she had met in her gym. When his big rough hand shook Taylor's hand, she immediately caught a flash of a disturbing scene in her mind's eye: a woman in tears with a black eye, cowering in a corner. Taylor felt the powerful, almost psychopathic rage directed towards this woman and sensed it was Mike's fury. The look of shock and revulsion in Taylor's eyes made Mike feel very uneasy and he felt the girl's small hand slip out of his square fist. She seemed to stumble backwards, and Mike could tell somehow that she knew about the dark and brutal beast that was hiding deep within him behind a façade of affability.

Taylor warned her mother that evening when Mike dropped her off after a night out at the cinema and a restaurant. Louise was flabbergasted at the warning and of Taylor's evaluation of the lovely Mike, but gradually, over the next few months, Louise discovered that Mike was very quick-tempered and quite possessive towards her. He was prone to all-out road rage over the smallest transgression from another motorist, and on one occasion had sped after a young driver who had given him the finger gesture at over 70 mph down a 30 mph road, almost crashing the car on a bend on Townsend Lane. Mike had seemed very considerate at first towards Louise, but now he seemed to treat her like some sex object that belonged to him, and he was very paranoid over any calls to Louise from any of her friends, but especially male ones. He would often pick up Louise's mobile and look at the name or number of the caller before he handed it to her. Louise began to realise that her daughter was very perceptive indeed, and regretted not listening to her that day when she first met Mike. Eventually Louise had to enlist the help of her brother Ken, a stocky man who worked as a bouncer, and Ken literally had to throw Mike out of Louise's home and her life.

Taylor came to look upon her talent of psychometry as more of a curse than a gift. Before, she had gone about life blissfully unaware of anything outside of her own little world. Now she felt like some psychic

Peeping Tom looking into the most intimate details of people's lives. She decided she wanted to get shut of her probing faculty, and this happened one Saturday morning as she was working in the boutique with Kate. Kate came into possession of a beautiful navy blue blouse with a daisy pattern all over it. It was size 8 – and Kate was a size 12. She told Taylor to try it on, but the teenager was cautious, as she knew she'd pick up on whoever had worn that blouse in the past, and it was supposed to date back to the mid to late 1960s. Kate had been given it with a bundle of similarly aged garments from a man who had found the clothes in his attic. Taylor tried on the blouse – and let out a scream as she clutched her chest. She saw a boy of about fourteen – perhaps a little older – appear in front of her, and as soon as he appeared he began to stab Taylor in the chest with what looked like a knitting needle. Kate recoiled in horror as Taylor fell back into a chair with such force, the chair tipped over, and the girl banged her head hard, knocking herself out. A woman in the shop was a first-aider, and she expertly put Taylor into the recovery position as Kate dialled for an ambulance. Taylor woke up in the ambulance and began to cry. She told the paramedics to keep the boy away from her. She said she'd been stabbed, and a paramedic assured her she hadn't, but then he noticed about a dozen red points of clotted blood on Taylor's cleavage area and one mysterious wound appeared at the bottom of her neck. These wounds were investigated and were thankfully found to be mere surface scratches on the skin, but what made them could not be determined. Taylor knew though. She had felt every single one of the fifteen stab wounds from the knitting needle as the boy attacked her.

Kate made enquiries about the previous occupants of the house where the blouse had originated, and months later she finally discovered that the blouse had belonged to a woman who had had a schizophrenic son who had stabbed her with a long hatpin, and luckily the woman survived, even though the pin had penetrated her heart during the attack. Taylor almost suffered a nervous breakdown through her uncanny ability, and she turned to a meditation group she saw advertised on a church bulletin board near her home. The leader of the group told Taylor that humans had about six senses: hearing, sight, touch, smell, taste, and a sense of time, and he explained how these few senses only allowed a trickle of the vast amounts of information of the universe into the brain; any more senses and the average person would be overwhelmed with a Niagara Falls of sensations and information. Over the course of many months of intense meditation, the faculty of hyper-sensitive psychometry was finally shut down, and Taylor was able to lead a normal "ignorance is bliss" type of life.

# WHEN WOMEN RULE THE EARTH

**One sunny lunchtime** in 1999 I was in the Lucy in the Sky with Diamonds café in Cavern Walks with Billy Butler and Wally Scott after I had been talking on their morning radio show about the supernatural. An oddly-dressed man seated at another table gestured with some urgency for me to go to him. In his outlandish, garish attire and wild hair he looked like a cross between Doctor Who and Ken Dodd, and as Billy and Wally chatted with ex-Beatles manager Allan Williams, songwriter Alan Crowley and several other friends at the table, I went to see what the man wanted. In a quirky hybrid Scouse-Welsh accent he introduced himself as Wesley Pole, and described himself as a Birkenhead grandfather to six children and a God-fearing Presbyterian who had never told a lie in his life, and then he nodded to the café radio and said: 'I heard you talking about timeslips before; I'm a walking timeslip.' He then explained. 'Over the past ten years I have had about seven timeslips, and a lot of lost time episodes, and I have people who'll back me up on this, because they lose time as well. I go in pubs and clocks stop dead, I go to bed at midnight and next thing it's light and I haven't even closed my eyes. My wife makes me sleep in another room because she loses time as well.' Mr Pole then told me about the timeslips. One drizzly morning in 1989 he was taking a brisk walk along the promenade leading to the Seacombe Ferry landing stage when he had a "funny turn". Suddenly a huge sun appeared in a cloudless blue sky – and where the Mersey had been, there was a vast tract of dry cracked land. All around was desolation. Most of the familiar landmarks were bleached ruins or completely gone. 'I kept pinching myself, thinking it was a dream, like,' Pole told me, and I could tell from the tremor in his voice that he was telling the truth. He descended stone steps from the promenade at some point and walked across what had plainly been the bed of the river, and the sun felt like a blow-torch on his skin. Semi-transparent scorpion-like creatures scuttled into the cracks in the yellowed dusty ground. Pole thought the whole thing was some unfathomable religious experience at first. He looked ahead at the post-apocalyptic moonscape of Liverpool shimmering on the horizon in the infernal heat. His heart almost stopped at the sight of a giant light-green bird lying on its side at forty-five degrees among the rubble – could this be the lone survivor of two of the city's world-famous emblems – a toppled Liver Bird? He thought, confused and sick with the heat.

'I've seen enough!' Pole shouted to the cloudless sky and his words echoed back. In the distance he saw the hazy outline of a shattered Anglican cathedral, and over to the left among mounds of sun-bleached rubble he saw huge trees growing out of the shell of St

George's Hall, and by the height and thickness of these trees, it was obvious that quite some time ago, something horrific had destroyed the North West – and possibly the entire country, and perhaps the whole civilized world. And then he saw the white dogs; a pack of wild canines, some resembling wolves, all of them with snow-white coats, heading his way. They vanished behind a hill of debris for a few minutes as Pole scanned a world laid waste by either a war that had truly ended all wars – or a natural disaster of planetary magnitude. He turned and headed back the way he came, but heard the pack of feral hounds closing in, and so he prayed like never before, and tried to run across the bone-dry river bed with his legs feeling as if they were made of jelly. He swore and used language he thought he'd forgotten. The snarling dogs were getting closer, but somehow he reached Wirral with his heart pounding and his head aching from the intense unrelenting solar blaze of what looked like an oversized sun. He ended up on his hands and knees, crawling through cacti up a slope of dusty shattered sandstone rocks where the landing stage should have been. To his right he could see a ghostly container ship lying on its side, embedded in the long-dried silt and sand of a vanished river. The hostile sun had roasted the paint from the vessel's hull and lent an eerie pale aspect to the metal. Mr Pole really believed he was about to die because the heat was now that intense he couldn't breathe, and he tried to get up, and saw ragged holes in the knees of his trousers, made from crawling on all fours. And then, the whole world started to tilt left and right as if he was on the deck of a storm-tossed ship, and he blacked out. He awoke on Victoria Place, suffering from chronic dehydration and was immediately taken to hospital by the paramedics. I heard brief accounts of the rest of the timeslips, took down Pole's number, and suddenly realised Billy and Wally were gone. I'd unaccountably lost two hours – but that could have been down to the engrossing accounts the old man had given me. What else did he see on his involuntary trips into the future? Well, there was the time in 1992 when Mr Pole was taken by his son and daughter-in-law on a fortnight's holiday in New York. Three days into the holiday, Mr Pole and his son were walking down the famous Fifth Avenue's Museum Mile when they both heard a rapid succession of echoing bangs in the distance followed by faint screams. People began running up the avenue from something, and Wesley and his son, sensing something bad was approaching, turned and walked back the way they came. Father and son then heard the gunshots become more rhythmical – like machine gun fire, and they turned and saw a surreal but terrifying sight. A triangle of about fifteen men with five men on each of the three sides, were walking along at a brisk pace, and each was firing a machine gun at people and vehicles. Mr Pole and his son were naturally frightened and horrified at the sight of the flickering flashes from the machine guns, the falling pedestrians, and cars that were crashing through store windows as the hail of bullets sprayed everywhere. In 1992, the Poles did not think the triangular formation of machine-gunners involved terrorists – instead they wondered if some bank heist had gone disastrously wrong and that the robbers were engaging in a running gun battle with the police and perhaps trying to cause as much mayhem as possible to affect a better chance at a getaway. The world-changing events of September 11 still lay nine years into the future, so Mr Pole and son did not consider the fifteen gunmen as terrorists and like most people of the time, they had never heard of Al-Qaeda. Mr Pole and his son heard a massive bang and felt a blast of air hit their faces – as if a bomb had been detonated, and there was no more gunfire after that. The two men managed to hail a cab and back at the hotel they told everyone what had just happened on Fifth Avenue, but Mr Pole's daughter-in-law said she had not heard of any such incident on the news. Radios were turned on and TV channels were rapidly browsed, but there was no news of any machine-gunning incident on Fifth Avenue. Only some time later that afternoon did Mr Pole suspect that he had once again somehow been transported into the future, only on this occasion his son had somehow shared the timeslip experience. Pole and his son returned to Fifth Avenue and saw there was no aftermath of any shooting, and one wonders if they somehow intruded into a future where a group of terrorists – possibly even an Al-Qaeda cell – were on the rampage in Manhattan. From the way Pole describes the gunfire ended with a bang makes me believe the nightmarish attackers were suicide bombers.

Pole's other timeslips after that were low-key and of a shorter duration in comparison to the ones where he stumbled onto a post-apocalyptic Merseyside and a Fifth Avenue under attack from a strange formation of mystery machine-gunners – but then in 1998, Wesley Pole had a very strange translocation into a bizarre future – or possibly a parallel future – a possible outcome of the future history timeline perhaps. This episode began when Pole was coming out of MacDonald's on the corner of Lord Street and Whitechapel. He felt dizzy, and a bit nauseous, and he knew these sensations were always felt before he had a timeslip experience. The people milling around on Lord Street became blurred, and suddenly, Pole was in the midst of a swarming group of extremely tall youths, aged about 15 to 20 perhaps, and they were all dressed in red and blue helmets, matching short-sleeved shirts, and white tight-fitting pants which finished halfway down the calves. The logos on the backs of these youths were some sort of odd version of the LFC and EFC badges, and each of these logos were underlined with the words 'Major League'. Pole realised that these young people were baseball players, and most of them were female. He was swept along by the throng of players up a Lord Street which bore no resemblance to the one back in 1998, towards a colossal white circular building at least 300 feet in height, and the arched entrance of this structure was where Derby Square now exists, Pole estimated. Above the entrance there was a golden oval sign upon which an intriguing symbol was displayed. Pole sketched this symbol for me, and it is an ancient symbol for Venus (a circle with a cross underneath – which represents the female) with a small symbol of Mars (a circle with an arrow pointing from its circumference at the 2 o'clock position) beneath it. Pole wanted to know what he was being herded towards, and he asked a few of the young people in the baseball gear but he couldn't understand their replies because they spoke too fast and seemed to be talking in either slang or some unknown language not unlike Polish or Russian. A shadow flitted over the gleaming mirrored thoroughfare, and Pole looked up to see a line of silent vehicles flying overhead, but they moved to fast and the sun was in the old man's eyes so he couldn't take in any real detail. Upon reaching a side street on this futuristic version of Lord Street, Mr Pole looked to his left, which in our day would be the site of the Liverpool One shopping complex, but in 1998, a bus station would have existed there. In this unspecified future era a huge pyramid of gold mirrors was present, and a long line of white marble statues – all of women – lined the long street there. The young crowd pushed on and soon Pole was going through the arched entrance to what looked like some ultramodern coliseum. A wall of cheering voices assaulted the elderly man's ears, and he saw he was entering a massive stadium. There in the centre of this circular stadium was some type of version of a baseball playing field with a diamond in the centre, the bases at each corner, and the sweeping crescent of the outfield. Another cheer went up, and all of the youths surrounding Pole threw their arms in the air, and at that point, Pole had another of his turns and felt very unsteady on his feet. He heard the screeching sounds of the brakes of a bus, and suddenly found himself outside the Queen's pub on Water Street where he had to lean against a wall to steady himself. Passers-by probably assumed Mr Pole was drunk. He went over to James Street Station and rode a train home to Birkenhead. He told his wife what had happened, but she was a very simple person who didn't know what to think of the timeslips, and in the end, Pole went to his doctor – who advised him to see a neurologist for a brain scan. Pole said there was nothing wrong with his brain and refused to go. He asked me what I thought of the timeslip. I'm not too sure what to think, but the symbol he saw in what might have been the future – Venus over Mars – could suggest that at a future date, some battle of the sexes between men and women was fought – and the males may have lost. We are currently living in a phallocracy despite the various sex equality acts that have been passed by a largely patriarchal Parliament, but perhaps some feminist firebrand will arrive on the political scene soon and redress the balance – and perhaps even go further – and would a matriarchal society be such a bad thing? The meaning of the baseball stadium is lost on me; perhaps the country will have become so Americanised in the future, traditional sports such as Football – and Cricket – might become as outdated as cockfighting. It's a medical fact that the children of today are, on average, taller and healthier than their parents, and where will this end? Football began over 2,000 years ago in China and became a forerunner of the game of soccer we recognise today, but once the players grow over a certain height, the game will possibly die out. Basketball on the other hand, is a sport ideally suited to players over six feet in height. Baseball may be another sport in which there is no height restrictions to impede the efficiency of the game.

Wesley Pole is not a fantasist and is telling the truth – he did have several experiences he cannot explain – and I have no cause to doubt him, because I have interviewed his son and various relatives and friends who have vouched for his honesty, and I even asked Pole to undergo hypnotic questioning; he did so and every detail of his stories were consistent with the accounts recorded by me months before. This doesn't mean he went into the future several times – the human mind is still largely unmapped and psychologists have made little headway in their field since the days of Ancient Greece. Pole could have entered some altered state of consciousness in much the same way most of us do when we dream, but it's equally possible that he did, through some unknown process, walk into the future at least seven times. I have interviewed people from all walks of life who have experienced timeslips, and it can happen to anyone. I don't expect you to believe these accounts without a healthy dose of scepticism – but should you find yourself experiencing a timeslip (as I have done on several occasions), I guarantee it will alter your view of clock and calendar time forever.

# AN ANGEL ON HAVELOCK STREET

**We all have** hunches and a sense of 'intuition' which guide us when we're making decisions, but throughout history many people have talked about having an "inner voice" which doesn't seem to be their subconscious or even a part of their mind at all. One of the earliest references to an inner voice is that made by the Greek philosopher Socrates in 399 BC. Socrates was one of the most brilliant and gifted men of his day and claimed that a strange, supernatural voice in his head prevented him from doing wrong. Another historical person who heard voices was Joan of Arc, although modern historians believe she may have been schizophrenic. In more recent times, the Nazi dictator Adolf Hitler said he felt as if he was being guided through his life by a higher intelligence. When Hitler was a Lance Corporal during World War I, he was sleeping in a trench when he suddenly had a terrifying nightmare about being blasted to death by a British shell. As he woke, what he described as "an inner voice" warned him to run from the position to another part of the trench. Minutes later the bemused soldier who sat down in the place vacated by Hitler was blown to smithereens by an enemy shell.

Hitler's arch-enemy, Winston Churchill, also claimed that an inner voice saved his neck on many occasions. One day, during World War II, Churchill was entertaining three government ministers before dinner at Number 10 Downing Street when he had a strange premonition of doom. The air-raid sirens sounded and, as usual, the guests at Downing Street ignored the sirens and continued to enjoy their drinks. But Churchill jumped up out of his armchair and rushed into the kitchen, where a cook and a maid were working next to a long plate glass window. Churchill ordered the cook and maid to put the dinners on a hot plate in the dining room and then instructed the kitchen staff to go at once to the bomb shelter. The maid and cook just laughed, but the Prime Minister appeared to be uncharacteristically deadly serious, and ordered them to go at once. Less than three minutes later, a German bomb fell at the back of the house and destroyed the kitchen. The plate glass window was shattered and long, razor-sharp shards of glass were embedded in the doors and walls of the kitchen where the cook and maid had been standing. They would have certainly died had Churchill not ordered them to leave.

In 1941, Winston Churchill had another premonition. He was walking to his staff car in Downing Street, about to commence a tour of the anti-aircraft battery units around London, when he suddenly stopped in his tracks. An official looked at him with puzzlement. The official had just opened the nearside door of the car for the Prime Minister, but Churchill walked around the car and got in the offside door, and he sat on that side of the vehicle throughout the journey. Five minutes later, as the staff car was speeding through the blacked-out streets of London, a bomb fell near the vehicle and the tremendous blast lifted the car into the air so that it was on two wheels. The vehicle would have rolled into a deep crater if Churchill had been in the nearside seat, but his weight in the offside seat balanced the vehicle, and it righted itself. The chauffeur later asked Churchill why he had chosen that seat in the car, and the Prime Minister told him, "Something said 'Stop!' when I was walking to the car that day, and I knew it wanted me to sit on the other side of the vehicle."

Closer to home, here on Merseyside I have looked into many other incidents where mysterious supernatural help has been given, and a case that immediately springs to mind is that of Brian King, who, in 1963, was a 21-year-old living with his parents in Dovecot. In the January of that year, the country was suffering from the coldest month of the 20th century, part of "the Big Freeze" as the newspapers called it, and recalled today with a shudder by the older generation as one of the most severe winters in living memory. The winter had started with a raging blizzard towards the end of December of 1962 and then the Mersey froze over; in fact the coastal seas of the country froze for a mile out. Everton's Havelock Street – widely acknowledged as the steepest street in Liverpool, was covered in a blanket of snow, and at 11.30pm, Brian King left the house of his girlfriend

Mary on that precipitous street, intending to drive to the home of his grandmother Gladys at Larkhill Lane in the district of Clubmoor. Brian had had just received word from a friend that his grandmother was seriously ill and the doctor had told him she mightn't make it to the morning. Mary wanted to go with her boyfriend but Brian told her to stay home as the journey would be a dangerous one because of the state of the roads. Mary insisted on accompanying Brian but he arranged for Mary's father to lock her in the parlour, and as soon as the girl was confined, Brian wiped the layer of freshly-fallen snow from the rear and front window of his Ford Consul. He had great difficulty starting the car because of the temperature was below zero and the cobbles of Havelock Street had a crusty mantle of snow seven inches deep. The wheels spun and the car slid backwards, so the handbrake went on – but the car continued to slide backwards because even though the tyres were locked into position, the surface was like a skating rink and the gradient behind the vehicle slanted down at almost forty-five degrees. The Ford Consul was sliding backwards from almost the top of the steep gradient, and there was nothing Brian could do to stop the vehicle. He thought of jumping out the car but that would be just as dangerous, and if he tried to swerve the car, it could possibly back into someone's front door and smash it off its hinges - and then the vehicle would probably explode from a ruptured petrol tank. As Brian's mind raced to find a solution to this terrible predicament he felt an awful sensation – his stomach was 'turning over' and he thought of Mary – would he never see her again? Was he about to lose his life in a freak accident when his car smashed into a wall at the bottom of this ski slope? All of a sudden, there were two loud thuds as something struck the car – and almost immediately, the Ford Consul came to a complete halt, seconds before it would have impacted into the walls of a house. There was nothing in the laws of physics to account for the way the car had suddenly stopped after gathering so much momentum sliding backwards down that sheer incline. Brian King got out of the vehicle and looked at the back of the car, thinking that something might have slowed it down – like a person's body or a large dog – but thankfully there was no one and nothing there which could have impeded the fatal course of the car. Then Brian noticed two palm prints in the layer of snow on the trunk of the Ford Consul . It looked as if someone had left those prints as they somehow exerted an incredible amount of force to stop the car as it slid down Havelock Street – but who one earth would posses such superhuman strength? Brian King had not seen any hand prints on the car when he had wiped the snow from his rear window after leaving Mary's house. Brian got back into the car but now the engine was dead; the subzero weather was to blame, and so he reluctantly left the car where it had inexplicably stopped, and he hiked up Havelock Street, gripping a handrail to steady himself for the treacherous ascent. He stayed in Mary's home that night, and on the following morning he visited his beloved grandmother, and was so glad to see that she had recovered. His Gran told him that as she lay ill in her bed last night, she knew he would try and brave the terrible weather conditions to visit her, but she had just known her grandson would be putting his life in danger if he went on the road with all of the iced and snowbound roads. Brian's grandmother Gladys had therefore asked an angel to keep him safe and to keep him indoors at his girlfriend's house in Everton. Only then did Brian tell his grandmother about his car sliding backwards down the length of Havelock Street and the mysterious hands that had stopped the vehicle from smashing into a wall. To this day, Brian King believes his life was saved that freezing night by an angel on Havelock Street.

# THE MORBA

**There is a class** of supernatural ghost called the Morba which are said to cause disease and sometimes death. I first heard about this species of entity from an old ghost hunter many years ago, but I have since read numerous accounts of mysterious outbreaks of diseases and plagues throughout both ancient and recent history, and it's possible that some epidemics as well as small-scale infections of a mysterious origin are but the work of the Morba. What do Morba look like? From the limited reports I've received I would say they range in form from cobweb-like strands (which often gather in corners over the sickbed of a victim) to a slithery snake-like creature which draws the very life-energy and sometimes the actual blood of its victim. It is even possible that the Morba may exist in microscopic form to mimic a bacterium or virus, and these paranormal pathogens would certainly explain the following medical mystery. Mary Mallon was born in Cookstown, County Tyrone (now Northern Ireland of course), in September 1869, and at the age of fifteen she emigrated to the United States, where she settled in New York City. Mary worked as a cook in New York from 1900 to 1907, and in the first year of employment as a cook in a certain household in Mamaroneck, New York, several of the people Mary prepared food for became ill with mysterious symptoms resembling typhoid fever. Mary had only worked at the house where the illness broke out for a fortnight, so no one connected the infection to her at first, but then she moved to Manhattan in the following year and people there went down with acute diarrhoea and fever, only this time, one of the infected – a laundress – died from the unknown illness. Mary left the house and found employment at the household of a lawyer, and eight people there developed typhoid. Still no one suspected Mary Mallon of being a carrier of the germs that were causing these outbreaks, and within two weeks of her taking up a new position at a house on Long Island's Oyster Bay, ten of eleven family members went down with typhoid and all had to be hospitalised. Once again, after the illness struck, Mary would move on to the next house, and wherever she was hired, the shadow of serious illness was cast upon her employers within a few weeks. When a wealthy New York banker named Charles Henry

Warren employed Mary as a cook at a luxurious rented summer house on Oyster Bay, six of the eleven people at the house capitulated to typhoid. There were more outbreaks in the other houses were Mary was employed after this, until, in the winter of 1906, a member of one of the families that had been left bedridden by the portly Mary Mallon got in touch with George Soper, an eminent sanitation engineer, and he investigated the outbreaks of what seemed to be typhoid, a disease that was very rare in the Oyster Bay area of Long Island. Soper drew up a list of all the people who had been in the houses were the serious illnesses had erupted, and one name kept coming up in all the lists – Mary Mallon. Soper searched in vain for Mary, and no one seemed to know where the unmarried Irish cook was, until there was a serious outbreak of typhoid at a penthouse on Park Avenue. At this upmarket address, two servants had been taken into hospital with acute typhoid fever and the daughter of the family had died because of the illness. Mary Mallon was being employed at this penthouse, and George Soper confronted her and requested urine and stool samples. Mary was outraged and refused to comply with his requests, and so Soper resorted to compiling a lengthy file on the last five years of the cook's employment history with the various families – who, it transpired, had all been plagued with typhoid. Soper paid more visits to Mary and strongly advised her to to be tested, and on one occasion he brought a doctor with him but Mary refused to be tested. Soper said he'd write a book on her role as an innocent immune carrier of the disease who was quite unaware of the illness she was spreading across New York, and what's more, Soper even promised Mary he would give her all of the royalties from the proposed book, but again, Mary firmly told Soper to leave her alone and she locked herself in a bathroom until he left. Mary was subsequently detained in a hospital for observation, and during this period of being in quarantine, the Irish cook had to undergo several tests. She had admitted she rarely washed her hands during cooking, and said that this was not at all unusual - most cooks she knew never bothered to wash their hands after handling various foodstuffs and items in the kitchen. Samples of Mary's stools and urine indicated that her gall bladder was teeming with salmonella germs, and so it was suggested to Mary that she should have the gall bladder removed, but she was horrified at the suggestion and refused to let a surgeon come near her. She still maintained that she was not carrying any disease and said the authorities were persecuting her. All the same, New York City's Heath Inspector branded Mary as a carrier, and as a result of his verdict, she was isolated for three years at a clinic. At the end of this three-year incarceration, Mary was offered a deal after it was deemed she no longer seemed to be a high-risk carrier: if she would promise to stop working as a cook, and if she would take pride in a programme of personal hygiene improvement as well as reporting periodically to the Board of Health, she would be released. Mary Mallon signed an affidavit promising to fulfil these stipulations and was duly released. She secured employment as a laundress, a job which didn't pay as well as that of the position of a cook, but at least Mary would have her freedom. But Mary missed kitchen work, and felt that she had been born to be a cook. She changed her name to Mary Brown and irresponsibly sought employment in a number of kitchens. Once again the very presence of the Irish cook guaranteed that the ugly bacillus of typhoid would manifest itself. George Soper went in search of the typhoid carrier but she kept going to ground too fast and took up new positions at other kitchens whenever he was getting near. And then, in February 1915 there was a massive outbreak of typhoid at New York's Sloane Hospital for Women (the first hospital in New York that was devoted to women's healthcare) in which 25 nurses and various attendants were affected – and two of those who went down with the disease subsequently died. The city's health authorities investigated the outbreak and soon discovered that a woman who matched the description of Mary Mallon had been employed in the kitchen of the Sloane Hospital – until recently; she had suddenly made herself scarce. Mary was eventually traced to a house on an estate on Long Island, where she was promptly arrested for violating her agreement, and this time she was quarantined for the rest of her life – a period of almost thirty years, until she died of pneumonia, aged 69, in 1938 – even during the autopsy, typhoid germs were found in her gall bladder. The body was cremated and buried at a cemetery in the Bronx. It's thought that Mary Mallon might have been responsible for the death of about fifty people in her lifetime, but there are many question marks hanging over "Typhoid Mary"; in the five years she used various aliases in her kitchen jobs, there were no known outbreaks of the disease, and she was deemed to be safe enough to be freed after she was released after the first period of quarantine. There are revisionists who believe that the experts of the day were using Mary as a scapegoat to promote their theories – some of them now discredited – about germ theory. One group of doctors said Mary was infected with typhoid germs and another group of learned medical men said she wasn't. In reality, outbreaks of various diseases seem to spontaneously erupt in communities without any apparent reason, even in hospitals where hygiene is the routine order of the day, we have had serious outbreaks of what the media terms as "flesh-eating bugs" that cannot be treated by regular antibiotics. The strange thing about these mysterious viruses and bacteria - which our drugs can't combat – is that they seem to occur in specific places out of the blue, and just when the media is warning of us of a doomsday pandemic, they vanish as mysteriously as they first appeared. A case in point is the SARS coronavirus – a deadly virus whose name is derived from Severe Acute Respiratory Syndrome. In the spring of 2003 the virus appeared in Asia and samples of it are now held in labs in Hong Kong, Manila, San Francisco and New York. The symptoms experienced by those who succumb to the virus are muscular pain, headache and a fever, followed by breathing problems two to ten days after the virus enters the body. The patient develops a cough which progresses to pneumonia, and 9 per cent of those who become infected with SARS die, although people over fifty have a much higher mortality rate. SARS is a coronoavirus – which means it belongs to the same family of viruses that cause the so-called "common cold" – but the way it appears out of nowhere and then 'goes to ground' means its difficult to trace and analyse this virus, although it does seem to originate in the Middle East, and has only reached Britain via people who have boarded a flight into the country. The Bird Flu virus is another example of these mysterious transient 'mutations' which flare up in an area of the world and pose a global threat, only to vanish into obscurity again. There have also been a lot of local cases where something which seems to be paranormal has seemingly affected the health of a person in a very sinister way. A nurse at a well-known local hospital once told me how, one evening in the late 1980s, she was attending a woman in her fifties who was recovering from a hysterectomy when the patient suddenly complained of feeling hot and unwell. The nurse took the woman's temperature and then called upon a doctor who diagnosed some sort of fever. The doctor told the nurse that the patient should be given nothing but water and bland food. The nurse assumed the patent was perhaps becoming delirious when she said something kept drifting down from the ceiling to crawl on her mouth, but then she noticed what she took to be a cobweb in the corner of the ceiling above the patient's bed. A cleaner with a ladder arrived to remove the cobweb but saw that it had gone. On the following morning the cobweb had returned, and the patient and several other people in the ward – both patients and visitors – said they had seen threads fall from the cobweb and land on the patient who was recovering from the hysterectomy. Another cleaner arrived with a fold-up aluminium ladder and a bucket of disinfectant and sponge – but the cobweb was suddenly absent again, and it was not seen for about four days. A nurse named Linda was the next to see this peculiar cobweb moving along the ceiling to another corner of the ward, and as soon as she pointed it out to a porter, the thing stopped dead, and seemed to drop down in slow motion as a bundle of threads. Linda likened this eerie entity as resembling a cluster of daddy longlegs, but when she went to look on the floor of the ward, there was no trace of the moving 'cobweb'. This cobweb-like entity has been reported to me time and time again, and this is thought to be the Morba as described by occultists. They are sinister thread-like beings that are often mistaken for cobwebs until the person tries to remove them. They then vanish or slowly move away and hide in whatever crevice or groove they can find. Once they land on a person, they feel stuffy and sometimes the throat closes up as if an allergic abreaction is taking place. Other people who have come into alleged contact with the Morba have stated categorically that the thing somehow enters the mouth either through the lips or through the nostrils, where it then makes its way to the tonsils and upper throat area. The victim then experiences a strange melancholic mood descend, and they begin to have morbid thoughts about their mortality. The medical profession will not recognise or acknowledge the Morba, but will often blame the equally mystifying ME, which stands for myalgic encephalomyelitis – a poorly understood debilitating medical condition which causes chronic exhaustion, muscle and joint pain, as well as a host of other symptoms. For years, people suffering from ME were branded hypochondriacs and malingerers because there is no way of clinically proving a person has the condition or not, but people have been affected with ME in bouts lasting typically as long as 6 months to almost a decade, and doctors haven't a clue what causes the condition and whether it is speared via a virus currently unknown to medical science.

In 2010 at a certain terraced house off one of north Liverpool's well-known thoroughfares, a 47-year-old woman named Claire became ill with flu-like symptoms and against her wishes, she was sent to bed by her husband Mike, who then had the formidable job of looking after the couple's three children. The youngest of the children was 10-year-old Shawney, and Claire was forever telling the girl not to leave the front door open whenever she called upon her friend's house, which was just next door. One evening in August 2010, Shawney left the door open after calling upon her friend to show her a new andoid phone she'd received for her birthday, and Claire knew her daughter had left the door open because she could hear the hubbub of noise from the street and so she shouted to her husband to close the front door, but he was watching TV and never heard her. Claire lay there on her sickbed and contemplated going downstairs to close the door herself, as she had been wary of the number of robbers knocking about in the area, thanks to news items on *Granada Reports* and articles in the *Liverpool Echo*. She tried to get up out of bed but felt very dizzy and nauseous. She looked for her mobile phone but couldn't locate it, so she settled back in bed, and every time she closed her eyes she felt the bedroom spin.

And then she heard something come up the stairs. A faint shuffling sound, and something which hit the bedroom door with a slight thump. That door was already open an inch or so, but now it had swung open a few inches further by the thing which had struck it. Immediately Claire had a bad feeling about the unseen invader; she wondered if it was a rat that had come into the house. This had happened at Claire's Nan's many years ago when she was a little girl; a rat had been chased into her grandmother's house by a cat in the back yard. The kitchen door was always left ajar by her Nan, and on that rainy afternoon a huge sewer rat darted into the kitchen and hid under the old four-legged cooker. Claire and her Nan had screamed the place down and a window cleaner had come to the rescue. He prodded the rat with the handle of a brush and the huge black rodent with red eyes flitted from under the cooker and out into the yard, where it scarpered under the backyard door and bolted down the entry.

As Claire listened, she thought she could hear something moving about under the bed. She yelled for her husband, and he never came, but her oldest son Daniel – aged fifteen – came to see what the shouting was about. He looked under the bed and said there was nothing there. Claire told Daniel to go and shut the front door, and he did.

Claire was convinced something had come into the house off the street to hide in her bedroom, and she told her husband Mike about her suspicions but he said there was nothing in the room and advised her to get some rest.

At around 2.40am, Claire awoke and felt something cold slither across her left ankle. She screamed, waking her husband with a start, and when she told him there was something in the bed he pulled off the duvet and saw nothing amiss. 'You've had a nightmare,' he told his wife, but Claire was sure she had felt something cold slide across her ankle in the way a snake would. By three that morning, Claire finally dropped off after telling herself that she had indeed dreamt of something being in the bed.

On the following night the same thing happened, only this time the incident took place much earlier than the previous one. Around 11.40pm, Claire was lying in bed alone as her husband watched the telly downstairs when she suddenly became aware of something touching the top of her head. She froze for a moment and looked sideways, and there on the wall was the shadow of her head in profile, cast by the light from the bedside lamp – and moving to and fro next to the shadow of her head was the shadow of a long worm-like 'thing' – and Claire could see it was protruding from over the top of the bed's headboard. She almost threw herself out of the bed and ran to the door. She pulled it open and without looking back to see what the thing was that had been hanging over the headboard, Claire ran downstairs and barged in on her husband. Mike, seeing the horrified expression on his sick wife's face, immediately got up off the sofa and asked her what the matter was, and when Claire told him about the "thing" in the bedroom he returned a doubtful look, because he really did think Claire's feverish condition was affecting her mind. All the same he went up to the bedroom and he looked under the bed, behind the headboard, and checked the wardrobe. He found nothing to account for the experience his wife had reported, and Claire was that afraid of encountering the thing that had cast its shadow on her wall she went and slept in the spare room that night.

On the following night, Claire returned to her usual bed after Mike convinced her that she had merely been hallucinating because of her flu, but over the next few weeks, Claire's health steadily deteriorated, and a strange fact came to light when she was take into hospital for an examination: she had lost quite a lot of blood, and the medical experts could not explain how this blood loss had come about. A specialist put an endoscope down Claire's throat, thinking he'd find an ulcer-like hole in her oesophagus known as a Mallory-Weiss tear. These tears often bleed and can cause what seems like unaccountable blood loss, but there was no such tear to be found in the oesophagus of Claire – so how had she lost so much blood? She was thoroughly checked for ulcers but had none – and then a very strange discovery was made: on her left foot, between Claire's big toe and the one next to it there was a sore spot, and upon closer examination a doctor found that it was a small puncture hole. Claire immediately thought of the slithering thing she had felt moving over her left foot in the bed; had this thing somehow been siphoning off her blood? If so, what the hell was it? Claire's mind went back to that evening when Shawney left the door open and something Claire could only hear came into the bedroom where she had lain ill in her bed. What in heaven's name had come off the streets that night to wander into her room? The doctor could plainly see the deep puncture mark between Claire's toes and yet, because he did not know what had made that mark, he seemed unable to accept that some creature had inflicted the wound. The doctor said the hole was probably the result of a deep rooted fungal infection and he prescribed Daktacort – a hydrocortisone cream to treat the hole, which eventually, over the course of three months, eventually closed up and healed. Claire refused to sleep in her bedroom after the discovery of the deep puncture mark, and she persuaded husband Mike to move their king size bed into the spare room. Mike and his brother Kevin carried the mattress and baseboard of the bed into the spare room, and as they did, Kevin noticed something very odd. Under the baseboard, in the corner, near to a castor, there was an elaborate spiral of toffee-brown fibres, as thick as knitting wool, and this domed spiral measured about 12-15 inches in diameter. The structure resembled a bird's nest only it was made of some unknown hard fibre – and it had a ghastly aroma about it too. When Claire saw the "nest" she naturally freaked out and told Mike to bin the baseboard and the rest of the bed too. The couple had to sleep in a single bed in the spare room until a new bed could be bought, and after that, Claire experienced no more strange goings-on in her bedroom. She asked me if I had heard of anything similar to her experience before, and I told her I had: a number of residents living on a housing estate off Earle Road suffered similar deep puncture wounds to their necks in the 1980s and some actually believed a vampire was at large. When I told Claire about my Morba theory she shuddered, but I did emphasise that it was nothing more than a theory. There was once a case reported to me which was alleged to have happened in the 1960s, and it makes me wonder if the Morba were responsible. People were sunbathing one summer – around 1964 or 1965 – in Abercromby Park, off Oxford Street on the Liverpool University campus, when hundreds of white threads dropped out of the clear blue sky. People assumed the threads were drifting dandelion seeds at first, but they soon saw that this was not the case: the white threads were like cobweb strands only a little thicker. When these strands landed on the bare skin of the people in the park, many of them began to feel an intense urge to scratch at the skin, and when the threads touched the face and nose, allergic reactions took place, mostly a tightness in the throat and sneezing. The lawns of Abercromby Park turned pale with the localised fall of the unidentified 'webs' as people termed the strands. Some ten minutes later, the white flimsy threads had vanished. This phenomenon reminds me of "Angel's Hair" – a type of material not at all unlike the filaments which fell over Abercromby Park – except that Angel's Hair usually falls from UFOs when they either materialise or dematerialise in the sky, and like the gossamer material which fell on the Liverpool park, it also evaporates without a trace shortly after it reaches the ground. One witness to the fall of the white irritant threads in the park that afternoon was Sheila Jones, who was 22 at the time. She told me that the material hung over telephone wires and television aerials and when some landed on her cleavage, it really irritated the skin there. A strand of the fluffy white material touched her nose and for days, Sheila felt as if there was something on the tip of her nose and as much as she scrubbed it, the sensation remained. For the next three weeks Sheila came down with a strange illness which her doctor diagnosed as flu, but it didn't feel at all like flu, and then she came down with chronic thrush, and she also had two blackouts. Other people who had been in the park that day also felt ill, but no one ever got to find out just what had fallen on Abercromby Park. Was it a species of the mysterious noxious Morba?

# WOOLTON ROAD'S PHANTOM PARK

**Behind the wall** of sleep our cares often melt away into a jumble of surreal imagery, but sometimes the concerns and worries of our waking hours follow us into the realms of sleep and haunt us as nightmares, and this latter state of affairs applied to a 39-year-old Liverpool man named Michael. He had lost his job in one of those mini recessions of recent times, and for the first time in his life he had been forced to sign on. His wife Emma's job, working in a college canteen was also being threatened by local cuts, so things were looking pretty bleak for the couple. The Government was 'clamping down' on people who were relying on benefits too much, and so, Michael was already being sent on 'back-to-work' courses within weeks of signing on, and he now had to log on to a website and prove he was actively looking for work. All of this totalitarian madness was taking its toll on Michael, and what affected Michael affected those who loved him – his wife Emma and their 5-year-old child Emily. One February morning in 2011 the dreaded manila envelopes came through the door: a letter from a debt collection agency, one regarding the unpaid phone and internet bill, a query from the local "compliance team" at the job centre who wanted to see Michael's bank statement to see if he had any savings stashed away and so on. Emily was at home on this morning because of a flood at her nursery, and the little girl was the only one in the family with a smiling face. She was too young to be aware of the misery hanging in the air, and she loved being with her mum and dad and she asked Michael if she could go out for a walk.

'It's too cold love,' Michael said, reading a threatening letter from a bailiff that had been stashed behind the clock (for out of sight is out of mind) for a week. 'We'll go out when it gets a bit warmer.'

'Maybe we should go out for a walk,' Emma suggested, standing in the doorway of the kitchen with a coffee in her hand. She had a horrible despondent look on her face and her eyes seemed to be searching for something – perhaps for a way out, Michael thought.

'Yeah! Let's go for a long walk!' Emily shouted and her little face beamed with optimism as if she was going to Disneyland. Michael couldn't say no to his daughter's glowing enthusiastic eyes, and he gave a brief forced smile, then nodded, and put the bailiff's letter back behind the clock.

They left the little semi in Childwall and walked through the cold but sunny morning towards Woolton Road. Emily's left hand clasped her dad's big hairy-backed right hand and her other hand held her mum's slender left hand, and the child skipped and defied gravity in her little world as her parents gently swung her up as she hopped along.

They walked past the Halfway House pub and intended to go to the Black Woods, and from there, perhaps they could afford a trip to a café in the area where Emily loved the cakes. They passed the pub and McNaughtons newsagents and a greengrocers, where Emily looked at the apples and the greengrocer always waved or said hello to her. The family passed the hairdressers and then they noticed something different as they passed the old white-painted cottages and Bishop Eton School. Something didn't quite look right, and when the couple later compared notes, it seems that both of them had noticed this; that something was missing, but couldn't say what. Emily pointed to an open gate of black railings, about twelve feet high, and beyond this gate a cobbled path ran in a sweeping curve around a tall hedge. Curiosity got the better of Michael; he had never noticed this gate before, and felt drawn towards it. He led his wife and daughter to it, then pulled it open a few more inches, and all three of them went down the curved path and turned at the hedge. Ahead lay three broad sandstone steps leading down to a lawn. At this point, the time was around 10.30am.

'Where *is* this?' Emma asked, and her husband shrugged.

'These flowers are all out of season,' Michael noted daffodils, roses, and a myriad of rainbow-coloured blooms which dotted the perimeter of the lawn. Some were wild.

'Daffodils come up early sometimes,' Emma reasoned, but Michael stooped down and looked close at a clump of glossy-leaved bluebells.

'Bluebells don't normally put in an appearance till April, not early February,' Michael murmured.

Emily crouched down beside him and looked at the bell-shaped flowers and asked: 'Do fairies live under them sometimes?'

'Sometimes,' Emma replied with a smile. She looked around and noticed that the steady hubbub of the traffic on Woolton Road could no longer be heard. A strange silence had crystalised all around them.

'Daddy, what are those blue flowers with yellow in the middle?' Emily queried.

'Ah, forget-me-nots they are, Emily,' Michael recognised the flowers, but then also recalled that the forget-me-not only appears between early June and late September. This was not making sense. There were buttercups dotting one part of the lawn, and thanks to his late grandfather, who had been a magician of a gardener - Michael knew his flowers, and he knew the buttercup appeared from May till October.

'Michael – look!' Emma pointed to a peacock strutting towards the trio across the lawn.

Emily was fascinated by the colourful bird and wanted to run to it but her mother restrained her, saying, 'No, Emily, leave it.'

'Who does it belong to?' the child asked.

'Good question – who indeed does it belong to?' Michael reflected on his daughter's question.

'I think we shouldn't be in here, Michael,' Emma suddenly said as she looked at something which had caught her eye in the doorway of a redbrick wall. It was a circular white structure, about twelve feet in diameter, with a bell-shaped roof with a weather vane at its apex, and it had a black wrought iron bench with wooden slats running around its circumference. 'A gazebo,' Michael spotted the building, and the funny-sounding word immediately caught the imagination of little Emily, who asked what a gazebo was.

'A place where we can sit,' her father told her.

'This is a private garden, not a park,' Emma said to Michael, and she felt as if she was trespassing.

'This is too big to be someone's garden – it's a park, love,' Michael tried to reassure his wife they were not invading anyone's privacy. 'We just haven't noticed it before.'

Now for a strange thing; as the couple and their child went through the doorway in the wall and on towards the gazebo, everything became warm, as if Emily, Michael and Emma had stepped into summer. It became so unbearably hot, hats gloves and coats were removed. It had been a glacial February minutes ago and now it seemed to be a day in the middle of a steaming August. It was very odd. The park was bordered with tall well-kept hedges, and some of them were sculpted into globes and the shapes of birds. Michael noticed straight away that the tops of the houses on Woolton Road outside could not be seen from within the park – not even a lamp post was visible, and that baffled Michael.

'This is what you could truly call a little oasis of peace and quiet,' Emma remarked, and she sat on the bench of the gazebo and smiled, eyes half closed, at the fierce sun above. She heard her husband cry out, 'Emily! Leave it!'

Emily was chasing a yellow and black butterfly across a lawn.

'Come here Em,' Emma called to her excited daughter, and Emily returned to the couple, all rosy cheeked and excited. The girl suggested that they should bring ice cream and sweets to this park next time and have a picnic.

The three of them sat there in a row on the curved bench, Emily seated on her father's lap, and a bee droned past somewhere. The stillness was hard to take in; still no sounds from the traffic outside, and no drones of a plane overhead, just a solid quietude and a warm drowsiness hanging all around. All cares were evaporating and all heavy concerns had been removed from the couple's shoulders. A faint ghostly morning half-moon hung high up in the blue vault of heaven, and Emily looked up at it before she dozed off. Michael yawned and did the same. He had not felt as carefree and blissful as this since he was a child.

Emma awoke first and turned to look at Michael, who was snoring lightly – and Emily was not with him. She was nowhere to be seen. Emma's heart went into freefall, and she opened her mouth and began to hyperventilate before she gasped, 'Michael – where's Emily?'

She grabbed her husband by the forearm and shook him hard.

'Wha – ' he woke and squinted at the noon sun.

'Emily's gone!' his wife cried out and as she got to her feet, she knocked the coats she and her husband and child had been wearing from the bench onto the gravel border.

'Don't panic,' Michael said, getting up off the bench and scanning the park, 'she can't have got far.'

'Oh my God!' Emma rushed from the gazebo and across the lawn. 'Emily!' she screeched, and Michael's stomach turned.

'Mummy!' said a familiar voice which floated through the air.

It came from the other side of the gazebo.

The parents rushed around the rotund building, one from each side, and they met 180 degrees on – and saw that Emily was sitting with a very peculiar little boy of around Emily's age. He wore a white sailor suit with navy blue stripes on the sleeves and one on his collar. On his head he wore a radiant white sailor's cap. His face was pallid and his eyes were brown, contrasting the pallid complexion like coal eyes on a snowman. He sat next to Emily with a purple ball – a bit smaller than a football – and it had animals printed upon it in yellow.

'Emily! We thought we'd lost you!' Emma ran to her daughter, threw her arms around her and dragged her to her feet.

'Mummy, this is Archie, he's my new friend!' Emily pointed at the pale boy in the sailor outfit. He hardly reacted to the introduction and he merely picked up the ball, put it under his arm, then made a curious gesture to Emily. He put his tiny index finger to his miniature doll-like cupid's bow lips – and Emily smiled and did the same, except she said: 'Ssshhh!' as she carried out the ancient gesture to symbolize secrecy.

The boy then ran off silently and disappeared behind a hedge.

'Where did he come from?' Michael asked.

Emily returned a blank stare, then gazed down at the grass, and her long eyelashes fluttered.

'What time is it?' Emma asked her husband, and as he got out his mobile to survey the time, Emma sighed and said to Emily: 'You gave us a real fright before, wandering off.'

'I don't believe it,' Michael said with a baffled expression as he squinted at the screen of his phone.

'What?' Emma asked, intrigued as she hugged Emily.

'It's 10.45am – but it can't be can it?' Michael looked at Emma and gently shook his head.

'No, it's wrong, we came in here around half-ten didn't we?' Emma replied with a vexed smile.

'Yeah, and we've been in here for more than fifteen minutes.' Michael put his phone back in his trouser pocket, and then he went and picked up the three coats and the gloves and hats.

The family left the park and when they came out onto Woolton Road they were greeted by an icy wind that stung their eyes and made their exhaled breaths visible. They quickly put on their winter clothing and hurried home to Childwall. Three missed calls from a debt-collection agency beeped on Michael's phone. Furthermore, the time on that phone now stated that it was half-past one. The couple tried to get information about "Archie" from Emily but the girl remained tight-lipped about her new friend. Michael went online and looked up information about Woolton Road to see if any sprawling gardens or parks had stood at the location they had visited earlier – but he could find no information whatsoever.

On the following day the couple and their child returned to Woolton Road and went in search of the beautiful garden which had been a blessed sanctuary from the cares of modern life – but they found not a trace of it. At this point I would like to add my experience into the mix. It's rare for me to mention my own experiences in these stories, but I feel I must on this occasion. Around 2007 I visited a friend who lived at an old house on Dudlow Lane, and during the visit I looked out of an upstairs window which afforded a sweeping view of the back of the houses on Woolton Road. I was intrigued to see a well-kept garden with stately-looking sculpted hedges, and a partially obscured structure with a cupola roof with a weather vane upon it. I asked my friend whose grand garden this was, and was told there was no such garden at the back of the houses on Woolton Road. 'There is, look,' I told him and pointed to the hedges and cupola, and he said: 'I've never seen that before.'

My friend brought a pair of binoculars into the room and we took turns surveying the massive garden. It was exactly the same as the one later described by Emma and Michael. I could see the magnified roof of the gazebo and its weather vane cross with what looked like a silhouette of Old Father Time on it and the letter N for north, and I could make out a bird sculpted out of a tall hedge. I could see no one in the grounds of what seemed more like a park than a garden.

About a week later I received an email from my friend in Woolton who told me how the garden we had both seen through the binoculars had now gone – it was nowhere to be seen. I visited his house and saw that it was true. Years later I was browsing for books in Reid's of Liverpool, an antiquarian bookseller on Mount Pleasant, when a man tapped me on the shoulder and asked if I was Tom Slemen. He then told me about the phantom park of Woolton Road. It was Michael, who walked into the mysterious green 'mirage' in February 2010 with his wife and young daughter.

To date I have not found any evidence of a park existing off Woolton Road in any of the old Ordnance Survey Maps, but the place must have existed there once, and a timeslip of some sort must have been involved in the park's transient reappearances. Emily, who seems to have shared a secret with the mysterious child Archie at the long-vanished park, is a little older now, and all she can remember is that the boy told her that she could stay with him and his father if she was "a good girl". Was this child a ghost of some sort? And if he was, what a chilling remark he made…

# JAGGAROO

**Here's a short** but intriguing story told to me many years ago by an Arabian friend.

In the 1970s there was a shopkeeper named Ali, who ran a newsagents in the Birkenhead area, and he was well-liked by all of his customers. If a customer enquired about a magazine or some new product, and Ali didn't have it, he'd go out of his way to find it and stock it, and he was also a very kind man, often letting his customers buy things on tick. In 1975 his brother-in-law Nadji passed away in north Liverpool, and Ali's sister-in-law Zora told him to go and collect her brother Nadji's belongings. Among the trunks of documents, books and other items, Ali found a little dark wooden chest which contained a bundle of papers full of romantic poetry and a dagger of some sort with a golden gem-studded handle which was jammed into an elaborate golden scabbard. Try as he may, Ali could not remove the dagger from this scabbard, nor could his cousin Jalal, a very muscular keep fit fanatic. Ali read the romantic poems and Zora recognised the handwriting as that of her late brother's, and the flowery prose was comparable to the work of the celebrated Persian astronomer-poet Omar Khayyám, and the object of the love poems was someone – presumably a lady – named Jaggaroo – although Zora knew no one of that name. The gist of the corpus of poetry was that Nadji had been in love with Jaggaroo since he had found her when he was a child and the poems described her 'gleaming eyes', her sleekness, her timelessness, and her previous lovers down the centuries and of Jaggaroo's demands for her lovers to sacrifice even their own souls to deserve her love. Zora found the poems absurd and eerie and told Ali to throw them away, but she suggested having the gold dagger valued. Ali took a close look at the scabbard of the dagger and made a strange discovery – in Old Persian there was one word inscribed in silver on the gold dagger's sheath: Jaggaroo. He whispered the word and thought he heard a woman sigh – and the scabbard slid effortlessly off to reveal a blade of gleaming metal which appeared to be chrome-plated – but upon closer inspection the blade seemed partially transparent – as if it was cut crystal. Stranger still, Ali felt an electrifying power emanate from this dagger, and the power coursed through the hands that held Jaggaroo and made him shudder. He felt as if he could do anything – any task at all! He could take on an army. He also felt as if he was not alone. He felt a female presence, her seductive hands on his shoulder and arm – and he was not imagining it. A raspy female voice was whispering, 'Yes, Ali, yes…'

Ali looked into the mirrored blade and there reflected he saw the faint grey faces of all those who had been slain by Jaggaroo, from the ritual slayings in the days of King Solomon to the shadowy victims in the festering gaslit warrens of London's East End during the Ripper's reign of terror. And Jaggaroo demanded more. Ali realised the bloodthirsty entity haunting this ancient knife was one of the Djinn – extremely evil spirits that have misguided and menaced mankind since time began.

Ali suddenly heard an echoing phrase in his mind's ear: *A running man can slit a thousand throats in one night!*

It was the voice of the entity which obviously haunted this ancient knife. That spirit screeched curses and threatened Ali as he sheathed the knife and took it to the waterfront through a sudden screaming gale. He hurled Jaggaroo into the Mersey, and there she lies to this day. I pity the unwary future archaeologist who finds her.

# A TRAGIC ECHO

**Way back before** MP3s and CDs, people used cassette tapes to create what was known as a "mix tape" to record a particular selection of songs ripped from either the radio or a record player. Some mix tapes where just a collection of popular songs of the month, but sometimes there was a theme to the collection, so the songs could have a sad theme and comprise of a collection of 'downer' songs about people breaking up or losing someone, and these bleak mix tapes were listened to when the person had been chucked by their partner. With the advent of the MP3 and iTunes, the mix tape seems like something from the Jurassic era, but there will probably be many readers out there who will remember the era I am talking about. Now, one rainy November afternoon in the Kensington area of the city in 1979, a 14-year-old lad named Kevin Patterson decided to make a mix tape, but he had no blank tapes, so he took one of his father's cassettes – The Best of Glen Campbell – and he stuck a piece of cellotape over the write-protect gap on the cassette so it was now possible to record over the songs on the tape. It was a mean thing to do, but Kevin believed his father would never find out because he hadn't played the Glen Campbell tape for about a year and probably wouldn't ever play it again. Kevin then sat in his bedroom with his cassette tape recorder's microphone positioned close to the speaker of his radio, waiting for one of his favourite songs of the month to be played – Message In a Bottle by The Police. Kevin waited and waited but the song wasn't played, but he recorded a song called Video Killed the Radio Star by Buggles, and during the recording, there was a knock on his bedroom door. It was his father, and yes, you've guessed it – he wanted to know where his Glen Campbell tape was. To distract his father – who was about to go into the bedroom – Kevin rushed past him and said, 'I've just seen your Glen Campbell tape down here Dad, and he hurried down the stairs – and his father fell for the diversion. Kevin led his father on a wild goose chase for the Glen Campbell cassette for about fifteen minutes, and had him turning over the cushions on the sofa and armchairs until the search was abandoned.

Kevin then sneaked upstairs to his bedroom and switched off the radio and stopped the recording. Around 7pm that night he played back the recording of the Buggles song, which was ruined by the taped conversation between Kevin and his father, and the teenager smirked when he heard himself lying through the teeth to his dad – but that smile was soon wiped off his face because Kevin suddenly heard the song stop dead. There was a pause of silence with a slight hiss present on the tape, and then came the chilling sounds of people crying and groaning and shouting for help. At first, Kevin thought that perhaps the radio station he had been taping from – Radio 1 – had switched to some feature within a show, but the recording of the people who sounded as if they were in distress went on for about twenty minutes, and during that time, Kevin heard women and children screaming, and what sounded like an old man saying he was bleeding to death. The teenager could also hear the sound of water gushing in the background in the strange recording. Kevin wanted to play the recording to his father but was afraid he'd give him a thump for recording over his Glen Campbell tape, so instead he played the recording to his mum and sister, and they were really spooked by it. His mother then told him that it sounded as if people were trapped in some cave-in, in a mine or something, and then she seemed to go pale. She went downstairs and had a talk with her grandmother, then returned and told her lad something that played on Kevin's mind for many years. In 1940, one of the worst civilian tragedies of World War Two took place when 300 people packed into the boiler room beneath the Ernest Brown Junior Instructional Centre in Durning Road, Edge Hill – just around the corner from Kevin's home. The people crushed into the basement because it was assumed it would be a safe and sound air raid shelter because it had metal girders running across its reinforced ceiling. However, that night a German high-explosive mine sailed down on a parachute during an air raid and destroyed the building on Durning Road, crushing and trapping the people sheltering in the basement. The boilers burst down there, scalding men, women and children to death as they lay trapped. The gas mains were fractured in the blast, and huge flames roared up, making any hopes of rescue almost impossible, but the firemen, wardens and local volunteers worked miracles that night, and while 166 people were killed or seriously injured, around 134 made it into the open air. The bodies of some of the dead were so inaccessible, the authorities could not bring them up and dumped quicklime over them before re-sealing the deep hole they lay in.When I researched this incident, I discovered that the recording had inadvertently been made by Kevin on Thursday, 29 November 1979, and the Durning Road tragedy had occurred on Thursday 29 November 1940. Was this an eerie case of the history-repeating-itself phenomenon which I have detailed in my books before? More recordings were made by Kevin and also his father, but nothing supernatural was captured. Perhaps some researcher familiar with EVP (Electronic Voice Phenomena) should make some test recordings around the site of the Durning Road tragedy on November 29th...

# THE SHADOW ON THE GRASS

**In the 1970s** there was a green square – a recreation ground to give it its official title – in Kirkdale, bounded by Brock Street, North Dingle Street, Garnett Avenue and Rumney Road West. Children from all over Kirkdale played on this little patch of green, and around 1975, two sports-mad lads – Steve and Billy – both aged thirteen – were playing football there as the sun began to set on the Mersey, throwing its long shadows across the grass. Steve noticed a very odd shadow that summer evening, and was at a complete loss to explain it because he could not work out just what was casting it. He called Billy over and said, 'Look at that!'

Billy shuddered, because stretched out across the grass was the elongated shadow of a hanged man. The rope ran from his neck to a gibbet of some sort. The young teens looked around, and seeing that there wasn't so much as a post or a tree that could be throwing a crooked shadow, they quickly left the recreation ground. Each lad told his mum and dad what he had seen but their parents either smiled, thinking imagination had gotten the better of their son, or that the hanged man was just some trick of light and shadows at sunset. However, in the following year, around spring, an art teacher and three pupils who had come to sketch the recreation ground and the surrounding streets also saw the sinister shadow of the hanged man. The art teacher tried to trace where the shadow was coming from without success. They did, however, sketch the weird stretched silhouette on the grass. The art teacher conducted a little research into the site of this ghostly shadow, and he discovered what any local Kirkdale resident could have told him, had he asked. The green square of the recreation ground was the present-day site of the long-demolished Kirkdale Gaol, built between 1821 and 1822. The first hanging at the infamous gaol was on 28 August 1835 and the last person to be hanged there met his fate at the end of a rope in August 1891. The grim history of the site surely must have had something to do with that shadow of the hanged man that was seen on the grass of the recreation ground by five known witnesses – and probably many more.

# SOME WALTON GHOSTS

**The Domesday Book** – the most comprehensive and detailed record of English and Welsh land and property in the Middle Ages – refers to Walton as Waletone, and at the time of the Domesday survey (1086) salubrious Walton was much more important than Liverpool, which was then merely a humble embryonic fishing village and just one of nine townships which Walton encompassed. Liverpool was not even mentioned in the Domesday Book because it was so tiny. Walton, then, has a longer history than Liverpool, but the latter eventually overtook it in importance because of a phenomenal rate of development in the later centuries as a prominent port. Walton Church is built on a very ancient and intriguing hill that was apparently regarded as sacred by the locals long before William the Conqueror set foot on English soil. Three churches stood on the revered hill at Walton and originally a menhir, or megalithic standing stone probably stood atop the hill, aligned with its stone brothers across Lancashire. The graveyard of Walton Church was once regularly haunted by a very dramatic ghost which was said to spout lines from Hamlet and several other plays, and the spectral thespian was allegedly identified as the being the ghost of John Palmer, an actor who actually died on the stage of Liverpool's Theatre Royal in 1798 after uttering the very apt line: "Oh God! There is another and better world!" All actors have periods of 'rest' when they cannot find work, but Palmer has been resting in a tomb in Walton Churchyard for over two centuries, and he still puts in an occasional appearance. There are other ghosts and strange lights that have been seen in the graveyard of Walton Church, and the same is true of another Walton churchyard.

I have a number of reports of a shadowy man in black prowling the graveyard on Rice Lane, Walton. The earliest one – if it's the same apparition – dates back to Thursday, September 14, 1876. In broad daylight (2pm in the afternoon), during the funeral of the Reverend Dr. Graham of Shaw Street Presbyterian Church at Walton Cemetery, Rice Lane, many mourners became aware of a tall oddly-dressed man in a long ankle-length coat, with a very pallid face, watching the graveside service from a hundred yards away among the gravestones. The presence of this eerie man is said to have made the horses that had drawn the hearse very uneasy. Major Graham, the only son of the deceased Reverend, was told that this individual was a prowler who had been seen in the cemetery for some months, and gave chase, but the figure is said to have vanished when chased. This vanishing act was witnessed by dozens of mourners, including the Reverend J. Nisbett Wallace of Shrewsbury. For many years after this, the same figure was seen, both day and night in that cemetery, and to this day, no one knows whose ghost it is. In 2009, a couple telephoned me at Radio Merseyside to tell me how they had literally bumped into the ghost one October afternoon whilst walking to a relative's grave. The married couple in their thirties said the figure looked two-dimensional, almost like a cardboard cut-out, and it flitted across the cemetery at a phenomenal speed and had slowly vanished when they inadvertently got in its way. There was also a report of a woman being followed out of the cemetery by a silhouetted figure in August 1976 around 7pm. The apparition she described had no features, just pure shadow. It followed her as far as Yew Tree Road and was seen by many other witnesses before it literally vanished before their eyes. The man in black is still said to be at large in the cemetery, and apparently he is not alone, for there are a few other chilling apparitions and presences at large. One gloomy afternoon in March 1988, two women who had just tended to their late brother's grave were chased out of the cemetery by a globe of blue crackling light the size of a football. Other people had seen this globe of energy whizzing about the cemetery after dark, and a ghost hunter who tried to capture the entity on camera was of the opinion that the electrified globe was just a form of ball-lightning, but how would ball-lightning remain at large in the cemetery over a period of a month, and how would a meteorological phenomenon possess the intelligence to chase people around the cemetery? Some of the older people living in the vicinity of the cemetery had recollections of a ball of light chasing children back in the 1950s. A 32-year-old woman named Barbara told me how, one day in 2004, as she was arranging flowers in a metal vase on her mother's grave at the cemetery, she felt a hand stroke her head. She half-tuned her head and looked up and saw the hand – but it was not attached to anything, and so Barbara dropped the flowers and ran out of the cemetery as fast as her legs could carry her.

Of course, not all ghosts hang around cemeteries, and you'll find the spirits of the dead in the most unexpected of places, such as a certain cellar at a house at the Breeze Hill end of Rice Lane. In the early 1970s an electricity meter reader – the "lecky man" – called at a house on Rice Lane, and the reader descended into the cellar of the nondescript terraced house via a wooden staircase. He shone his torch at the meter, and, after he had jotted down the reading indicated by the meter dials, he unlocked a black metal box containing a small fortune of shillings. The reader would then routinely go upstairs and count these shillings in the kitchen on the table and give the householder a rebate – paid in shillings of course – and it was something most people in those days looked forward to. On this occasions, as the Lecky Man was about to go up the steps he saw a strange figure silhouetted against the doorway at the top of the staircase, and instinctively shone his torch up at him. The torchlight revealed a man of about six feet in height, wearing a purple dressing gown and striped pyjama trousers. His head was swathed in bandages, and in his hand he held a hatchet! The hands of the unidentified man were also wrapped in bandages. He quickly descended the wooden steps as he raised the hatchet in a threatening manner, and the meter reader backed away into the dark reaches of the cellar in terror, expecting to be dismembered, but as the hatchet came down and struck the Lecky Man's left raised arm, the bandaged figure vanished in an instant. The meter man had somehow suffered no physical harm, but psychologically he was left a deeply scarred man, and he was so afraid, he dropped the black metal box full of shillings, bounded up the wooden cellar steps two at a time, and ran straight out of the house. The middle-aged couple who had lived at this house for three years had also encountered the bandaged man in the dressing gown on numerous occasions, and each time he had a hatchet in his hand, but not once did he act in a threatening manner. The 13-year-old daughter of the couple went down to the kitchen one morning in January 1972 and walked straight through the ghost and blacked out. She recalled an icy sensation passing through her before she felt her legs collapse under her with fear. The girl's parents also bumped into the apparition one afternoon as they hurried into the house during a downpour. On this occasion the couple saw the ghost standing in the hallway looking at the hatchet in its hand, but the eyes of the ghost, set in its bandaged head, were just two black holes. The ghost vanished abruptly when the couple switched on the hallway light to get a better view of the figure. I have researched the history of this house off Rice Lane and cannot find any incident to throw any light on the hatchet-wielding "mummy", which, thankfully, in recent years, has not been that active.

Next, we move a little further north across Walton next, to a house on Northfield Road, just a stone's throw from Linacre Lane's cemetery. Here there stands an unremarkable residence which I personally investigated in the early days of my ghost-hunting. A woman named Barbara who had lived at the house for 18 months told me how, even during the day, the doorknob of her front parlour would turn all by itself, and sometimes the door would open a few inches to allow something to peep in with its shadowy head. I visited the house in 1999 and while I was there, the doorknob squeaked, and began to slowly turn, only the door did not open, but rattled on its hinges. As the knob turned, I tip-toed over and grasped the handle and wrenched that door open with some force, convinced I would catch some practical joker on the other side of it – but there was no one there, the hallway was empty, and a mouldy odour greeted my nostrils. I had felt that doorknob being turned as I grabbed at it, and there was no way for a prankster to go to ground within the moment it took for me to overenthusiastically yank open that door. Barbara was in a terrified state when I opened the door in this way. She told me how, about three months previous, her 7-year-old daughter Joanne had been sitting with her in the parlour one evening reading a book when she noticed the doorhandle turning ever so slowly. Mother and daughter gazed apprehensively at the turning handle, and Barbara wished it was merely her husband George coming home early from the pub, but the door opened about five or six inches, and Barbara could not see who was behind that door from her position near the other side of the room, but Joanne saw something unearthly and fainted with the shock. The door then slammed shut again and Barbara took Joanne in her arms and gently tapped her face until she came around. Joanne couldn't speak for almost half an hour, and when she did, she spoke gibberish. She mentioned a skull and kept bursting into tears. In the end, Barbara, George and Joanne moved out of the house around the year 2000 and three male students moved in. Out of curiosity I visited the house during the tenancy of the students and after explaining my job as a researcher into the paranormal, I asked them if they had witnessed anything unusual at the house. All three mentioned the door of the front room opening and closing by itself, and also the voice of what sounded like a demented woman reciting nursery rhymes somewhere upstairs. The woman would laugh hysterically or scream halfway through the rhymes of 'Three Blind Mice' and 'Wee Willie Winkie' and sometimes she would come out with some shocking bad language, on one occasion describing Wee Willie Winkie as a c**t. On one occasion, one of the students was reading a book in a hot bath when something took the plug out and wound its chain around a tap. The book was then knocked out of the startled student's hands into the bath by something. Another scary incident took place one morning around 1.30 am as a student named Paul turned off his bedside lamp, put the book he'd been studying on the bedside cabinet, and tried to get some shut eye. As he lay in his bed he felt breath on his face, and so he opened his eyes – and someone spat in his right eye. He groped about in shock for the bedside lamp, clicked it on, and saw the bedroom was empty, but the book he had been reading had been placed on the floor, just a few inches from the door.

I asked the neighbours of this house if they knew of it having a supernatural reputation, and many of them said the house had been the scene of a suicide in the 1970s; a woman in her twenties supposedly hanged herself from the banisters and was afterwards seen gazing through the front window of the house. To date I have not been able to pinpoint a suicide at the address but I will keep on searching.

These are just a few examples of ghosts that haunt the Walton district, and I will include some more in future publications.

# THE EYE IN THE SINK

**There's a terraced house** on Lorenzo Drive in Norris Green which has been the scene of a particular grisly supernatural incident for over forty years now. In 1972, Mrs Martin, a widow in her sixties, and her 27-year-old son Colin, moved into the house in question, and had only been there three days when something shocking took place. The kitchen at the house had an old stone sink, quite unlike the newer aluminium ones that were in use in most kitchens around that time. Mrs Martin however, thought the stone sink was fine for doing her washing-up in, and it reminded her of the one in her grandmother's kitchen in fact. One Sunday afternoon in October 1972, Mrs Martin was preparing the Sunday dinner for her and Colin, and she went to fill her kettle over the stone sink when she noticed something in it, near the plug hole. At first she thought it was a globular white sweet known as a gobstopper, but when she looked closer, Mrs Martin saw it was in fact a human eyeball with traces of blood around it and a piece of ragged red muscle protruding from beneath it. The widow screamed and backed away from the sink, and moments later, Colin, who had been watching a film on the telly, came running into the kitchen to see what the matter was. He too saw the eye in the sink, and reached into the sink to pick it up, but his mother gave a yelp and told him not to touch it.

'Where did it come from?' Colin asked his mum, 'Whose eye is it?' He hoped that it had perhaps been a sheep's eye from the butchers that had accidentally been wrapped up with the chops currently sizzling in the frying pan.

'I don't know,' she replied with her hand over her mouth. She felt she was going to throw up.

'Is it a sheep's eye?' Colin asked, somehow knowing it wasn't.

'No, that's a person's eye!' Mrs Martin put her hand to her mouth and in horror and confusion she gazed at the edge of the sink, wondering what to do.

'Should we call the police Mam?'

'We'll have to lad, come on,' Mrs Martin turned off the gas ring and left the chops frying in lard as she headed into the hall with Colin in tow. 'We'll have to use Mrs Jones's telephone to call the police,' she said, thinking through the grim task at hand.

Well, when the Joneses were told about the eye in the sink, Mr Jones was very unconvinced about the so-called eye, and believed some kids had probably thrown one of those plastic joke shop novelty eyes through the window into the sink. It was late October after all and children got up to all sorts of macabre pranks around Duck Apple Night (nowadays known as Halloween). Not so long ago, Mr Jones had seen a chicken claw opening and closing at his window, operated by a mischievous kid using a chicken foot from the butcher's and a piece of string.

'It's not a joke, it's a real eyeball Mr Jones,' Colin assured his neighbour, and even invited him to go and see for himself – which Mr Jones did. His wife shouted for him to come back but he went with Colin next door – and upon reaching the sink, Colin said, 'See – '

There was no eyeball to be seen anywhere. He rushed back and told his mother just in time, because she was about to tell the operator on the telephone that she required the services of the police.

'It can't be gone,' Mrs Martin asserted with a baffled look, 'how would it be gone?'

'It's gone Mrs Martin,' Mr Jones said with a slight smirk, 'I told you it was all tomfoolery; the kids are cases round here.'

Mrs Jones accompanied Colin and his mum back to their house, and they all looked into the empty sink. 'But it was there, wasn't it Colin?' Mrs Martin said, and she went to point close to the corner of the sink where the eyeball had been but withdrew her hand as if she feared touching that part of the sink. Colin had to clean the sink before his mother would do any washing up.

On the following Sunday, around 5pm, there was a scream and a clatter in the kitchen. Colin ran down the stairs from his room and saw his mother rushing across the hallway from the kitchen to the living room.

'Mam! What happened?' Colin asked, and he somehow knew his mother would tell him the eye was back.

'It's there again! That bleedin' eye! Oh God it must be something to do with ghosts this, Colin!' She said, and this time Colin saw his mother's hands tremble as she buried her face in them.

On the floor in the kitchen was the frying pan Mrs Martin had dropped and seven sausages scattered on the black and yellow chequerboard floor. Colin stepped over them and inched towards the stone sink. He peered over the edge – and saw that eye again, only this time the iris was facing him and he could see a small stream of blood coming from it. Colin and his mum were soon round at the Joneses, and this time Mr Jones ran around to the Martins' kitchen, determined to catch the imagined hoaxers – but he too saw the eye. He picked it up for a moment and realised it felt very realistic. He dropped it back into the sink and returned to his own house. He picked up the receiver of the telephone on its crescent table in the hallway and dialled 999 without saying a word. 'Did you see it?' Mrs Jones kept asking her husband but all he did was nod in answer. Two policemen came to Lorenzo Drive in a Panda car and went straight into the kitchen with Mrs Martin and her son – and by now the eyeball had vanished. 'I would swear on a stack of Bibles that there was an eye in that sink, officer,' a red-faced Colin assured the flint faced policeman who was not at all happy about being called out on A Sunday afternoon by cranks. Luckily, the Martins and Mr Jones were not charged with wasting police time, but they were determined to somehow prove that a human eye was mysteriously appearing in a sink, and Mr Jones even bought film for his camera, and he hoped to provide photographic proof of the eye's existence next time it appeared – but it never did. Mrs Martin and her son kept watch on the sink throughout the week, and on Sundays Mr Jones would come around with his camera, but the accursed eye never put in an appearance. That should have been the end to the baffling matter, but in 2011 I received an intriguing query one day from a student named Emma, who (with two fellow students) had lived at the house where the Martins had once resided on Lorenzo Drive. Emma said that she and two other students had got up late one Sunday afternoon and it was left to her to cook up a meal. As Emma was filling a saucepan with water over the sink – and by now the sink in the house was an aluminium one – she was freaked out by the sudden appearance of what looked just like a human eyeball resting near to the plughole. The eye still had blood running from it and the two other students who had been alerted by the scream from Emma ran into the kitchen to see the same macabre sight. What's more, the piece of muscle hanging from the eye was still twitching, which meant that the eye had only just been excised. The girls ran out of the kitchen and decided to call the police, but before they did, one of the students had another look into the sink and saw that the eyeball was nowhere to be seen. The students were that shook up about the incident they moved out a week later when the rent for that month was due.

I briefly mentioned this incident on a radio show and afterwards received a phone call at the radio station. The caller refused to give me his name, and said in a low voice that he knew why the eyeball was seen in the sink of the house on Lorenzo Drive. Many years ago in the mid-1960s a man in his twenties had been trying to fix a television aerial on the roof of the house in question. He fell and when he landed – headfirst – onto the pavement below, there was an horrific mess, and the man's eye came out of its socket and lay there in a pool of blood. In shock, the man's mother picked up the eye and put it in some water in the sink, thinking the eye could perhaps be reattached by a surgeon – even though this would be impossible in the 1960s when microsurgery was unheard of. The man was already dead anyway, but because his body was twitching heavily with nerves, his mother perhaps thought he was alive. In shock, people have done things which would seem senseless to most rational people. When President Kennedy was assassinated, his wife tried to retrieve a large piece of his skull that flew out the back of the limousine after the second headshot. There was also a case many years ago in Widnes where a man who had his arm blown off in a factory explosion initially ran away in shock from the scene of the explosion, but then ran back to pick up his severed arm, which he carried to rescuers. Again, this was before microsurgery would have made reattachment possible.

# THE OTHER ONE

**It's possible that** many of you reading these words have lived before in a previous life and will go on to another life when this one is through. The incorporeal true self – the soul – call it what you will, is, according to ancient sacred texts such as the Bhagavad-Gita: 'never born nor dies, nor does it exist on coming into being. For it is unborn, eternal...although the body is slain, the soul is not.' Reincarnation is when the soul returns after bodily death into a brand new body, and according to several polls, just over a quarter of people in the UK believe in reincarnation. I once interviewed two nurses who were present when a baby boy was delivered in Oxford Street Maternity Hospital many decades ago, and both of these nurses stated that a newly-delivered baby had cried out: "Why have I come back?'

How far back into your life can you remember? The inability of adults to recall memories before the age of 2 to 4 years is known as childhood amnesia, and most people find it hard to go beyond a mental wall to access memories before the age of two, but there are some people who claim they can remember being born and there are also people who state that they even recall being in the womb. In 1910 a six-year-old Liverpool girl named Martha Jones asked her mother one day: 'Mamma, what happened to the other one?'

Mrs Jones asked her daughter who she was referring to, and little Martha said, 'The baby I was in your tummy with.'

This shocked Mrs Jones because she had given birth to identical female twins, but sadly one of them died a few minutes after she was delivered, and the other one was, of course, Martha. Mrs Jones could not work out how her daughter had learned of her twin sister, for she and no one else ever talked about her. Martha said she remembered 'the other one' and said that they often hugged one another in mummy's tummy. Furthermore, in 1910, 6 year-olds were not told the facts of life – so how had Martha known she had come from her mother's 'tummy'?

Mrs Jones discouraged her daughter from talking about the deceased twin, for she found it quite unsettling, but a fortnight later, something very peculiar took place. Martha came into possession of a little doll, and it looked just like the child; the facial features and hair and eye colour – and even its clothes – made her look like a miniature version of Martha. Mrs Jones asked Martha where she had got this exceedingly lifelike doll from but the girl said she found it in her room. Martha refused to be separated from it, and would be heard talking to it at night after bed. One morning when Martha was seen trying to feed the doll porridge on a spoon, Mrs Jones tried to wrench the sinister toy out of her daughter's arms and Martha screamed, booted her mother in the shin and fell down face first. The dropped doll cracked its face on the fender of the fire, and in that split-second the very same jagged pattern of that crack appeared on Martha's face in blood. Martha screamed and fainted. Her wound was thankfully only superficial. Martha cried and shrieked for her beloved doll, but her father put the doll on the fire and as it burned, Martha had a seizure, and she burned up with a mysterious fever and made strange howling noises as she suffered a series of fits. She took days to recover from the baffling illness. The origin of the creepy doll was never traced, and Martha eventually stopped talking about "the other one".

# HELTER SKELTER

**One rainy Sunday** afternoon in September 1969, a 9-year-old girl named Marion was standing on the front step of her terraced house of Walton Breck Road when a 7-year-old girl named Tina walked past, looking bored in the inclement weather as she headed to her home on Oakfield Road. 'Hey, do you want to go on the waltzers?' Marion asked the girl, and Tina returned a puzzled look, because as far as she knew, there was no fairground in any of the local parks.

'The waltzers?' Tina asked, stopping in her tracks.

'Yeah, come in, come on, hurry up before me Mam gets back,' Marion beckoned Tina inside with a sideways tilt of the head and hurried down the hallway. Tina gingerly followed her, wary of a little black and white mongrel dog that was looking at her under the stairs.

'Come in here!' Marion shouted from the parlour and Tina walked in, expecting to see an actual waltzer car, but instead, she saw just two padded green leather armchairs – one in each corner, and a matching sofa. 'He'yar, sit on here – ' Marion pushed Tina into one of the armchairs, and then she closed the parlour door and began muttering something to herself, and Tina found the words unintelligible; it sounded like Welsh speeded up. Tina felt a bit frightened the way Marion's lips were moving so quickly, and then, all of a sudden, the armchair Tina sat on moved up and down. Tina was about to jump off it in fright when the armchair began to spin around and simultaneously lift off the floor. Tina clung on to the arms of the chair and sunk into it in terror as Marion laughed. The chair flew across the room and then curved back to where it had become airborne – and the sensation Tina was experiencing really was just like the waltzers at the fair – only this was not natural, and Tina began to cry.

'Shut up you stupid girl!' Marion shouted at the twirling child and seemed to be directing the flight path of the armchair with her hands, waving them about and pointing towards the ceiling.

Tina threw up and the sick went over Marion and also an arm of the sofa. Marion let out a stream of swear words and the armchair slowly stopped gyrating and came down onto the middle of a rug with a bump. Tina staggered towards the door of the parlour, and felt as if the room was tilting back and forth. Marion shouted to her: 'If you tell on me you'll die in the middle of the night!'

Tina opened the door, ran down the hallway towards the front door, and fell upon reaching the doorstep. She threw out her palms instinctively and skinned them as she landed. The poor child then got up, winded by the fall, gazing at the pale peeled-back broken skin of both hands and the emerging blood, and ran screaming to her home. Tina told her mother and grandmother what had happened but they found the child's account of the armchair sailing through the air as rather far-fetched. That night, Tina went to her parents' room in tears three times, saying she could hear 'horrible voices' in her head. In the end, the child was allowed to sleep between her mother and father, and kept bursting into tears. I came upon this peculiar case whilst investigating why, in 1969, two women, both aged 33, died within a week of one another at their homes off Walton Breck Road after waking up at 3am and letting out a scream before they died, apparently of heart failure. I mentioned the strange incident on a radio programme and was afterwards contacted by several people in the Anfield area who remembered the two bizarre deaths. One caller told me to check out the reports of a 9-year-old chid named Marion, who lived off Walton Breck Road, because there were rumours in circulation for years that the girl had something to do with the deaths of the women. Expecting the claims to be some urban legend, I slowly discovered that the more I dug into this case, the more intriguing it became and more and more locals in Anfield recalled Marion and said that without a doubt, the child was possessed. It transpired that five priests had tried to exorcise Marion between January 1970 and March 1971, and all attempts had failed. Schools were disrupted by Marion's powers and she and her mother (her father had died in the early 1960s) moved to St Helens for a while. They moved to Speke around 1974 and were known as "the witches" by the community on a certain housing estate there. Marion and her mother were persecuted by members of the community who set out on a literal "witch hunt" to drive out the mother and daughter from the housing estate by smashing their windows, painting crosses on their door and on one occasion, posting lit newspapers through the letterbox. The city council moved Marion and her mum to West Derby, and here the mother changed her very distinctive surname by deed poll to a much more common one. At this time, 1977, Marion had turned seventeen and was nicknamed "Helter Skelter" by the few friends she had because of her wild unearthly talents and almost psychopathic personality (hence the Helter Skelter surname, this being a Beatles song infamously misinterpreted by Charles Manson). Marion was said to be absolutely stunning at this time and had a huge mane of red unkempt hair which added to her outlandish reputation. A girl named Hope Robbins became Marion's best friend, and it was said that Hope herself was a witch, originally from Crosby. There were eerie black tales of these two witches pointing at cars on a certain secluded road in West Derby and causing many fatal smash-ups as they chanted: "Crash, Crash, Crash!" I had heard of the stories many times from West Derby residents over the years, and I once spoke to a "cocky watchman" named Mick Vaughan-Edwards who said he was somehow blinded by the girls once as they trespassed on a building site one evening near Finch Wood (an old coven meeting place), close to Deysbrook Lane. Mick warned the girls – who were throwing bricks through double-glazed window frames on the site – that he would call the police if they didn't leave, and all of a sudden, everything became blurred and his eyes began to water. He felt as if he had a "blast" in both eyes and found it impossible to open them, as if they were glued together. He could hear the girls laughing at him and using coarse language as he staggered towards the gate of the building site. He somehow managed to unlock the padlock on the gate and he was almost knocked down by a car on Hall Lane as he tried to get help. Eventually his vision returned, and he went to St Paul's Eye Hospital where he underwent an examination. Nothing could be found to explain his temporary blindness, but Mick believed the girls had somehow blinded him with witchcraft, as he later heard of their sinister reputation.

By 1980 the reports of the West Derby witches Hope Robbins and "Helter Skelter" died down, and I assumed they had perhaps moved from the area or decided to lead a "normal" life, but in 2006 I was told that the witches had been welcomed into a huge coven in the Knowsley area, and they are now perceived as respectable pillars of their community – at least during the hours of daylight.

# YOUNG LOVE

**There are things** staring us right in the face – right under our noses – that could make us billionaires and change our lives for the better if we could only open our eyes and minds to them. We are like the stone-age people who died during the Ice Age from a lack of wood fuel, unaware of the rich coal seams that existed under their very feet. It's the same with medicine; people despised moulds which ruined good food for centuries until some bright spark discovered that a certain mould contained the life-saving antibiotic penicillin. Most of us look at flowers as pretty-coloured plants without realising some metaphysical pharmacist up there put those countless plants in the earth as a medicine chest to cure every disease and condition human flesh is heir to – even ageing. In recent years some notable advances into the quest for indefinite life-extension and rejuvenation have been made through manipulation of the genetic code and the application of stem cells. It's only a matter of time before an Age Management Centre is opened in all major cities – including Liverpool, where people with age-related conditions and diseases will receive rejuvenating treatment to knock decades off their life-clocks. Ultimately DNA repair and many other techniques currently being developed around the world will allow us to reverse the ageing process and return a patient to his or her physical and mental prime. What effect this will have on population growth is another matter of course, because natural death will become a rarity. Here's a strange but true story about alleged age-reversal.

In February 1991, during a heavy snowfall, 55-year-old Fiona Herricks lost her 90-year-old spinster aunt, Morwenna – deemed the eccentric of the family and a lifetime dabbler in witchcraft. Morwenna had died in a car crash, and Fiona tried to drive through a blizzard to her cottage in Heswall before the other family vultures descended, but they had already removed the old woman's biscuit tins packed with money. Morwenna had said she would never leave anything in a Last Will and Testament, and indeed, she died intestate. Fiona found nothing of value in the cottage, but she did find an intriguing veneered walnut box, almost a foot square full of compartments and drawers lined with green baize. The chest contained Jars of dried sunflower leaves, tiny bottles of strange purple granules, eyedropper phials, green lipstick tubes, and pots of cream. Auntie Mary, Morwenna's younger sister, casually told Fiona that the chest contained a witch's make-up kit – to reverse ageing, and advised her to try the products.

'What? No way!' Fiona shook her head and pushed the chest away across the table, and yet she was so intrigued by Mary's claims.

Mary told her things she had heard from the late Morwenna. 'There was a witch who lived nearly a thousand years back named Poppea; she was the wife of the emperor Nero, and she used to make face masks from bread crumbs and asses milk, and when she began to age, Nero began to look at young maidens, and this really upset Poppea , so she sought out an older witch and asked her if it was possible to use her craft to reverse ageing. The old witch gave her the recipe to make a special cream, and Poppea looked fifteen after she had used it, and her husband the emperor almost had her killed because he thought some young impostor had taken the place of his wife. That recipe for the cream that smoothes away wrinkles and firms the skin was passed down through the centuries, and Anne Boleyn - the second wife of King Henry VIII, and, incidentally, an amateur witch – was said to have used it.'

'If this was all true,' Fiona said with a broad smile, 'the cosmetics industry would go bust overnight – it'd become obsolete!'

'But it is true,' Mary said calmly, 'but fortunately for the make-up industry, most people are unaware of things like this.'

'I'm sorry Aunt Mary, but I don't believe it,' Fiona admitted, and she felt so mean, doubting her favourite old aunt.

Mary shrugged. 'Try it yourself then.'

Fiona recoiled at the suggestion – she didn't believe in witchcraft. 'Why did Aunt Morwenna use this anti-ageing kit? She died a spinster – she never met anyone, did she?'

'She used it, or so she told me, but she said it only attracted lusty men who had one thing on their minds. She told me some long-winded story about a man she met when she made herself younger, and she thought he was Mr Right, but it turned out he was married and already had a mistress too. I can't recall the details now,' Mary told Fiona with a grimace and a dismissive wave of her hand.

'Well. That snow's getting worse, and I'm getting back before I end up being snowed in here,' Fiona said, looking through the window at the ghostly white wintry street.

'You're a spinster too, like Morwenna, I only just realised that, Fiona,' Mary suddenly said, and Fiona thought it was such an insensitive thing to say. Fiona had been engaged to marry a few years ago but he had second thoughts.

'And what made you think of that, Auntie Mary?'

'Nothing; just you wanting to hurry home, and no one being there to go home to. It isn't right, Fiona – '

'Well, that's the way it is,' Fiona felt so choked up as she put on her coat. 'I prefer being alone sometimes, no one to answer to.'

'Try it, it'd be a laugh, go on,' Mary picked up the strange Make-Up Kit and handed it to her niece. 'I told you, I don't believe in witchcraft, it's all ridiculous,' she said, and yet she kept hold of the kit, and that night after a glass of gin, she went to her mirror and saw hair salted with grey, that cruel eye sag under the eyebrows, parallel lines across the forehead, bags under sunken eyes, the start of a drooping lizard neck, crow's feet, and that cleavage; the breasts were elongated now and almost down by her navel. What use did ageing serve?

Fiona started to get a bit deep. She thought that, instead of ageing, it would be better if a person dissolved or dropped dead on their 30th birthday without all of this long drawn-out crap of ailment after ailment.

Fiona returned to the so-called Witches Make-Up kit, and tried to smile. What had she to lose? Auntie Mary was not a woman to tell fibs, so why did she say that the concoctions in this walnut box could arrest ageing? Was it possible that Aunt Morwenna had somehow discovered some ancient technique for turning back the body's clock? She applied the cream, and her face blistered. She cursed Mary, washed her face and then drank herself asleep – but in the morning she looked in the mirror in the bathroom – and saw the Fiona from her 20s looking back. She swore and almost cried; the cream worked! But the eyes still looked 55 years of age Fiona recalled the eyedroppers in one of the compartments and hurried to the make-up kit. She applied the drops to each eye, took a chance and applied the bottle of green goo to her hair – and yes, by God, it worked. The sparkle of youth returned to those jaded eyes and the original hair colour – chestnut – had returned to a thick head of hair. She had dyed that hair a hundred colours over the years, and had forgotten its original shade. The green lipstick resurrected those 1957 cherubic lips. The rejuvenating cream was applied to her cleavage, her varicose areas on the back of her hands and legs. And then, Fiona stood there naked before the wardrobe mirror in tears. 'I never thought I'd see you again,' she told her younger reflected self. The jealous neighbours spread rumours about Fiona blowing an inherited fortune from her late Aunt Morwenna on extreme plastic surgery, so Fiona moved to a quiet corner of Wirral and started a new life. She met a 22-year-old student named Dale in a pub and they really hit it off; he thought she was "beautiful but so different, so wise," he said. Fiona felt a fraud, a cradle-snatcher.

But she continued to see Dale, and one night he pinned her against a wall in an entry behind a pub and asked if she was on the pill. Fiona was a little drunk and she laughed at the question and said 'Oh, don't worry, nothing's gonna happen there.'

Dale was puzzled by the reply and he asked her what she meant.

She had to think fast - which can be hard when you're drunk. 'I-I mean erm, I'm already on the pill – to er, regulate my periods; but er, I don't sleep round, in case you're wondering why I'm on the pill,' Fiona told him as he kissed her neck. 'And I don't sleep with someone until at least a month – '

'Oh shut up Fiona,' Dale said, and made love to her there in the alleyway, and for some reason - probably nerves - Fiona had a fit of the giggles throughout the act.

Sometimes she forgot her fake date of birth – she pretended she was born on 9 April 1970, but sometimes she would forget and say it was 1972, and Dale suspected something but couldn't put his finger on it. Fiona seemed to know an awful lot about Modern History, and she knew the words to some of the old songs his mum knew. He never once suspected that he was seeing a woman old enough to be his mother. She thought about leaving him so many times because she thought it was so unfair in a way – Dale deserved a girl he could age with, and how long would Morwenna's make-up last? What then? She knew she should leave, but Fiona was having the life she had missed out long ago when she was in her twenties. A love like this had never come her way. Sometimes she would cry as she thought of the day when she would no longer be able to keep up the illusion, when Dale would see her for what she really was – a woman in her mid-fifties.

Then one beautiful summer's day on the ferry over to Liverpool, Dale hugged Fiona, looked her in the eyes, and said he wanted a baby, and Fiona's heart went into freefall. He told her to stop taking the pill, and she told him he should pursue his career first, for he wanted to be a teacher, but Dale said he loved her so much he wanted to start a family with her right away. 'I don't think you know how much I love you, Fiona,' he told her one night not long after this, and once again he spoke of becoming a father, and even mentioned the baby names he liked the sound of.

Fiona buried her face in her hands and cried non-stop.

'What's wrong with you?' Dale asked, becoming angry, 'Don't you love me? Don't you want to give me a baby?'

Fiona knew it was over. The make-up had given her a youthful appearance – but she had not had any periods since she started using it, so it seemed it only worked to a certain extent. If she had had one period, she would have risked having Dale's baby, for she loved him so much, but she knew this was the end now. He was determined to have a son or daughter, and Fiona couldn't provide him with a baby. She believed he would not stay with her now. She went home, and stopped using the make-up kit, and within days she had returned to 55. She cut her hair and became a recluse for a while, unplugging her landline and shutting herself off from the world. She tortured herself though, and in dowdy clothes she started visiting the places she used to go with Dale, and one night her heart stopped when she saw him being comforted by a friend outside the pub where they had met.

'I loved her,' he was saying, and tears were streaming down his face.

Dale's friend Sean said, 'Ah, there's plenty more fish in the sea mate.' And the young men went into the pub.

Fiona walked on into the night, hardly able to breathe because her throat was so choked up with emotion. 'Goodbye Dale,' she whispered, and through her tears she glanced up at the moon and stars, and sighed, 'Goodbye young love.'

Printed in Great Britain
by Amazon